AF327829

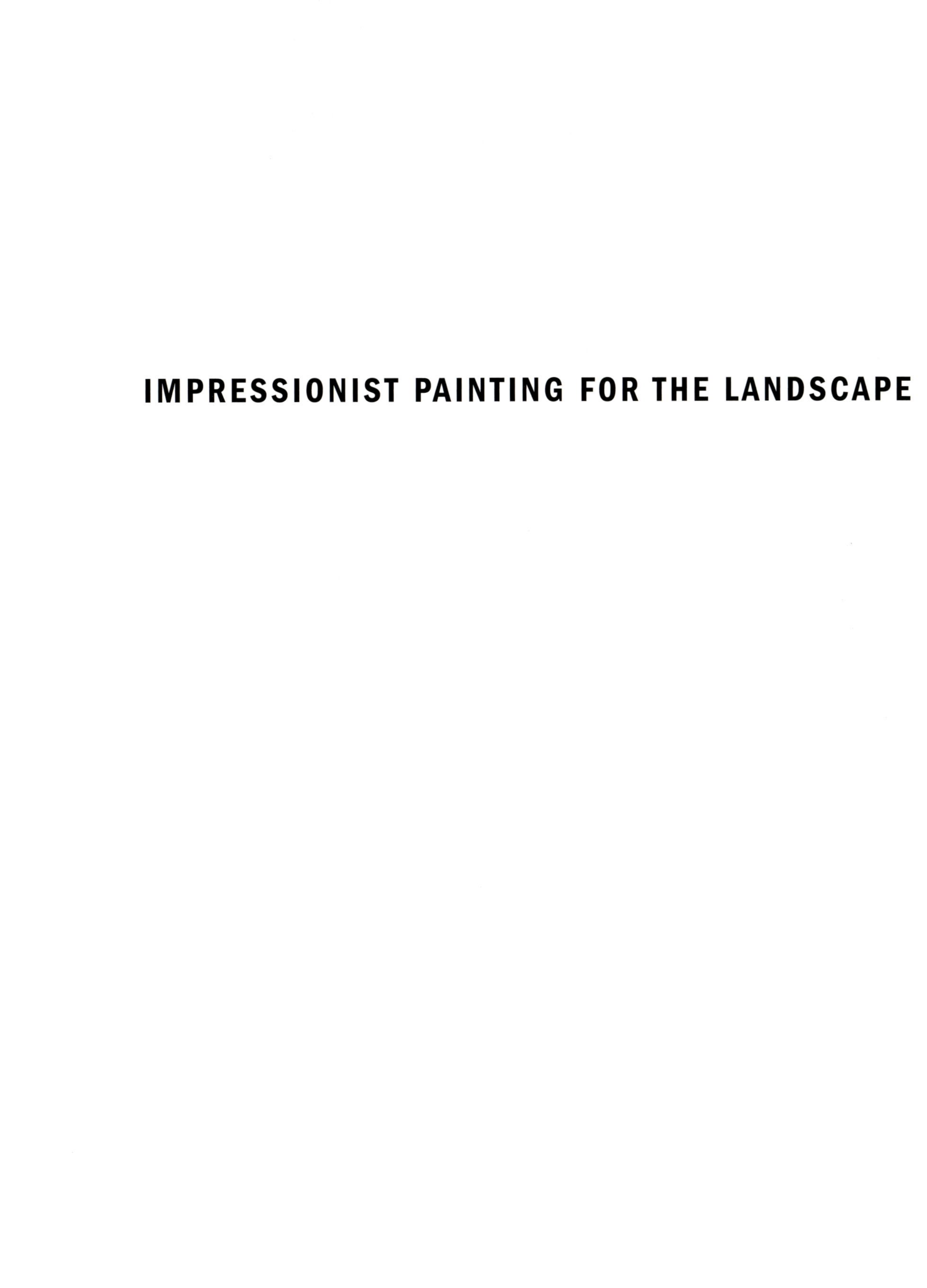

IMPRESSIONIST PAINTING FOR THE LANDSCAPE

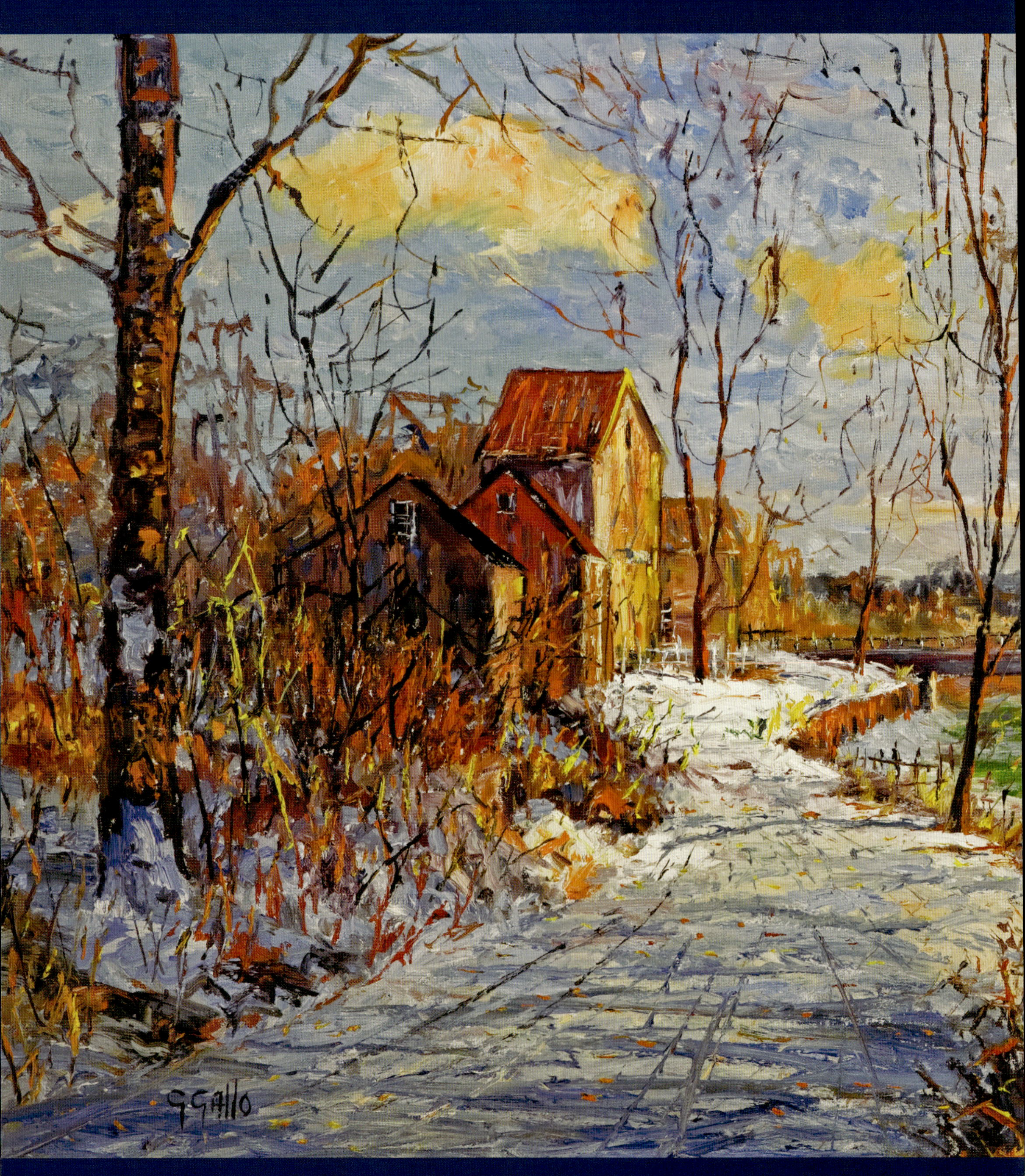
G Gallo

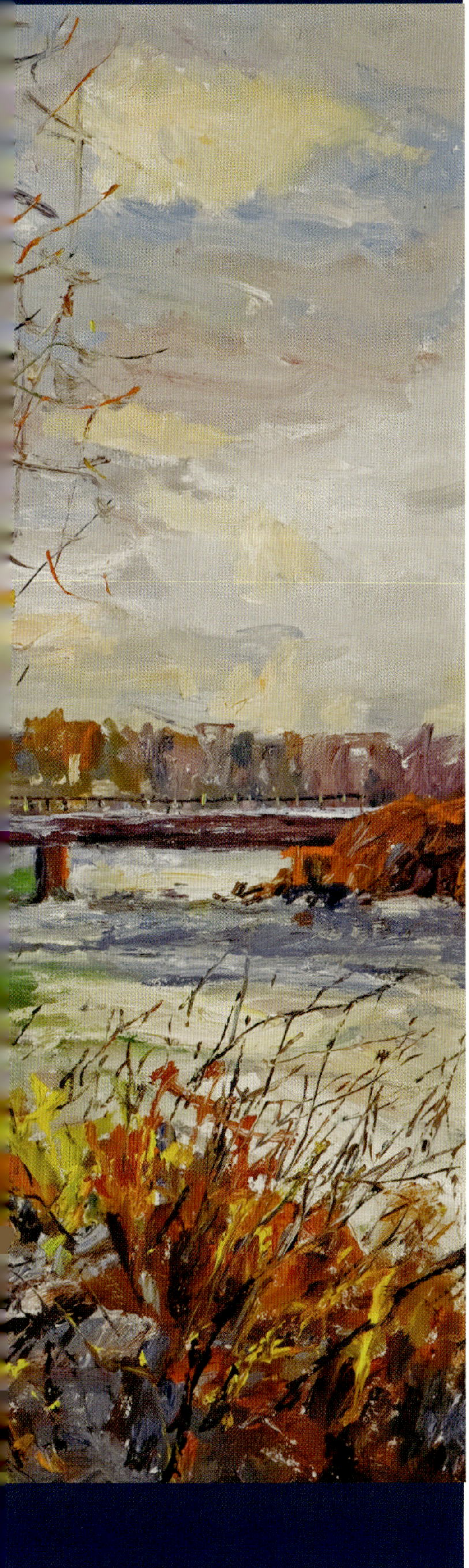

IMPRESSIONIST PAINTING for the Landscape

Secrets for Successful Oil Painting

George Gallo and **Cindy Salaski**

NORTH LIGHT BOOKS
CINCINNATI, OHIO
www.artistsnetwork.com

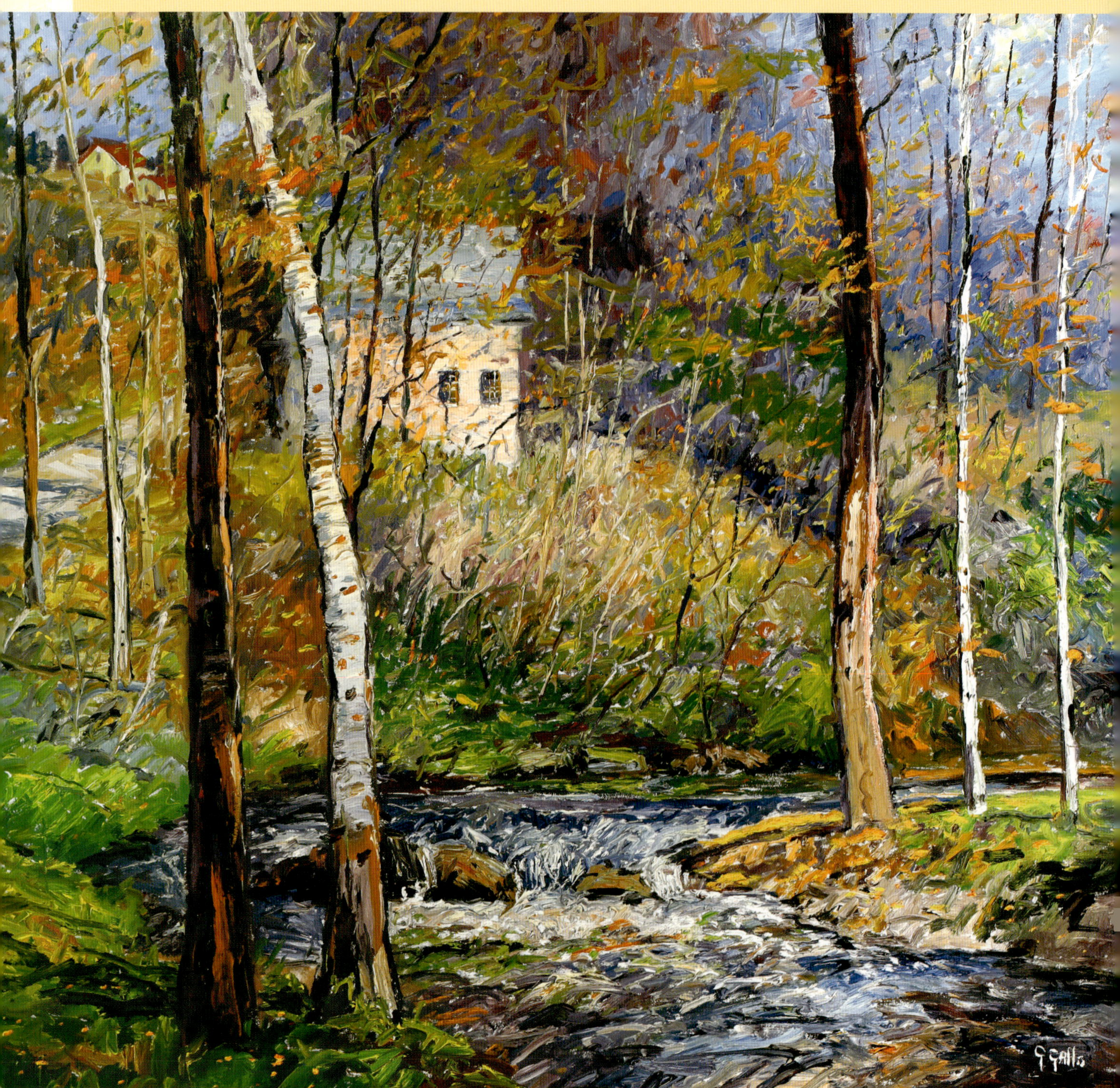

SEPTEMBER, NEW HOPE · Oil on Canvas · 50" × 56" (127cm × 142cm)

Previous page: **PRALLSVILLE MILL IN WINTER** · Oil on Canvas · 36" × 48" (91cm × 122cm)

Contents

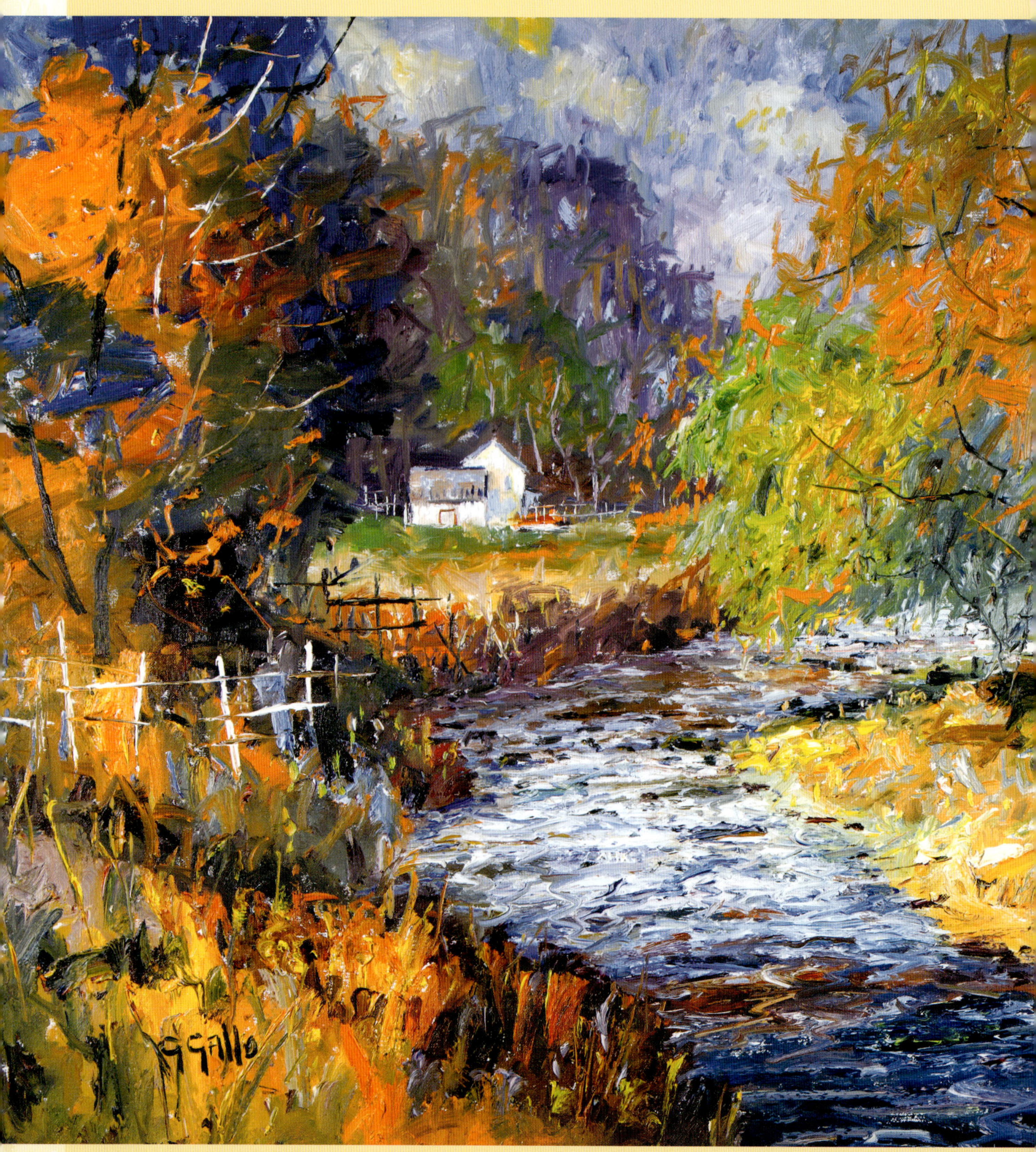

BETWEEN SHOWERS, NEW HOPE · Oil on Canvas · 36" × 48" (91cm × 122cm)

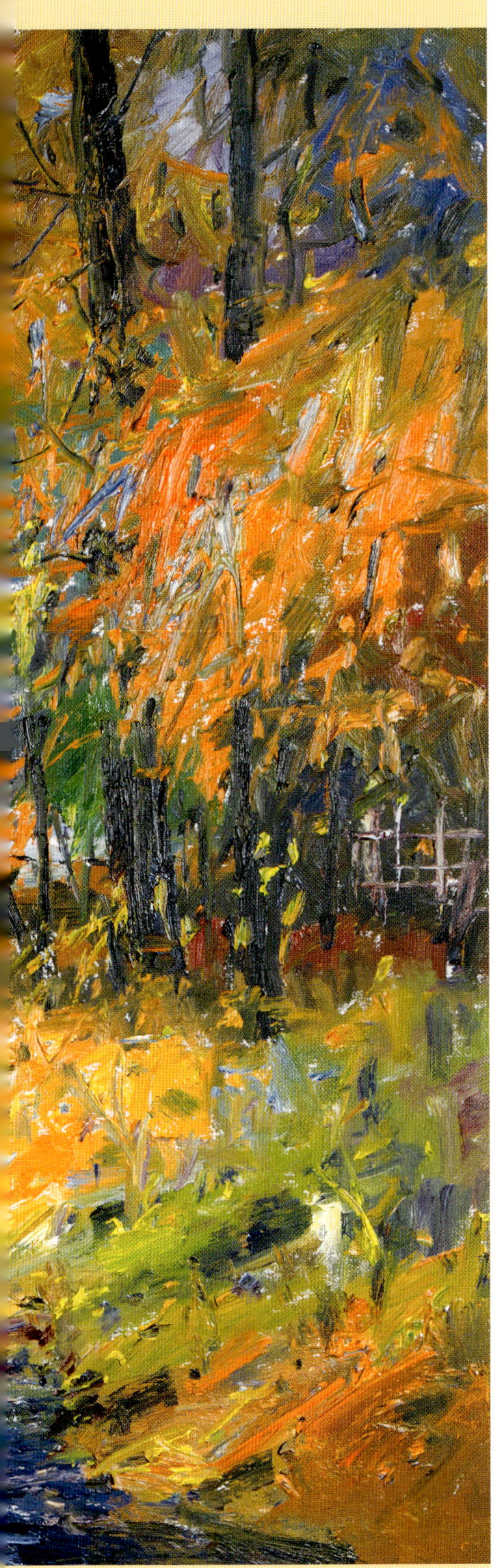

Foreword by David Leffel

If every painting is a self-portrait, then American Impressionist George Gallo exemplifies that premise. Both the man and his paintings are large, colorful, ebullient and full of expressive emotion.

George, one might say, is a Renaissance person. A musician, writer, director of movies, he still finds time to turn out large, eye-filling canvases in the tradition of his mentors: Edward Redfield, Daniel Garber and Edgar Payne.

And while somewhat following in the path of these plein-air forebears, George has distanced himself from them. He follows his own drumbeat.

First, his method of paint application is his personal invention. He will use any part of the brush or no brush at all if a stick of wood proves the more expressive tool. Palette knife, wood, paper—anything is fair game in conveying his emotional state of mind.

Second, his color palette is driven, comes out bursting from that same deep wellspring of feeling that is called George Gallo.

He uses color to define his compositions and to form the shape of the landscapes he loves to paint.

And while he has the enormous ability to create paintings from his vast storehouse of mnemonic images, George has returned to his roots. He has come to the realization that painting on location has no equal. Communing with nature in a one-to-one atmosphere is a different experience for the artist. Conveying the subtleties and nuances of nature can be the determining factor in considering whether a work is ordinary or transcendent. This can only be realized when one is in touch with the real, the actual.

So there is George Gallo, a multitalented person, but painting is his true passion. Painting is where his heart is. Through his canvases, his impossible impasto, his brilliant color, George engages his audience that they might see what he saw and feel what he felt.

David A. Leffel

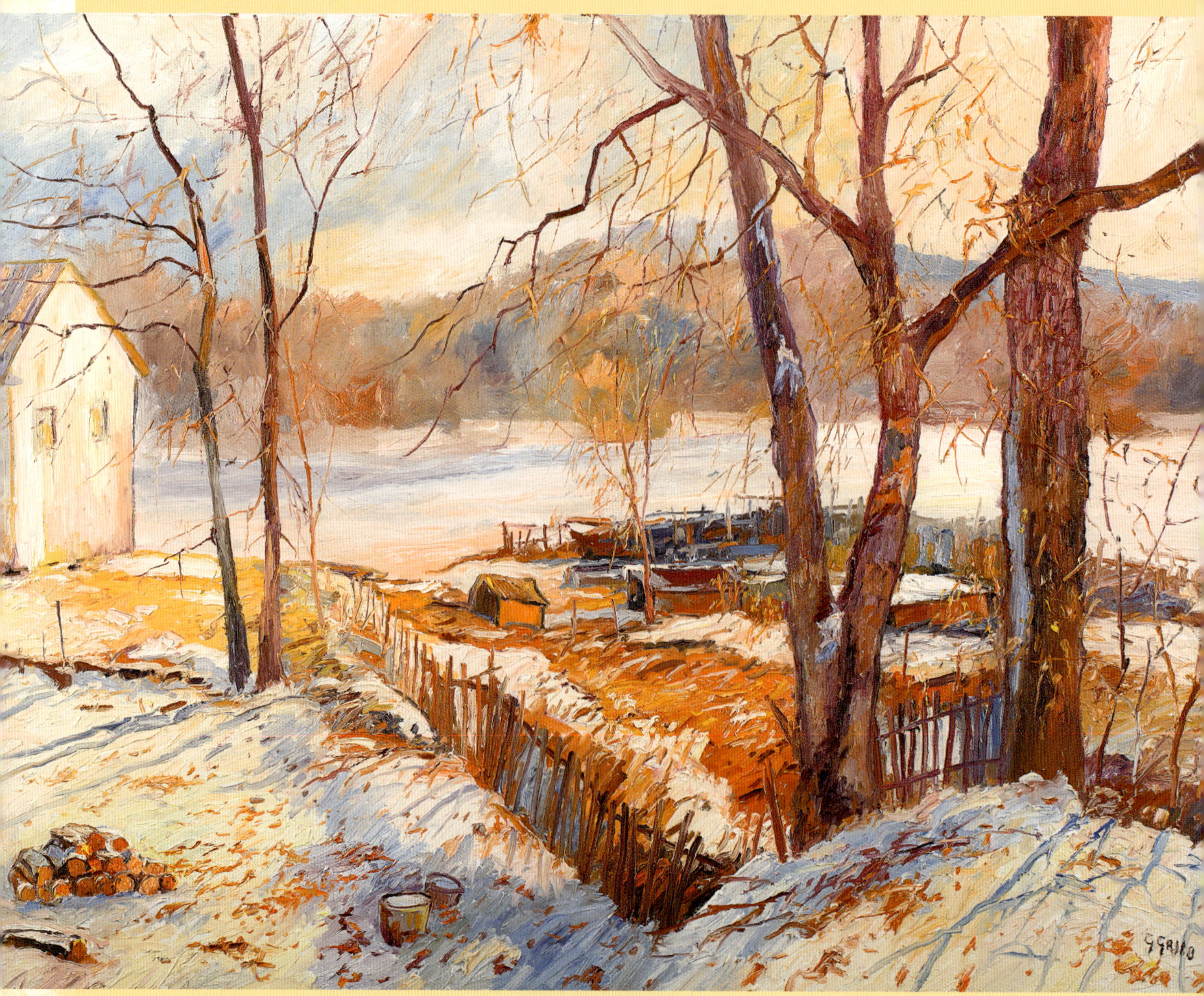

TAOS BACKYARDS IN WINTER · Oil on Canvas · 36" × 48" (91cm × 122cm)

Introduction

As far back as I can remember I have loved to draw and paint. Growing up as an only child in Port Chester, New York, my fascination with creating images became my best friend. At twelve my mother bought me an oil painting set, and I have been painting in that beloved medium ever since.

I have always been hungry for information about painting. Over the years I have read countless books by artists, especially those who paint landscapes. And what is amazing to me is that many painters I meet have very little knowledge about the great master painters of the past. Anyone involved in representational painting should not only know about these artists but also immerse themselves in their work.

Claude Monet, Pierre-Auguste Renoir, Alfred Sisley, Camille Pissarro, Vincent van Gogh, Edward Redfield, Daniel Garber, Walter Schofield, William Merritt Chase, John Henry Twachtman and Childe Hassam are some of the Impressionists you should become familiar with. These people were giants, and to not be completely familiar with their work is to shortchange yourself of great knowledge.

The problem with most student painters is not that they don't know how to paint; it is that they don't know how to see or think in a painterly manner when creating a painting. The act of painting itself does not require any great amount of manual dexterity or even a particularly steady hand. The fact is that as we age, our eyesight weakens and our hands become less steady.

Many of the great masterpieces were created when the artists were advanced in age. So forget the notion that all you need is some secret swipe of the brush. All you really need to know in order to do successful work is to learn how to translate what you are seeing before you and put it down on canvas. That's easier said than done, but hopefully after reading this book you'll be closer to your goal.

The point of this book is not for you to learn to paint like me, but for you to *learn to paint like you*. All of us learn by copying others, the same way that we learned to walk by imitating the people around us, but eventually all of us develop our own swagger. I implore all of you to take risks as you work. When you are reaching—that is when you're at your best. Learn to paint with expression and don't be afraid to mess up, because you will, just like every great master before you. No one starts out at the top. And even painters who have completely mastered their craft can still paint something rotten. Recently David A. Leffel said to me, "It doesn't get easier." Knowing that is powerful because it keeps you sharp.

I don't paint because I want to. I paint because I have to. There are times when I wonder why I find myself carrying my painting gear through the great outdoors. I've come to the conclusion that it is a spiritual experience, sometimes less about the painting than a need to express thanks for being on earth. I have a deep need to share this joy and celebrate the beauty I see all around us.

We live in a time when that type of pursuit and mind-set is ridiculed. I find this attitude to be sad, but it shouldn't be taken all that seriously. As someone once told me years ago, "Cynics are merely romantics who have gotten their hearts broken." My wish is that this book inspires all who read it in the same way other books on art have inspired me. The journey of an artist is one of the noblest roads a person can take. If you do it right, every day will bring you joy as you get closer and closer to the truth. The truth, as far as I can tell, is that simplicity in art, as in everything else in life, is best. I ask all of you to continue to learn, continue to grow and continue your pursuits to paint beauty and the best that we are and can be. May your hearts and brushes chase away the darkness.

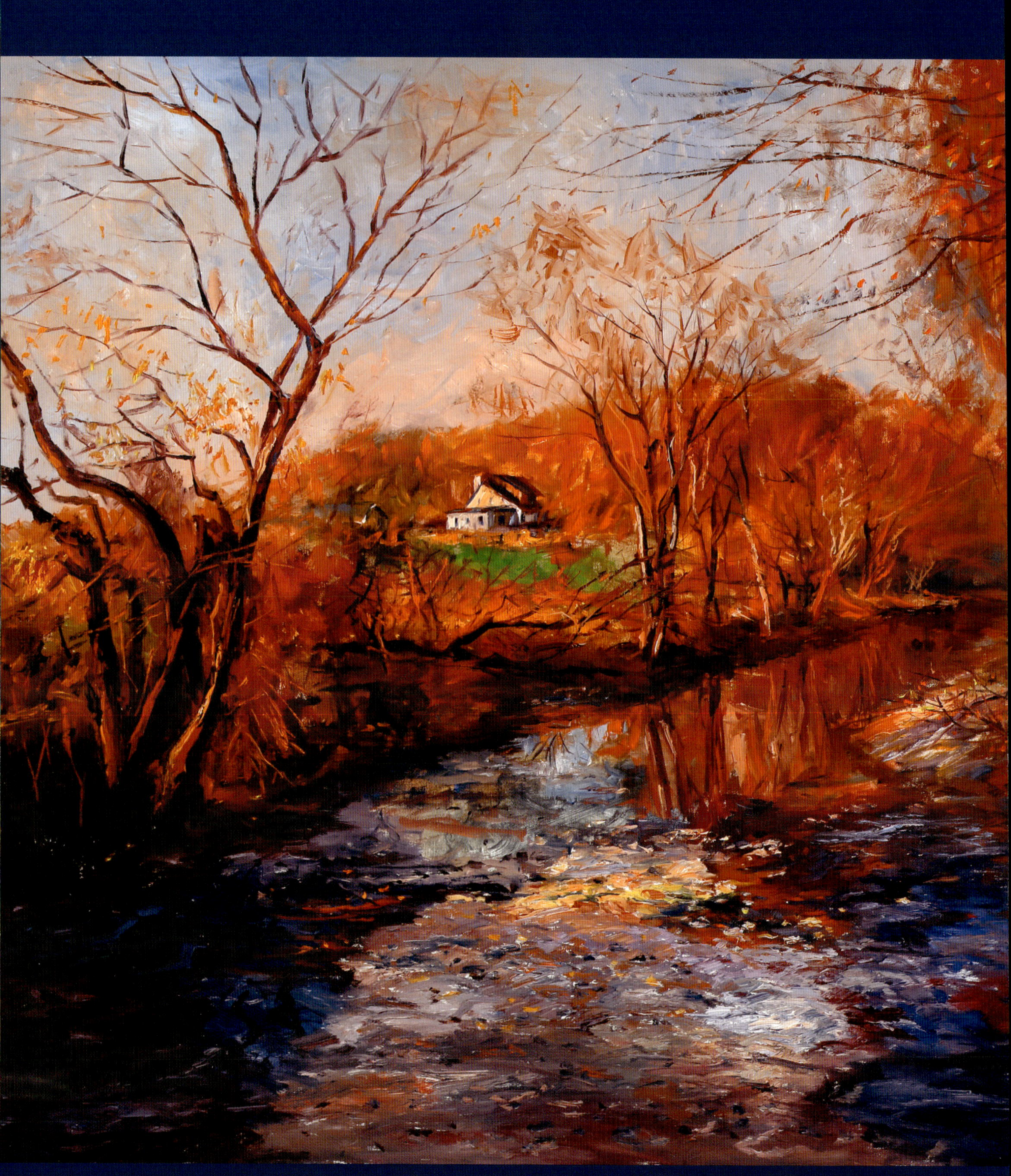

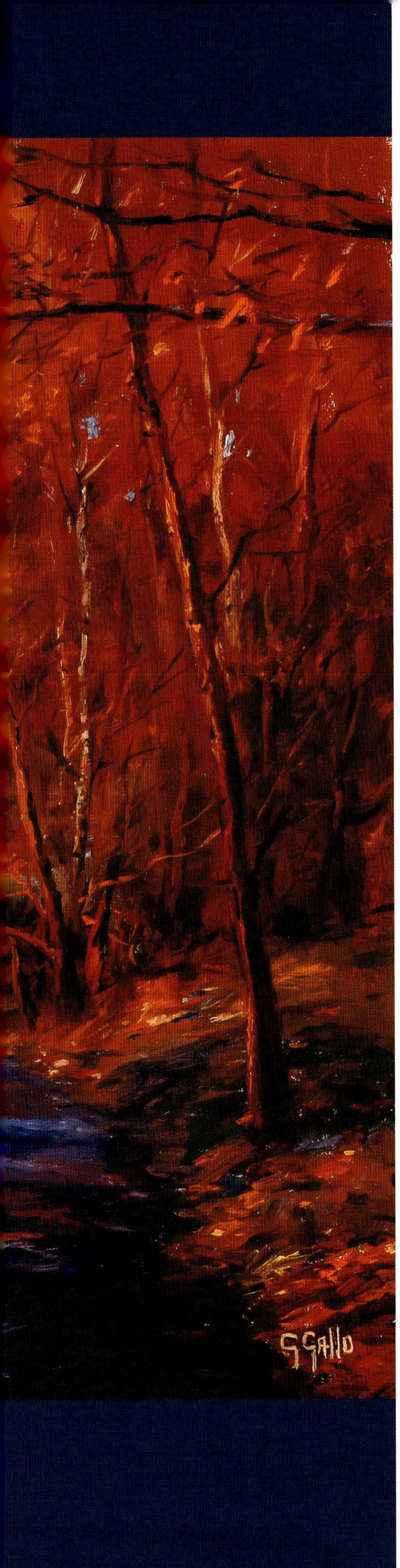

CHAPTER 1
WHAT YOU NEED

If you're embarking on the journey of plein air painting, it's good to have gear that allows for a quick setup. You want to boil down your painting necessities so that you have only what you need and can travel lightly. After years of outdoor work I've found that I need nothing more than the following materials.

PAINT RECOMMENDATIONS

Michael Harding Artists Oil Colours

BRUSH RECOMMENDATIONS

Rosemary and Company white bristle brushes

ADDITIONAL ITEMS

canvas/painting panels
easel
electrician's box, fishing tackle box or backpack for
carrying paint and other supplies
graphite pencil
medium cup
mineral spirits
painting knives
paper towels
plastic bag for trash
small sketchbook
umbrella
wood or paper palette

NOVEMBER · Oil on Canvas · 36" × 48" (76cm × 122cm)

Materials for Painting Outdoors

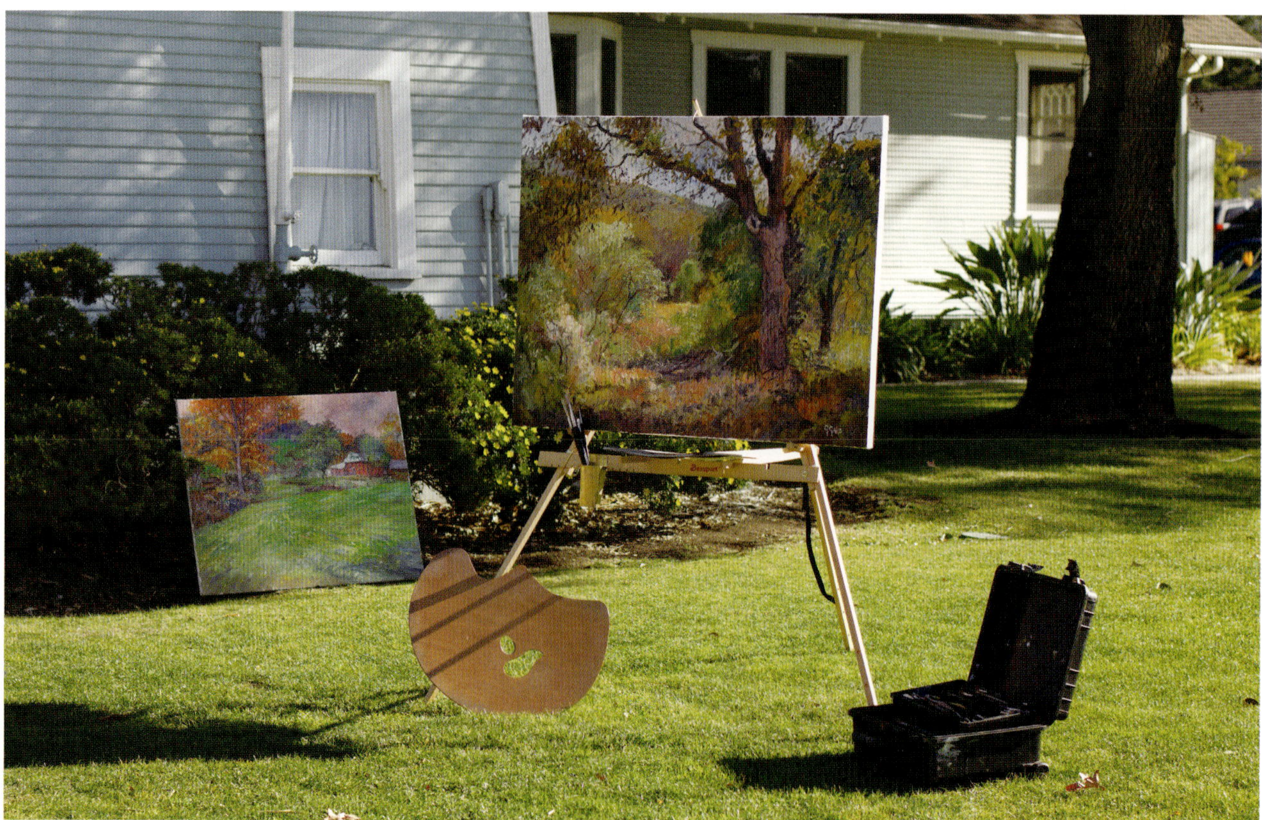

▲ GEORGE GALLO'S BASIC OUTDOOR SETUP

▲ **Easel:** This is my basic outdoor setup. I want the option to paint large pieces outdoors, and the Beauport easel is perfect for this. It is an improved version of the old Gloucester easel that was used by many of the great American Impressionist painters. I can also paint as small as I want with it, but again, the easel's strengths are that it can hold a canvas as large as 48" × 60" (122cm × 152cm) with no problem. It also sets up very quickly, and I've never had it blow over. In heavier winds I recommend weighing it down with either a sandbag or a piece of equipment.

▲ **Paint Box:** My paint box is an electrician's case. It's incredibly durable and large enough that I can fill it with lots of big tubes of paint. I use the foam divider to hold all the paints in place and I have a brush tray from an old paint box that I place on top. My mineral spirits and a mixing cup can also be stashed inside.

▲ **Palette:** Sometimes I use a wood palette. Sometimes I use a paper palette pad. The pads I recommend are from New Wave Art. The paper palettes that New Wave makes

OUTDOOR EASEL RECOMMENDATIONS

Beauport Large Format Outdoor Easel
Open Box M Palette/Panel Holder—12" × 16"
(30cm × 41cm)
Jullian Original French Easel—Full Box

are great because of their gray color. Outdoors sunlight can hit your palette and if the palette's white, the sunlight will bounce off the palette and reflect into your eyes. The gray tone eliminates that problem. Also, colors tend to look darker against white than they do against gray, so it's much easier to get proper color mixes using a gray palette. New Wave's wood palette is also terrific, and it is treated in a way that allows excess paint to be easily wiped off with a paper towel. In the studio I use both paper and wooden palettes, whichever is more convenient at the moment.

◄ **Paint:** I use Michael Harding oil paints because they are simply the best paints on the market. They are highly

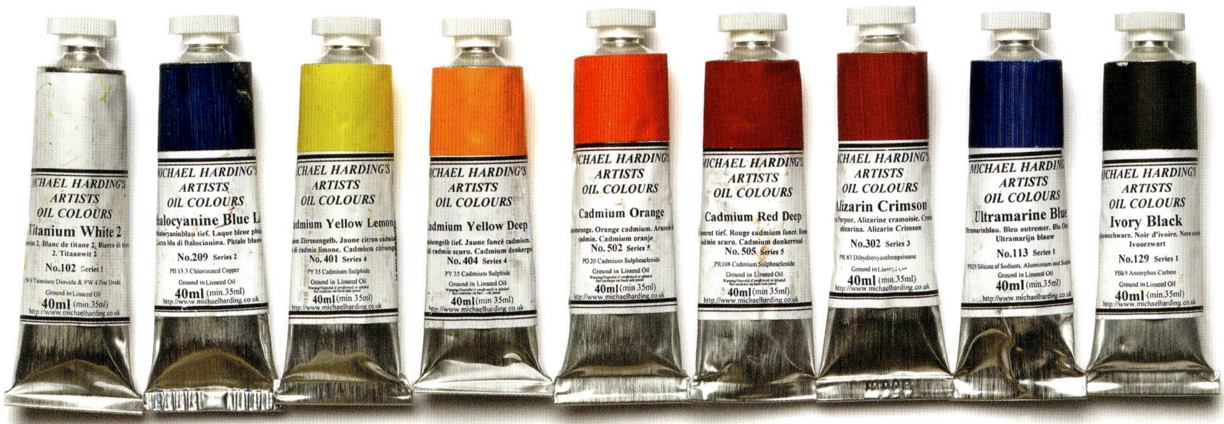

concentrated, and the colors are wonderfully intense and have a very buttery consistency. This is important since I don't use medium after I do the initial sketch. I want the paint to be consistently workable so I can dip from paint to paint without overmixing. It is often better, after dipping your brush into the various piles of paint, to do the actual blending on the canvas itself. Simplicity works best, especially when painting outdoors where you have to carry your equipment to the desired location. I use a limited pure color palette consisting mainly of two blues, two reds and two yellows with the addition of orange, black and white. We'll get more into that in Chapter 3.

▼ **Brushes:** The brushes I use are all white bristle and are either flats, filberts or my new favorites, daggers. All of these longer bristle brushes hold a great deal of paint, and that is what you will need to paint expressive brushstrokes. For details, I recommend riggers. They have extra-long bristles, come to a fine point, have a lot of snap and are capable of creating a myriad of delicate strokes. The brushes I use are all manufactured by Rosemary and Company. I feel that these are the best brushes on the market today.

▼ **Painting Knives:** Painting knives come in a variety of shapes. The thing to remember when using them is that they are capable of creating the sharpest of all edges, but as a general rule only one side of the stroke you make will be usable. You'll have to make an adjustment on the part of the stroke where you pull the knife away from the canvas. They are very versatile tools and can create effects that are impossible to do with a brush. Combinations of strong-edged knife work and soft brush work can create incredibly dynamic contrasts in paintings. They can be used to blend brushstrokes and create great transitions between the edges of objects. They can also be used to blend various colors with one or two swipes. A word of caution: If knives aren't used with restraint, your painting can take on a very stilted and mannered look. The knives I use are made by Creative Mark.

Additional Items: I hook a brush holder to the crossbar of the Beauport, which makes things very convenient. Also, don't forget to bring plenty of paper towels and a plastic trash bag that you can easily attach to the easel as well. Never leave your painting site a mess. It's an insult to nature and you don't want the next artist to come along and catch grief for your sloppiness.

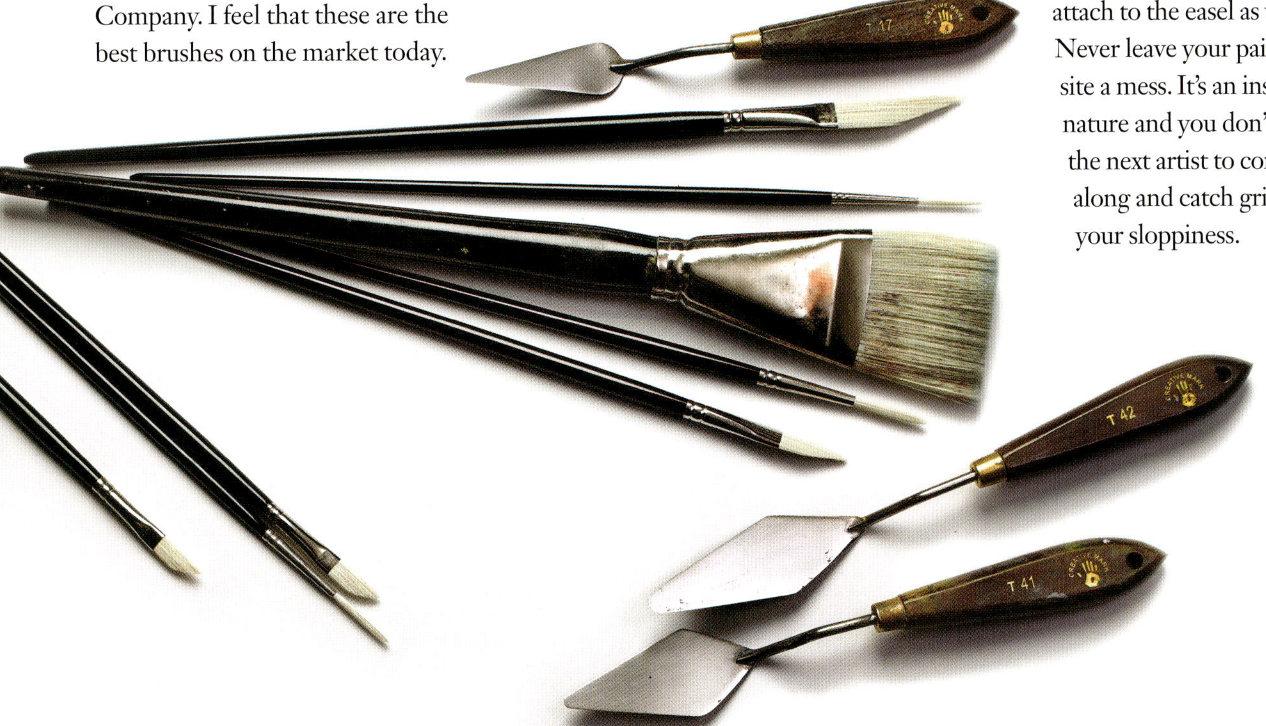

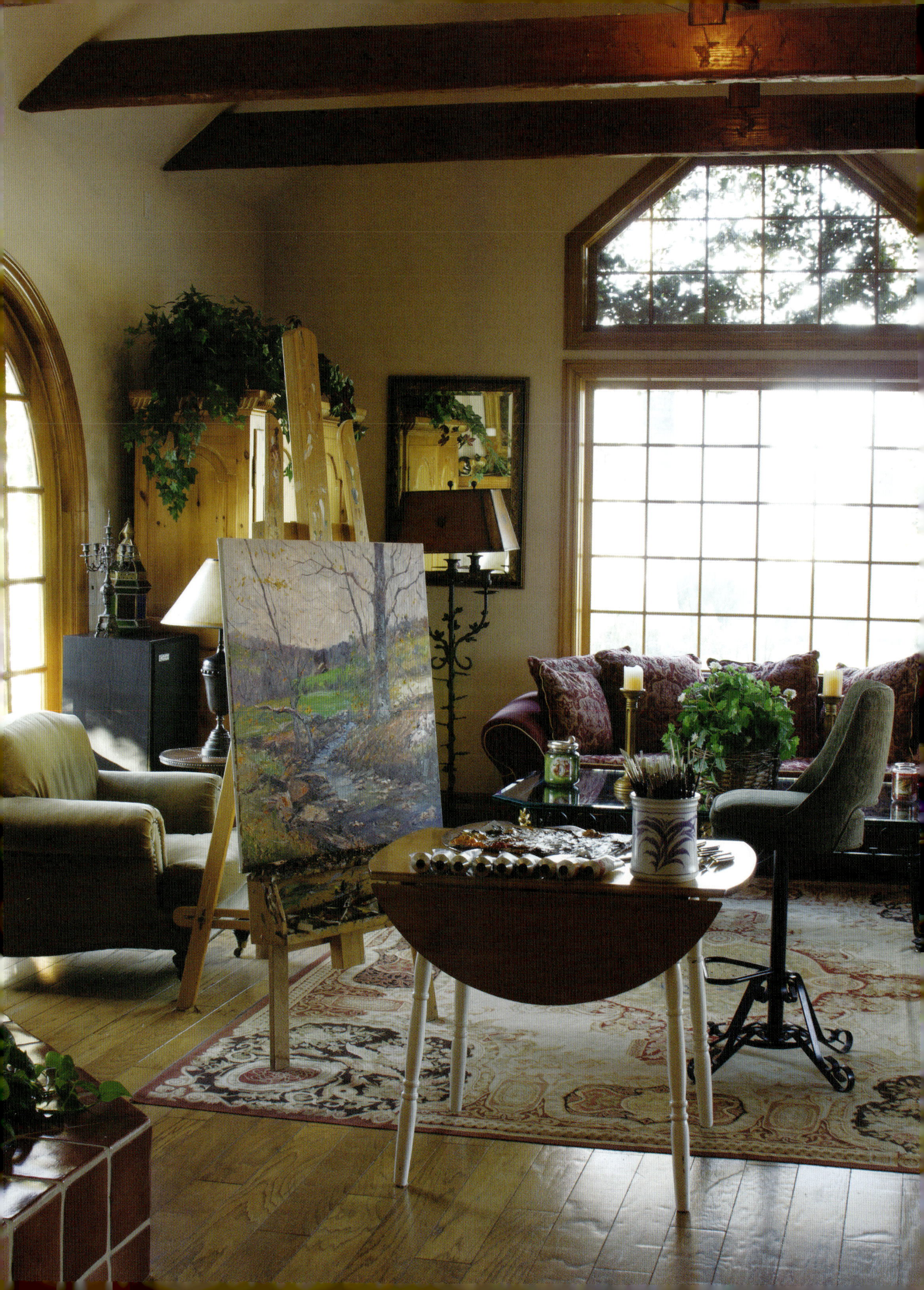

Materials for Inside the Studio

Other than a solid indoor easel, both my indoor and outdoor materials are identical. I don't add extra colors for my studio work as some other artists do. When I paint in the studio, I also try to work at about the same speed I would outdoors. In regards to my palette, I find that I can mix anything I want, so there's no need for me to add anything else.

▶ **Wooden Palette:** The wooden palette is great if you work standing up, which I have a tendency to do. The one that I use, by New Wave Palettes, is designed in a way that causes virtually no fatigue. Not only is it very light, but the palette hole is shaved at an angle so your thumb never scrapes. Also, it's designed so you can hold it against your body, making it a lot easier to hold for long periods of time.

▼ **Brushes and Knives:** I almost exclusively use bristle brushes. They hold a lot of paint. Sometimes I'll use a sable to blend things, but as a general rule, I find bristle brushes to be the best for painting landscapes. They are designed to create heavy, thick strokes. I stick with flats, filberts, egberts, swords and daggers. Brights are better used for portraiture since they create very chiseled and accurate strokes. I find that landscapes are better when the brush has a little more play and the longer bristle brushes help you create that effect. I use painting knives when I want a shape to have a very hard edge or to flatten and blend a group of brushstrokes together. The ones that I use, regardless of the sizes, come to a point at the tip. Look for knives that have a little play in them also because if you're not careful, your knife strokes can begin to look mannered.

▼ **Additional Items:** I use everyday graphite drawing pencils and a simple small sketchbook for sketching out my compositions before I begin painting. Make sure your sketchbook has good quality paper. Sometimes I sketch with a black Pilot G-2 pen. Working with ink and paper forces you to be more accurate because you can't erase it once you put it down. I find this to be a very useful exercise. As for canvases, I use Centurion Oil Primed Linens in sizes 12" × 16" (30cm × 41cm) to 48" × 60" (122cm × 152cm).

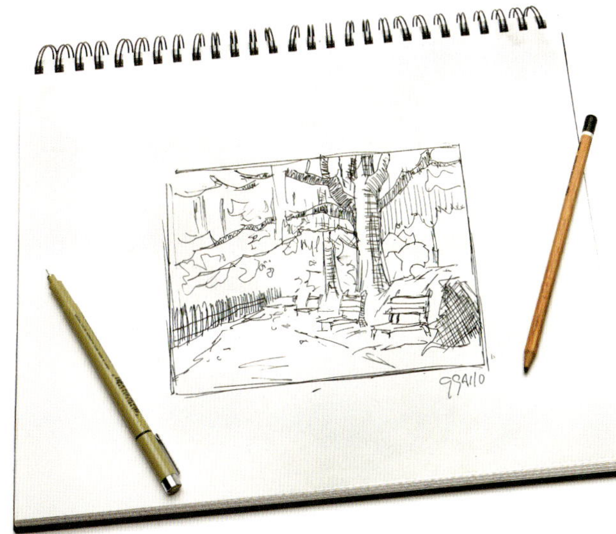

◀ **GEORGE GALLO'S BASIC INDOOR SETUP**
While George usually paints outdoors, he works in his garage or family room to add the finishing touches to a painting.

Painterly Secrets

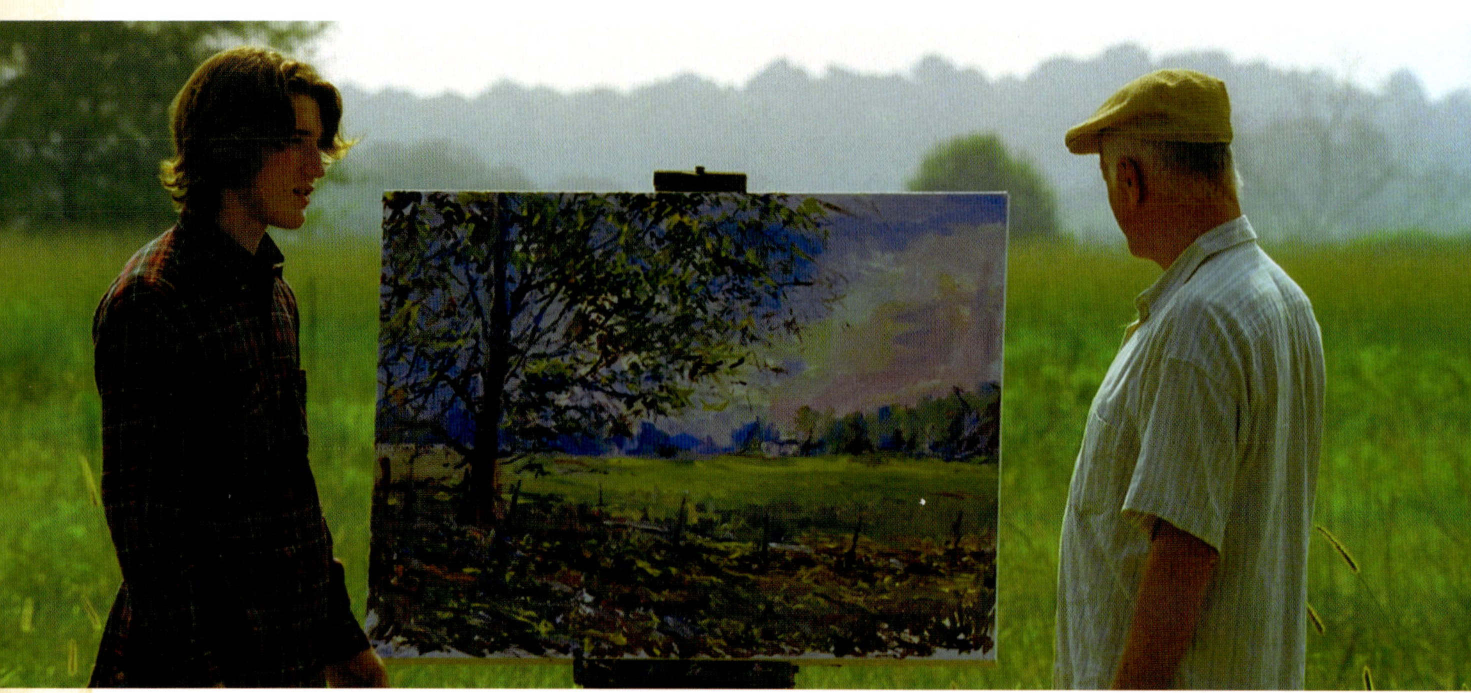

In the feature film *Local Color*, Russian master Nicholi Seroff (Armin Mueller-Stahl) shares his painterly secrets with John Talia (Trevor Morgan).

Much of what I know about representational painting goes back a hundred years or more. A lot of that knowledge was lost when the modernists took over and there seemed to be little interest in learning about more traditional work. I was lucky that when I was younger I encountered a few teachers who were around when representational painting was at its height; they passed their secrets onto me. Of course these secrets are really just lost knowledge. To paint well necessitates a thorough understanding of your palette. That's one of the real secrets.

I am not a big advocate of just painting what I see in front of me. After years of work it's nice to know that I can generally paint everything I see, but leaving it at that isn't something I find very interesting. Too many artists, especially today, are too caught up in just rendering what's in front of them. Even though it is essential to learn to do

so, eventually an artist must move past that if he wants to create unique work. The same way a writer uses certain truths about human behavior in order to make a point in a dramatic piece of writing, the painter must take certain visual truths and interpret them in a painting to make a strong statement.

Part of the landscape painter's craft is knowing how to take the visual elements he sees before him and edit them to make a cohesive statement. I have rarely, if ever, come across a scene that was simply *perfect*, a scene in which I did not have to make a single compositional change. Being able to see what's in front of you, to digest it, and then to have the knowledge of what to move, subtract or add is one of the great joys of being a landscape painter.

Knowing what you want to say and how you are going to say it is the strongest tool you have. I ask students when we are out on a painting location why they are painting a particular subject. A lot of times I hear, "I don't know" or some other vague answer. You can never achieve a successful painting unless you know exactly what you are going for. You should know it before you put down the first brushstroke. It is the only way to paint with verve and style because each brushstroke is there to support your original intent. I will bet that many of you who are struggling are much further along in your abilities than you think. What you are lacking is the ability to see the finished painting before you begin it.

Once you master this skill, you will have a very clear, defined idea of what you want to say and how you will say it. Remember this: If you don't know what you want to say with your painting, how is the viewer ever supposed to know?

We've all been wonderfully awed in museums and galleries upon seeing delicious, juicy, bravura brushwork. Here's another secret for you: You're not being awed by the brushwork. You're being awed by the confidence. Confidence comes from having a very clear picture in your mind before you start. If you see it clearly, you can paint it with authority. These things are as close to secrets as I know.

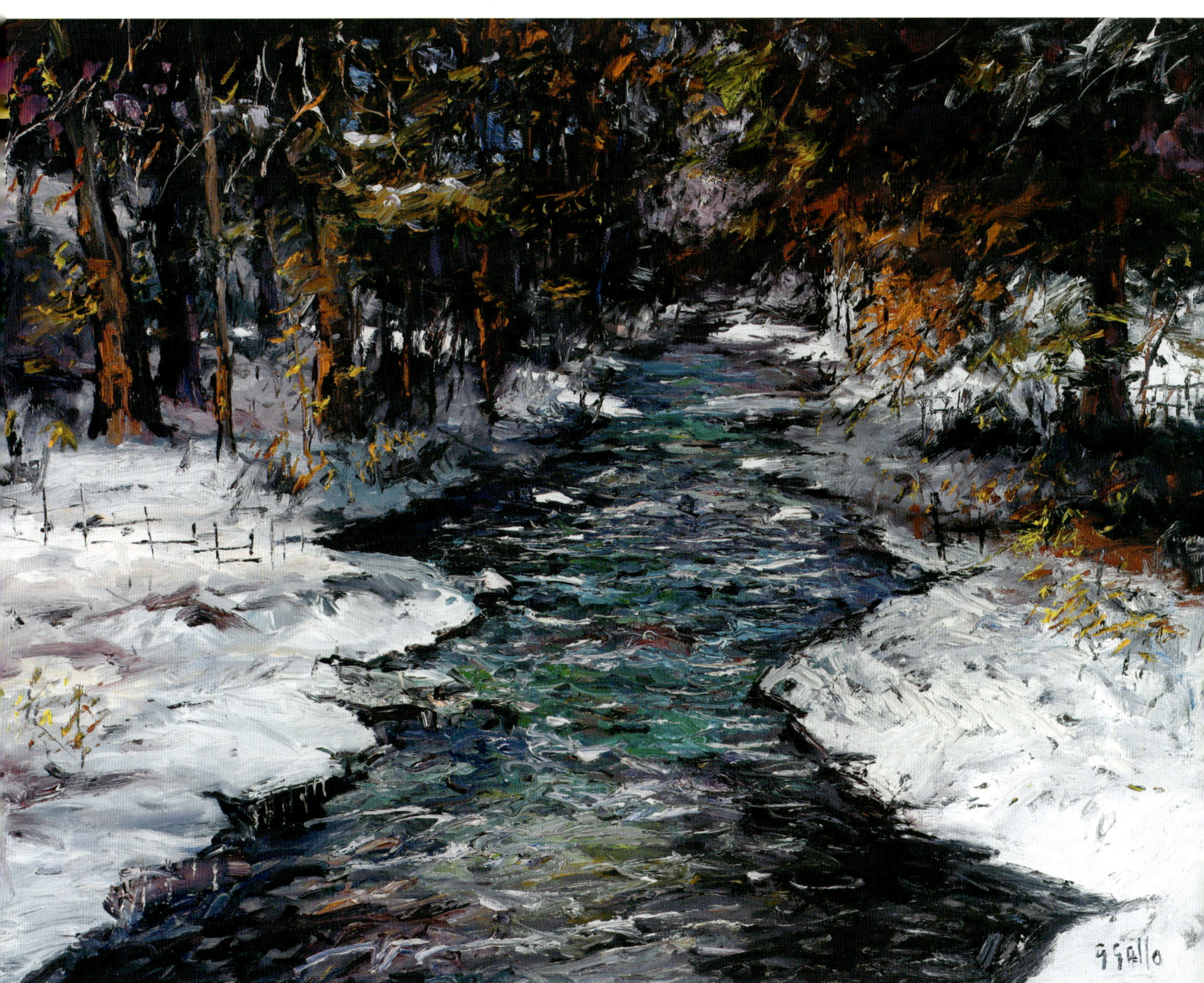

FEBRUARY · Oil on Canvas · 36" × 48" (91cm × 122cm)

Find Your Own Voice

What I am about to say may sound like a contradiction, but trust me, it is not. One of the best ways to develop your own voice is to know as much as you can about the Great Masters and how they achieved their goals. Many times when I am working I look upon a group of rocks and think of the way Winslow Homer painted them. It's impossible for me to stand by a snowy creek and not think of Edward Redfield. This list of painters and associations goes on and on in my mind, and having become familiar with them and how they painted has helped me discover who I am as an artist. Every great singer, writer, musician, actor or poet has learned by emulating the artists who have touched them. It is like standing on the shoulders of giants, and to not take advantage of their hard work is silly.

The idea that painting begins with just you is an absurd concept that was fostered by many in the modern art movement. I am not going to go on a rant about modern art. I happen to like some of it a great deal. I just think the notion that painting is a singular experience with no prehistory is ridiculous. If you are trying to be different, you are already acknowledging previous work. Therefore, the way to find your own voice is to collect knowledge from the painters who move you and ask yourself, "Why?" As you continue to delve into this question, you'll find a theme developing in terms of the work you're attracted to.

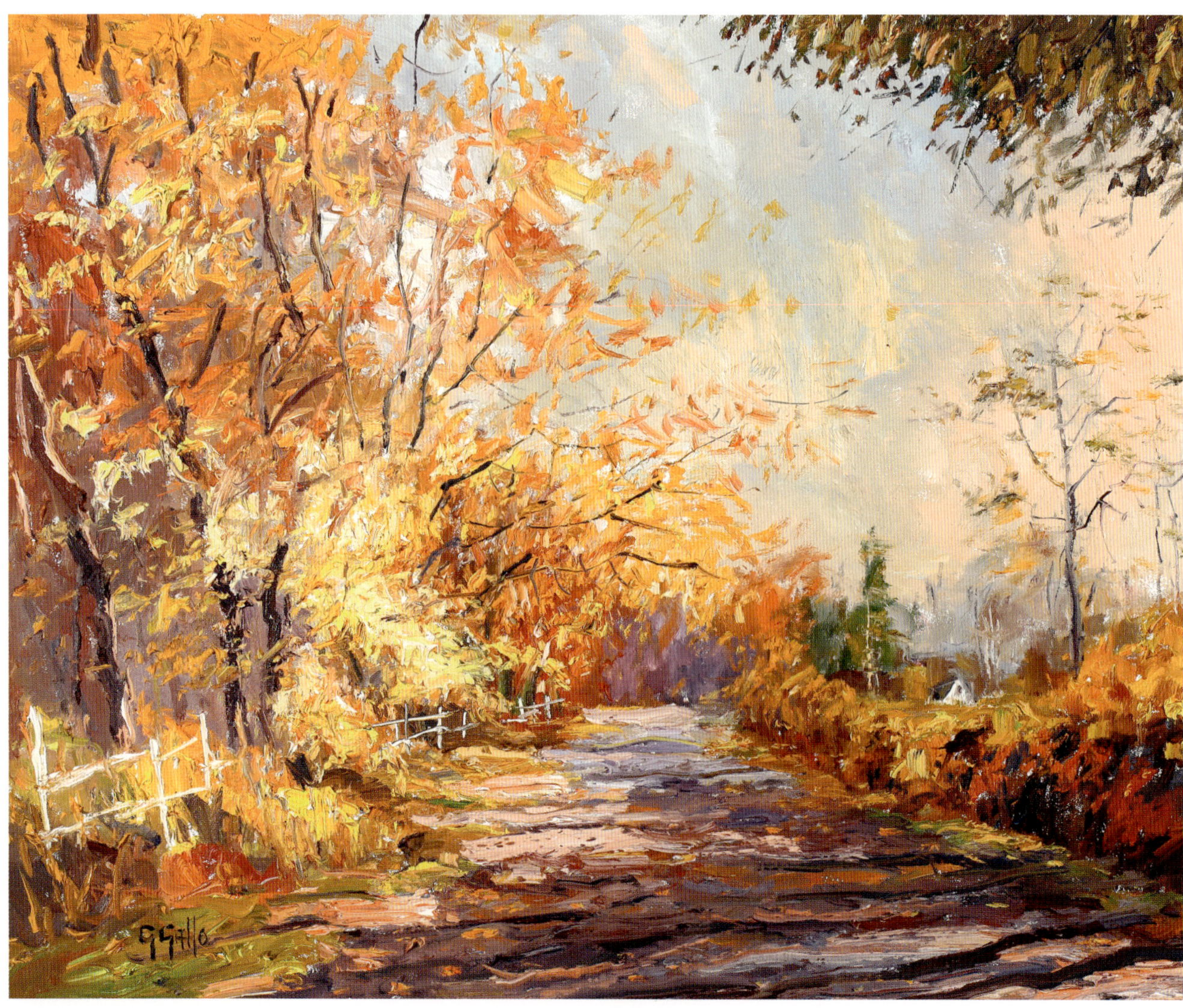

COUNTRY ROAD IN AUTUMN · Oil on Canvas · 24" × 30" (61cm × 76cm)

From there you'll be armed with the knowledge of why you like certain things and, as a result, you'll be on your way to developing your own personal version of it.

Perhaps the best way to really find your voice is to paint large canvases outdoors. This was a practice of many of the Pennsylvania Impressionists, especially Edward Redfield. When an artist is painting a large canvas outdoors, time is limited due to shifting light and shadows. Because of this, the artist is forced to work rapidly if the goal is to finish the piece *alla prima* or *all at once*. Some painters will tell you this is foolish. Don't listen to them. Part of making great art is being in control. An even greater part is being comfortable with the fact that you are partially out of control. As you chase the work, maybe even feeling unsure of its outcome, not only will you be forced to stay highly focused, but you will have to solve all of your problems quickly without overthinking and respond in your own unique way. This is when your personal voice will develop and eventually shine.

Also, you can get away with a lot more on a small canvas. An evergreen tree in middle distance on an 18" × 24" (46cm × 61cm) canvas can be achieved with a few swipes of a brush. When you get into larger paintings, you have to paint many of the nooks and crannies of that same evergreen. If you have to do so in limited time, you will find your own way to render it. Too many landscape painters, especially today, are painting works that look similar to one another. A surefire way to avoid this and break away from the pack is to paint larger to find out who you are.

A word of caution: This is not easy. In fact, it can be very daunting. I have done it many times and even I can get overwhelmed standing in front of a blank 48" × 60" (122cm × 152cm) canvas on my outdoor easel. If you can harness that fear and turn it into positive energy, you will find a whole new wonderful excitement happening in your work. If you're unable to do this at first, don't fret. Failure is part of the process. I've failed many times on my way to finding my voice. In fact, we often learn more from our failures than we do from our successes. But if you stick to it and don't get into negative thinking or self-recrimination (an artist favorite), you will find your way through to the other side.

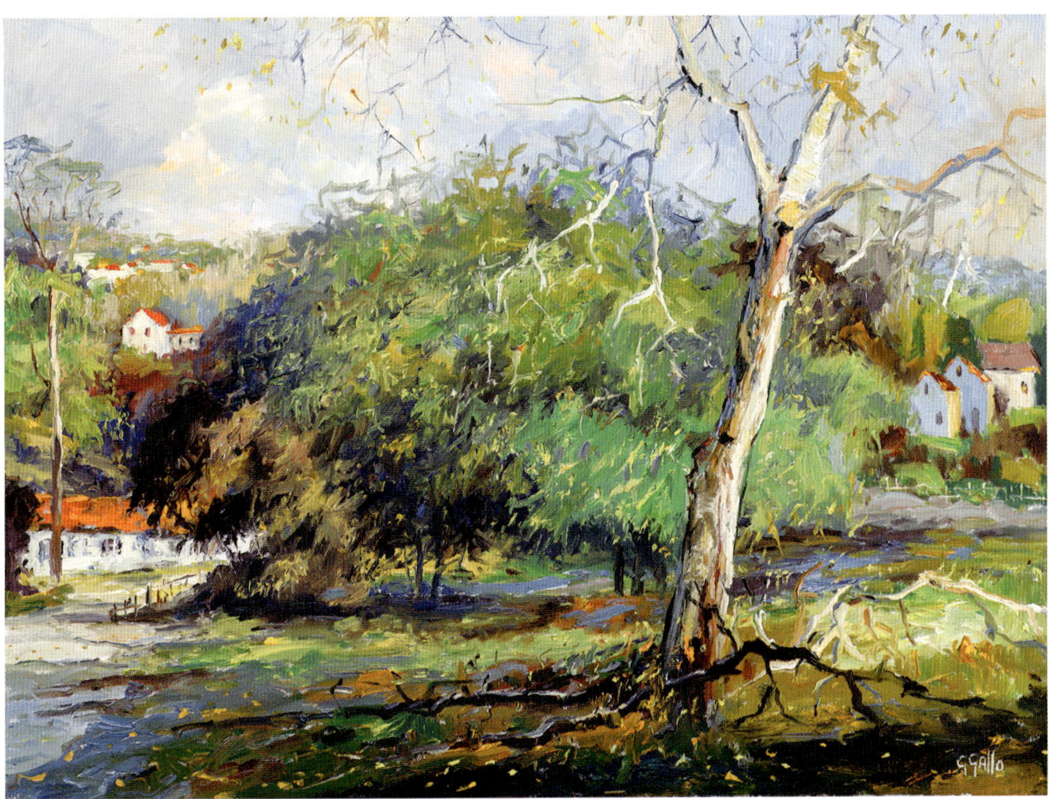

TOPANGA CANYON · Oil on Canvas · 36" × 48" (91cm × 122cm)

Abandon Negative Thoughts

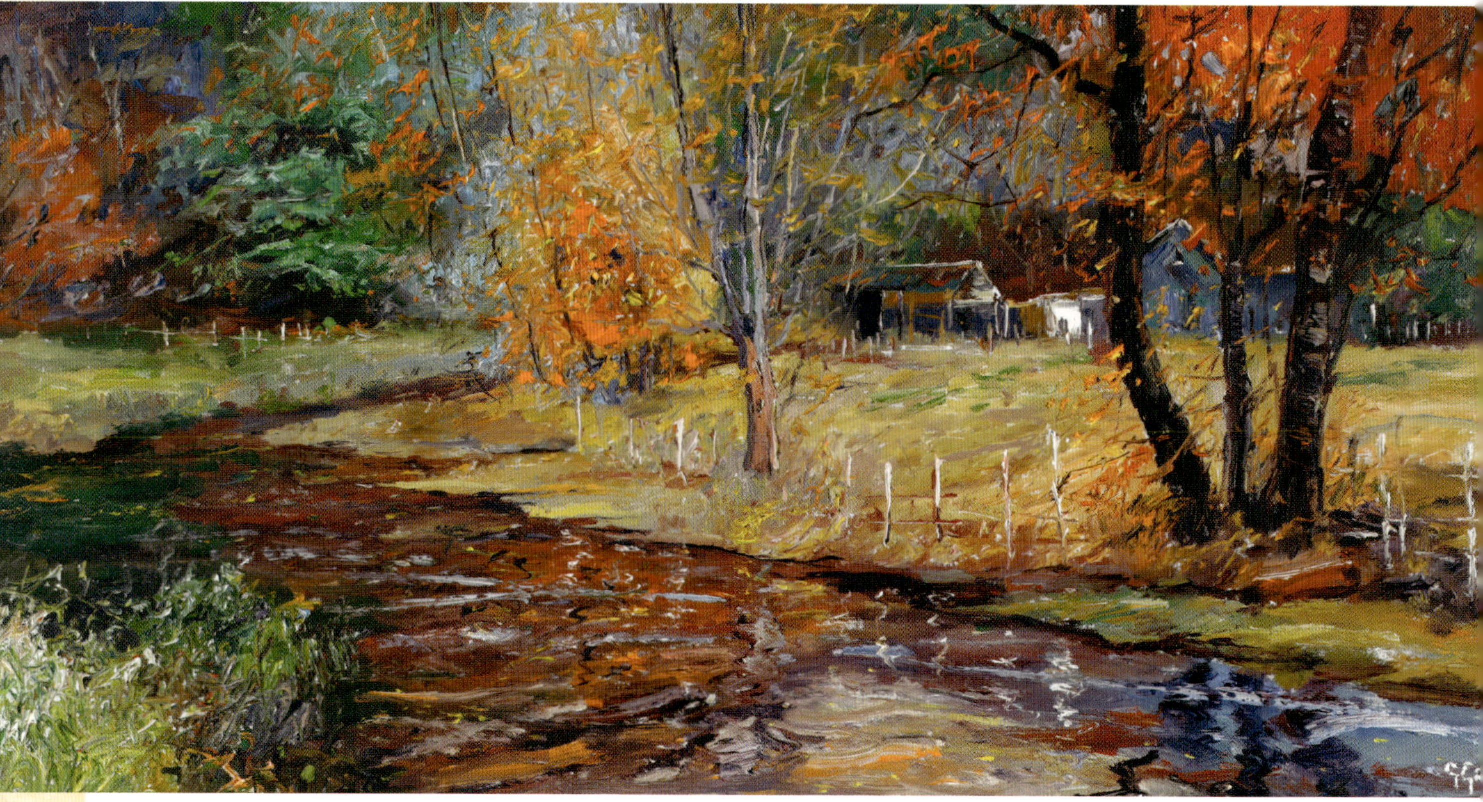

VERMONT STREAM · Oil on Canvas · 24" x 48" (61cm x 122cm)

For years I have wondered why human beings seem more apt to embrace negative thinking than positive thinking. I have come to the conclusion that it is not a flaw in our characters. It is nothing more than an emotional comfort zone we get into in order to avoid growing as artists. Growing takes responsibility. As we get better at painting—and also as individuals—we have to redefine ourselves in the process, seeing ourselves in a new and more positive light.

I used to think I was nervous when I was about to work on a painting outdoors. After a lot of self-examination, I came to the conclusion that I was misreading my feelings. I was, in fact, excited, not nervous. The two feelings can sometimes feel nearly identical. If you feel that shaky rush of emotion that can happen as you work, it might be a good idea to redefine it as excitement, harness it and put that into your work.

People forget that painting should be fun. Critics love the idea of the tortured artist who lives in a world of self-doubt, a loner desperately seeking something just beyond his grasp and killing himself to get there.

Although this is terrific drama, it has little to do with the reality of painting. I am not saying that it shouldn't be taken seriously. I have spent decades trying to get to my own personal truths about what is good art and what is bad art. What I am getting at is that I don't believe you can paint beauty (if that is your goal) and see things through the eyes of a child if you are beating up on yourself while you work.

The fun—and I do mean fun—of all of the Impressionists is that their work is full of freedom and abandon. It's the primary reason we are drawn to it. It speaks not only a truth about what is beautiful but asks us to see the world in a more joyful way. It is nothing short of a celebration. If you are going to be part of that celebration, I advise you to enjoy the party as you work. Loosen up, enjoy yourself, swing your arm around as you paint! Put your feelings into the strokes.

If you have a strong start in mind, you can create your painting with confidence. Try not to get so caught up in the result. You're not walking a tightrope, where a bad day at the office could kill you. You're painting a painting. If you mess up, there's always tomorrow and hopefully you will have learned something from your mistakes.

I hear from students things like, "I can't paint trees." Or, "I can't paint water." This isn't helpful at all. I promise you if you can't paint a tree, it's because you've convinced yourself you can't. What you need to do is study trees. See their movement. How they reach for the sky. How they are rooted in the earth. How they don't encroach on each other's space. Understand them. Grab a sketchbook. Draw them whenever you get a chance. Trees, like water (and everything else, for that matter), are nothing more than shapes, colors and values.

There is another kind of negative thinking that artists suffer from. As we work, we begin to become more proficient in the way we paint and tackle our subjects. Sometimes as it becomes easier for us, we suddenly doubt that the work is good because we aren't suffering through it the way we used to. This is also folly. What we should strive to do is get to a place where the act of creating a painting becomes effortless.

On good days it should be as effortless as other things we've been doing for years such as speaking, walking or driving a car. Don't diminish the work if it becomes less difficult. Embrace it and give yourself new challenges.

The idea is to let go and react freely to what you are seeing and experiencing. Then put it all down. You, of course, need to be proficient in knowing your craft and how your materials work, but just as important, you need to learn to trust that you will get more control by letting go rather than holding on tightly. Abandon all negative thinking. It doesn't serve you. See things in a positive light. Trust that you can do the things you want to and jump in. Like everything else in life, if you work at it, you'll get there.

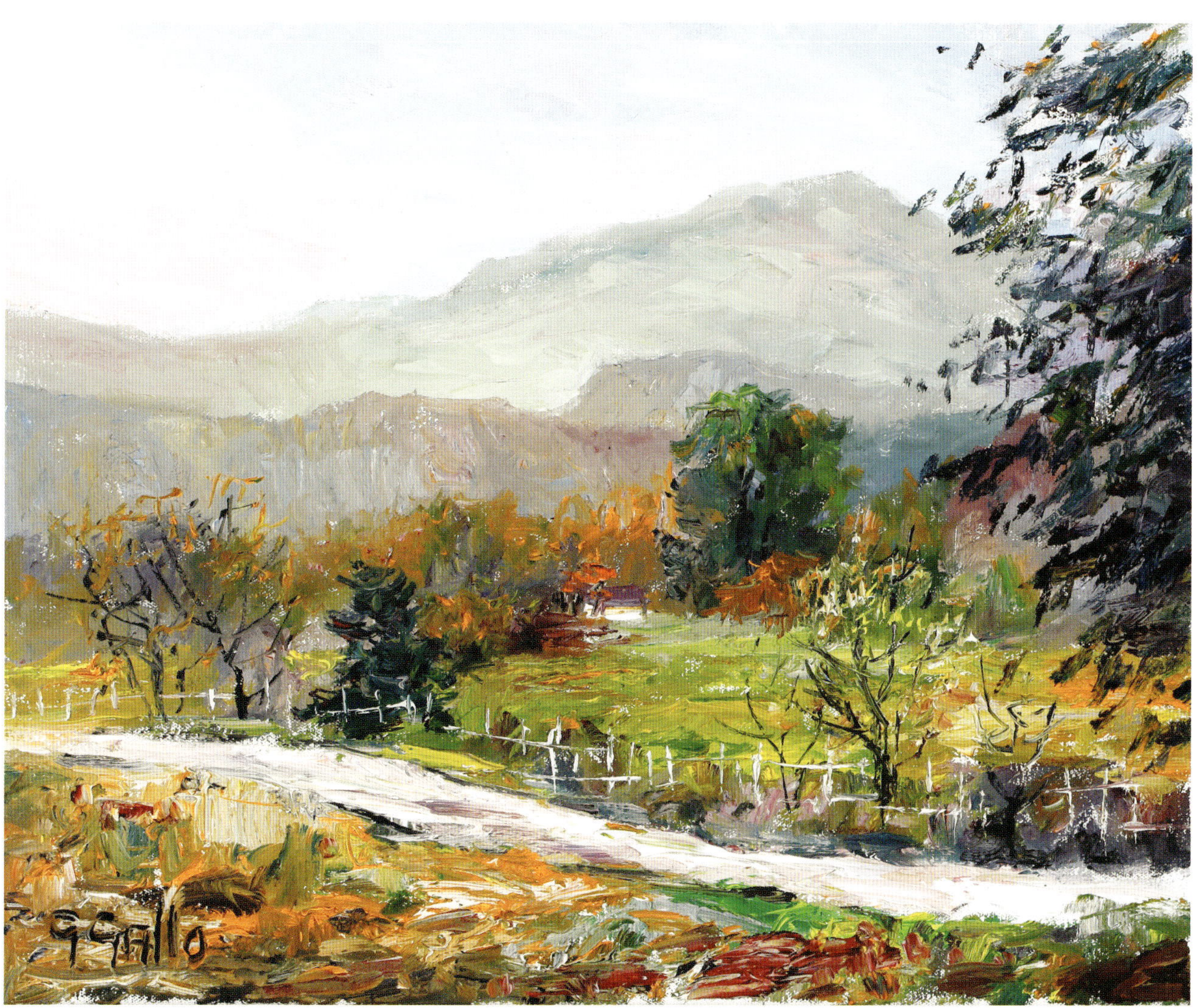

OLD ROAD, LAS VIRGENES CANYON ·   Oil on Canvas ·   18" × 24" (46cm × 61cm)

Take Yourself Out of the Process

One of the main reasons I advocate letting go as you work is that you will create without ego. Ego is about showing off your skills, and that is, without a doubt, the death of anything creative. Your ability to draw and paint should be harnessed to freely express yourself concerning what you are seeing and feeling about those images around you. It should not be a means to itself. Try to remove the idea that the work is about you. It isn't. Painting is an act of giving, not taking. If you remember anything, remember this: Creating a terrific painting should be the by-product of your enjoyable and wonderful experience in the field. We've all had those great moments when as we worked, time elapsed, and suddenly we found ourselves working happily, almost in a trance. Then, after stepping back, we find that we're pleasantly surprised at how good the work is, not even certain where it came from. This is the state in which we do our best work. We've let go and surrendered to the work without ego or judgment. The more often we can get to this place, the better.

There is little in Impressionist landscape painting that could be considered a massive feat of technical draftsmanship. You are merely laying down luscious dabs of paint to simulate the effects of light on objects. Your daily signature requires more deftness and a steadier hand. You sign your name without thinking because it has become second nature and it's uniquely yours. This is what you need to do as you paint. I am not saying that thinking is not a part of the process. I do a great deal of thinking as I work. Much of my thinking is done up front so I can work with abandon later. This is akin to jazz. Jazz musicians freely improvise, not knowing what note they will play next, but they decide up front what song they are playing before they improvise.

As you remove yourself from the process of painting, you will find that you have surrendered to some inner voice that will guide you. Trust that voice. It's like a muscle. The more you use it, the stronger it will get. I am sure you will find some artists who will disagree with this philosophy. I implore you not to listen to them. There are many painters, even successful ones, who are stuck in a world of formulas, who believe that rigid control is the only way to create good work. Rigidity in any aspect of life is counterproductive, and painting is no different. Have you ever watched a great chef at work? They work with the speed and grace of ninjas. They work rapidly and skillfully. They may taste their food as they go and add spice the same way we as painters pause and add an edge or a highlight. But they move quickly. This is not an idea I invented. It actually goes back to several painters I admire.

Emile Gruppe, one of the most outstanding landscape painters of his time, worked rapidly because he felt it was the best way to stick to the essentials of a scene. Edward Redfield, perhaps the painter I'm most influenced by,

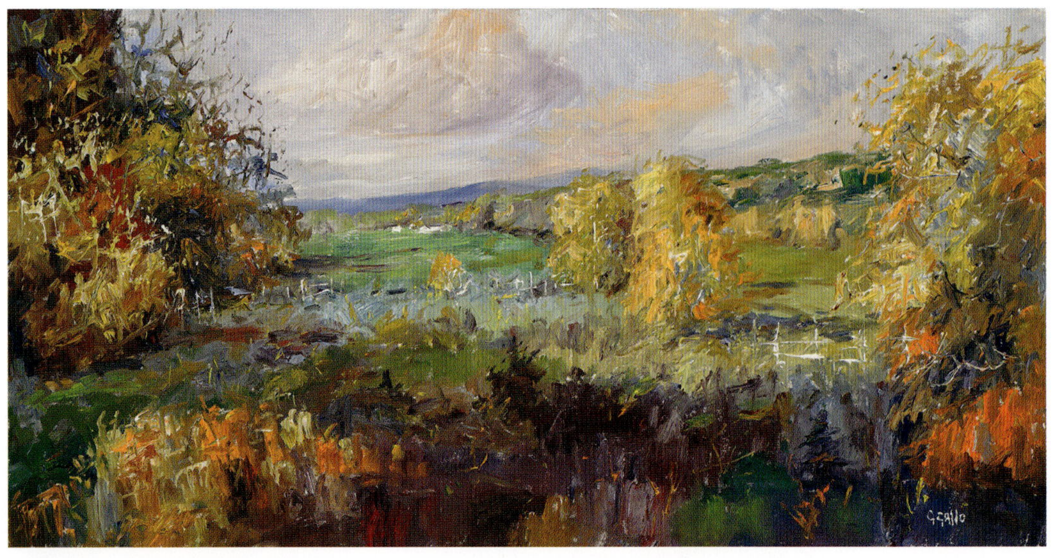

NORTHERN NEW MEXICO AUTUMN · Oil on Canvas · 24" × 48" (61cm × 122cm)

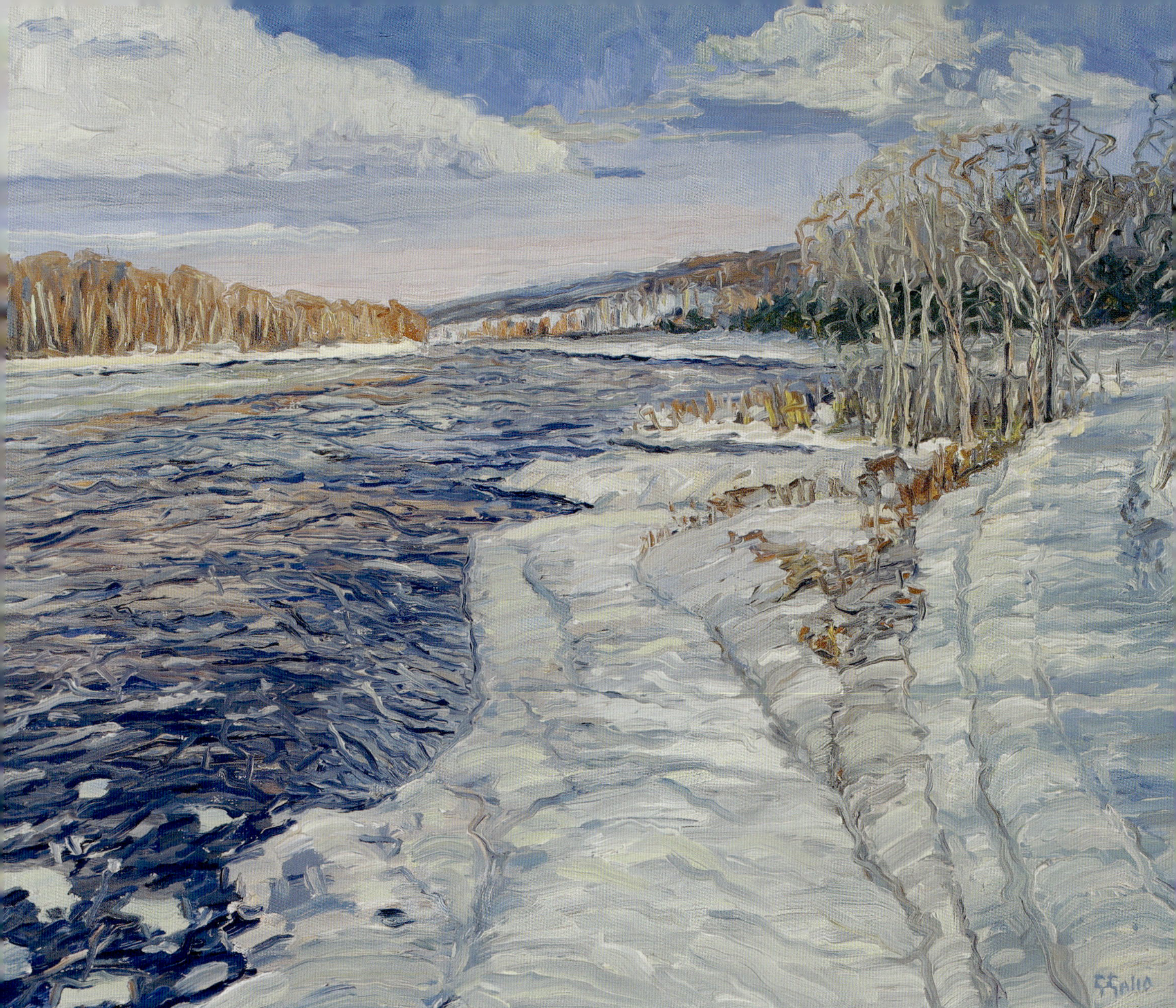

THE RIVER IN WINTER · Oil on Canvas · 21" × 26" (53cm × 66cm)
This painting won the Art for the Parks Top 100 Award in 1991.

believed painting was a performance. As a result he worked on massive canvases outdoors, racing against the light and shadows, which were forever changing. In doing so he had to let go completely, trust what he was doing and, as a result, he discovered new ways to put down what he saw. Working in this manner is thrilling because it's performing without a net. As you continue to paint for the rest of your life, you will do consistently better and more personal work. Working in this manner will keep you fresh and forever on your toes. If don't know enough about your materials and the technical aspects of painting to cut loose, you may be right. So let's discuss what you'll need to paint in the field and learn some great tips on composition, value and color to help unleash your inner artist.

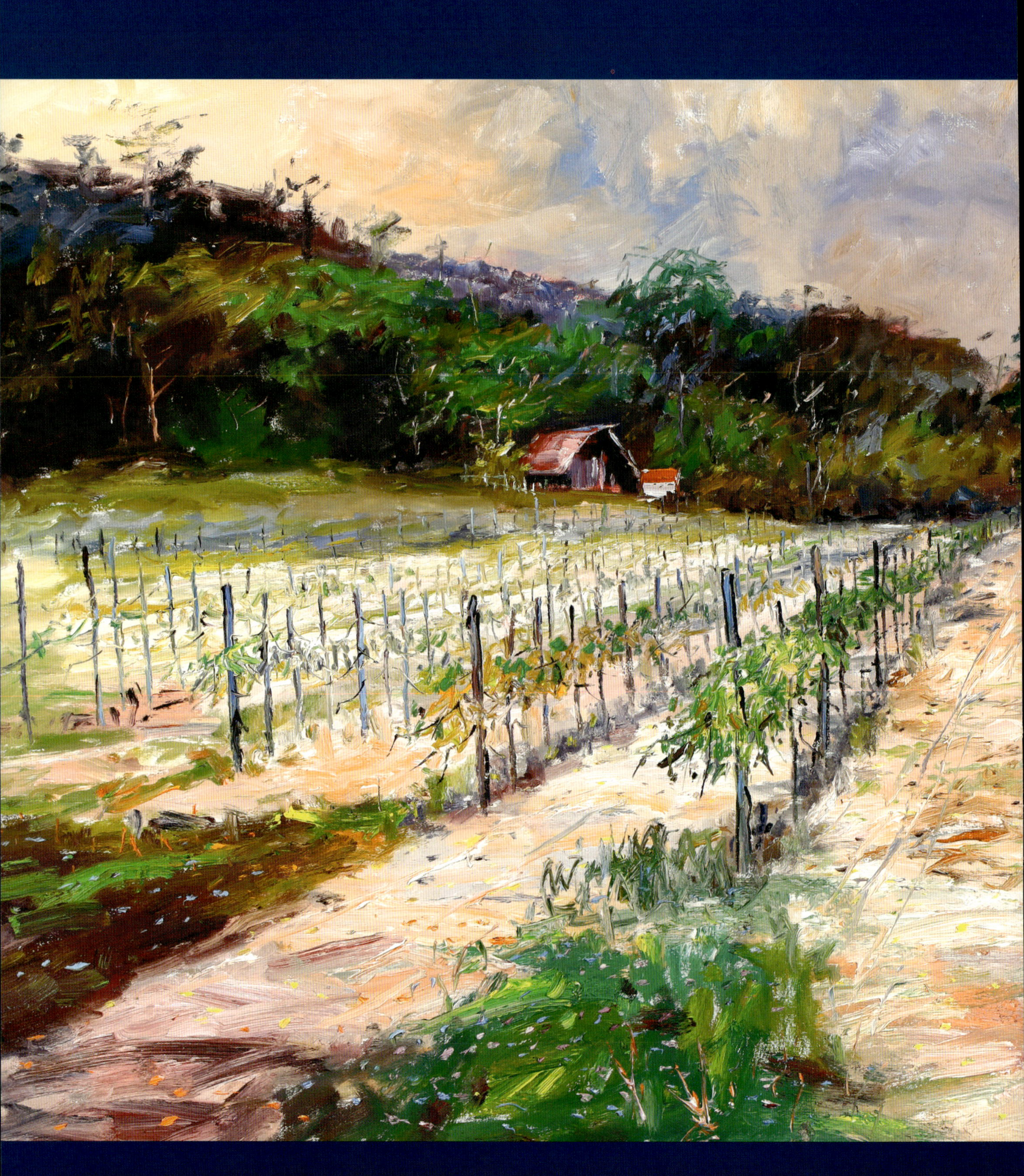

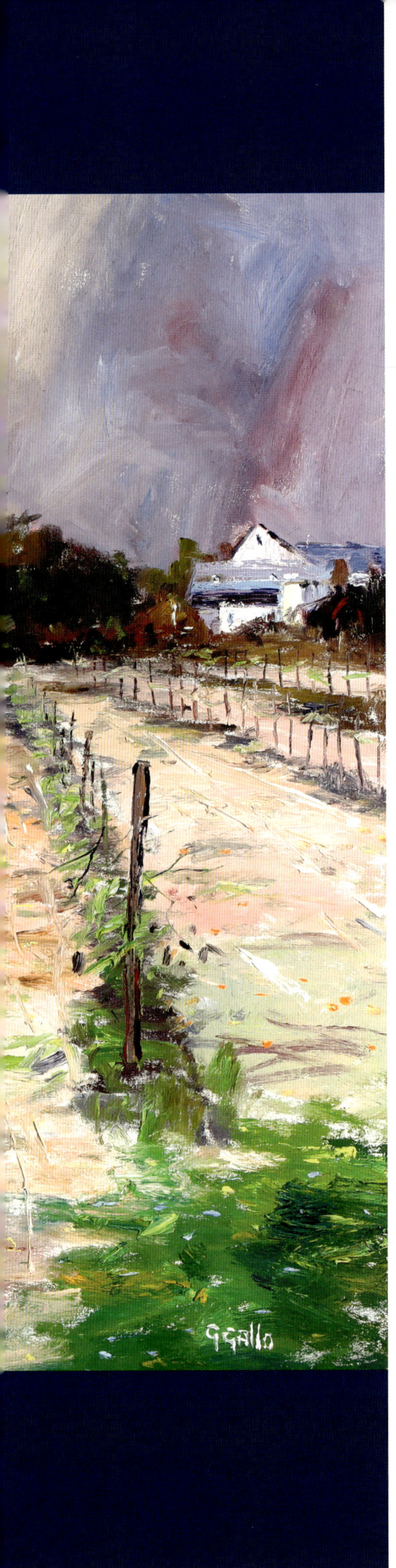

CHAPTER 2

DESIGN BASICS

We've all made ourselves dizzy looking all around and in every direction while outdoors, trying to figure out what to paint. Settling on a subject is the first step in considering design. What to leave in or take out in interpreting what we see before us is another aspect of design. Nature is wonderful, but she throws everything she has at us. It is the artist's job to discern what is necessary and what is not. Let's discuss the various ways to compose paintings and to see nature through the discerning eye of an artist.

Design or composition is the placement of shapes on your canvas. It starts when you choose your subject and build a composition around it so you can begin to tell the story you want to tell. A forest is not a subject. A large oak tree catching light while the other trees are in shadows is a subject. Design is about picking something specific, making it the focal point and letting everything else be of secondary importance. You cannot and should not paint every tree, every cloud or every wave with equal interest. Otherwise the viewer will be confused because everything will be fighting for equal attention.

JUDY'S VINEYARD · Oil on Canvas · 36" × 48" (91cm × 122cm)

Why Design Is Important

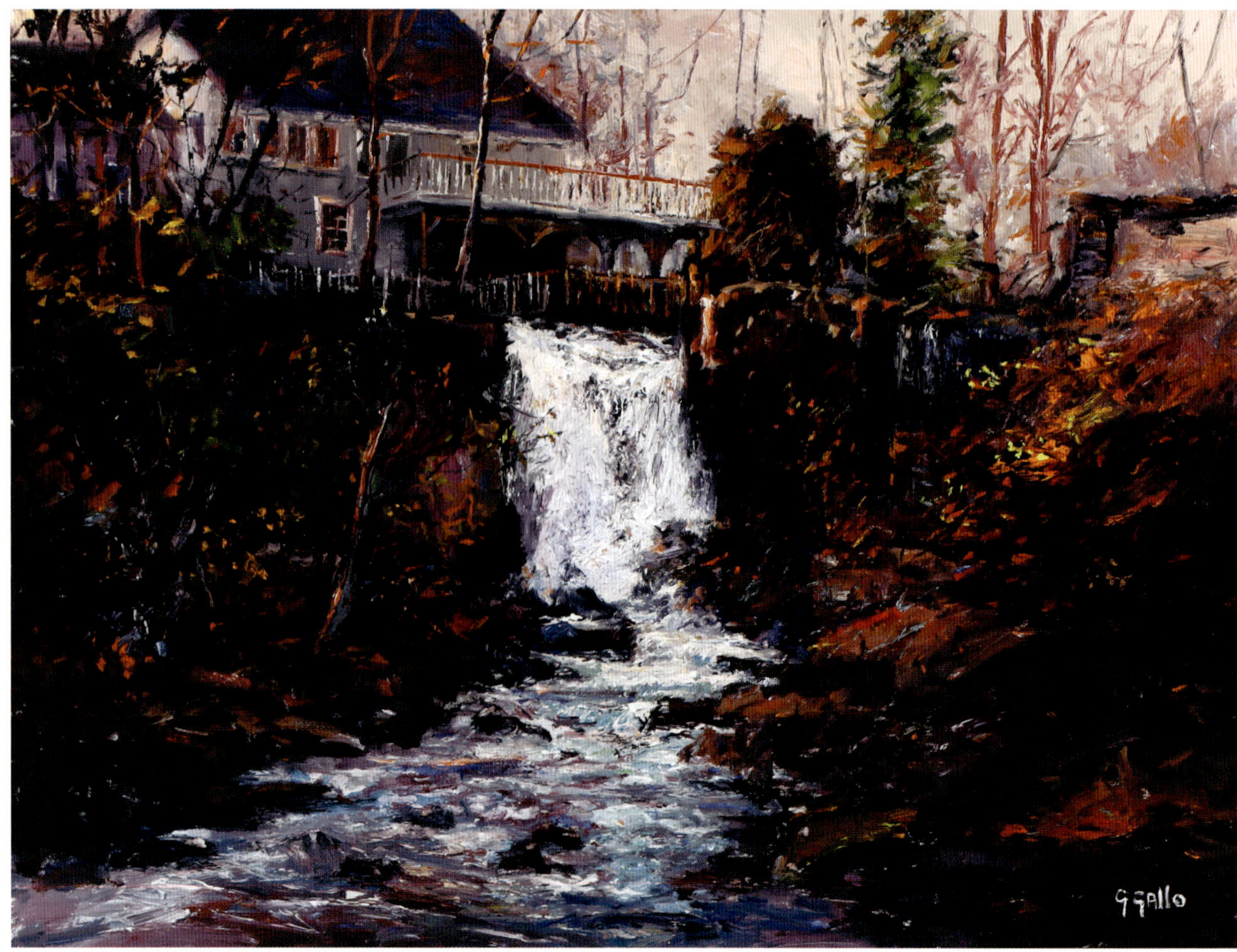

NEW PRESTON FALLS · Oil on Canvas · 36" × 48" (91cm × 122cm)

Design is the single most important element in painting. It's the first thing that grabs you and ultimately it is what will continue to hold you. The reason is simple. Design is the element that has to work from across the room in order to draw you in. Color alone won't do it. Nor will drawing or value. Only design will. Abstract paintings are entirely about design. The reason some of them work better than others is the placement of shapes. We've all seen well-composed paintings that looked good from a distance. Then as we move closer, we see that they lack something in value, color or drawing. But remember, it was the design that drew us in. A beautifully rendered painting with great drawing and color but poor design will never hold our interest for long. The design has to be strong, enticing and simple. It is the spine on which everything else you add will hang.

Design also has to inform the viewer as to what the painting is all about. Many times when I come upon a place I wish to paint, I ask myself first, *What do I want to say about this place? What feelings does it bring up in me?* Does this place appear spacious? Cozy? Does it bring up feelings of loneliness? Is it chaotic? Settling? Unsettling? And so forth. Then I ask myself, *How do I best design my canvas to express the thoughts and emotions I wish to convey?* After I arrive at a clear design, I must then choose a canvas with proportions that will further help my design choices. For instance, if the scene before me begs to be expressed in terms of vastness, a canvas with less height and more width is recommended. If intimacy needs to be expressed, it would be done better in a square format. These are just general thoughts, though, and not hard, fast rules.

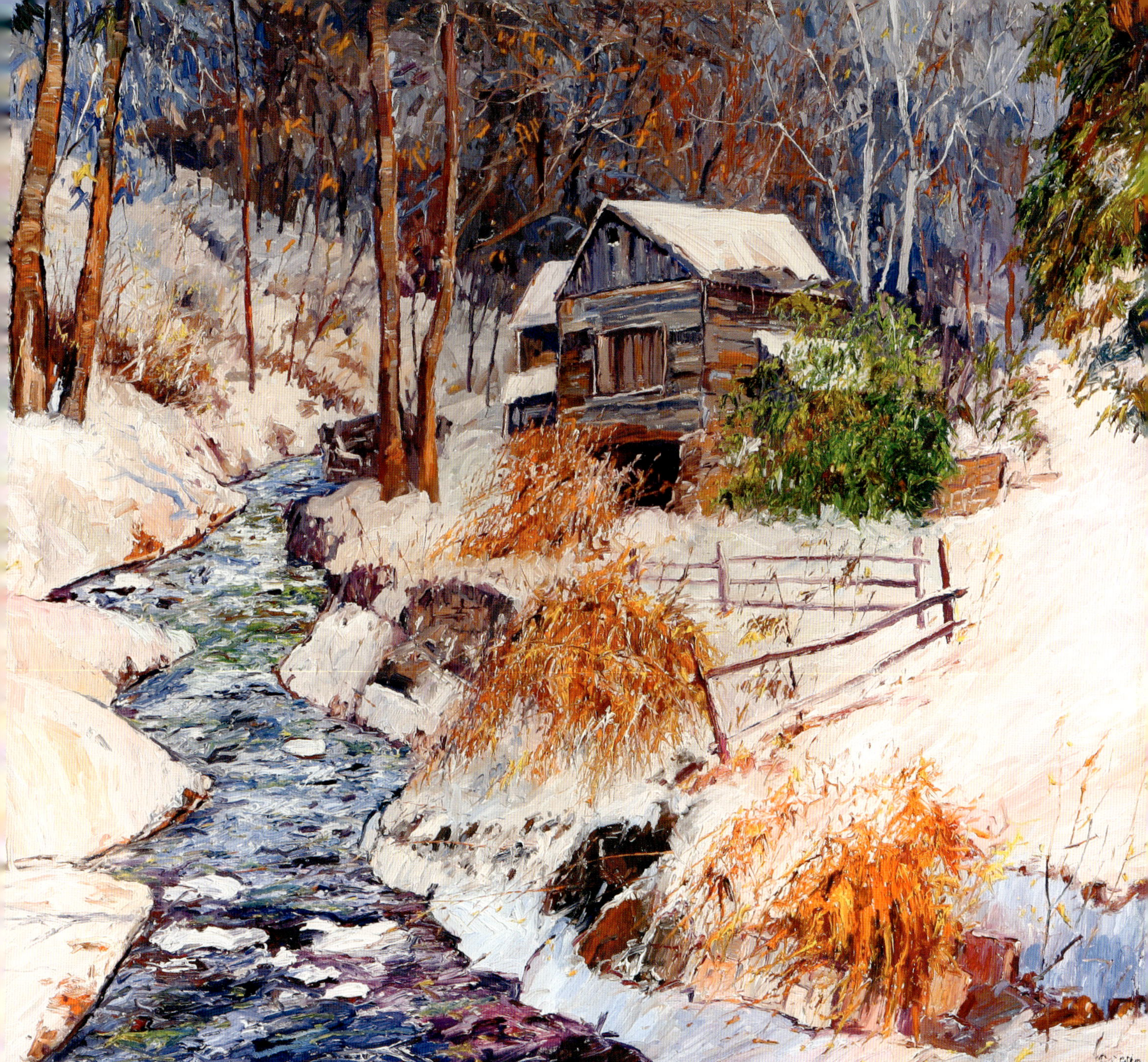

DIRECTING THE EYE

The creek, which is widest at the bottom, leads your eye through the painting and up to the farmhouse. The fence leads your eye back down toward the creek, creating a circular pattern.

CUTTALOSSA CREEK IN WINTER
Oil on Canvas · 50" × 56" (127cm × 142cm)

Line, Value and Color

What is good design? It is, first and foremost, the clearest way to state what you want to say. It is usually built around a subject or some kind of center of interest. That center of interest can be whatever you want it to be, from a tree in the forest to a creek with a romantic and interesting vanishing point. It can be a group of dark rocks against the dappled light of the ocean. Whatever it is, you must choose it and then build the rest of your composition to support it. The center of interest, or focal point, is the star of your painting and everything else is the supporting cast. For example, if you're making a painting about the sky, make the sky your star by making your horizon line low. The opposite is true if your painting is more about the land. Then the sky would be the support, not the star.

There has been a trend in the last thirty years or so to create paintings with very obvious focal points by, for example, blasting light into one small area while other areas remain grayed out. Although this can be highly effective (and I've been known to use this device from time to time), it is a bit of a trick. My biggest concern with this approach is that once the viewer gets past the razzle-dazzle, there is little left to enjoy in the painting because it doesn't keep you coming back for more. It's also a substitute for thinking and seeing because it reduces the landscape to a formulaic approach. I advise you to look for new ways to paint nature and all of her glory. I also ask you to look at the works of the Old Masters. They had hot spots in their work as well, but they didn't clobber you over the head with them.

Paintings are made or broken from the onset. Design is akin to the structure of a building. If it isn't strong, it will come apart quickly. Here we will discuss not only the placing and arrangement of shapes but also the placement of value, color and line, which are all essential ingredients in the creation of strong design.

LINE

Design can be about a series of lines that lead you merrily through a piece. Imagine the shape of a tree line that leads to a group of rocks. The line then takes you down to a foreground shadow that takes you back across the painting and to another tree whose branches lead you through the painting again. These invisible lines join the various objects in a painting and lead the viewer's eye in order to create one cohesive statement.

Keep in mind that you have to decide what is of primary importance in your piece. If you paint everything with the same importance, then nothing ends up being important. Look at any of the great portraits by the Old Masters. One eye is always a bit more rendered than the other so they don't fight for attention.

Edward Redfield and Daniel Garber, two of the Pennsylvania Impressionists, painted works that were extremely strong in terms of design. They created heroic compositions with many pictorial elements, such as mountains, clouds, rivers, farms and figures, all on one canvas. These paintings are all joined together by a wonderful series of lines that connect the various objects. They also hit their edges hard, even using lines that are not in nature to separate the various objects. This has become a no-no as of late; today's landscape painters seem more attracted to the idea of making edges romantic or soft.

I am personally not so militant about using lines to express edges when creating a landscape painting. I am attracted to very strong design and have absolutely no desire to make my work look like a photograph. The larger, more heroic canvases I mentioned generally have stronger lines and dynamic compositions because they have to work from a great distance due to their larger size.

In life, objects meet in space before our visual plane. Artists refer to these meetings as "edges." A tree line against the sky is an edge. A sharp rock in front of soft grass is another edge. Where the cloud meets the sky is an edge.

While there may not be lines in nature, there certainly are lines in art. Many artists begin their sketching with lines. I have a tendency to start that way because I like strong composition, and a great way to set the rhythm of a design is to use expressive line work. This is a concept that was used by the Old Masters, who created canvases with very strong design. They thought in very abstract terms of triangles, squares and circles before they put down their subject matter.

As you work out your composition, look for lines and shapes. Are they hard? Jagged? Angular? Or are they curvy? Soft? Sinuous? Different lines say different things. In general terms, a curved soft line will say something gentle, whereas a sharp decisive line will say something severe. In most cases you wouldn't render the edge of a cloud and the edge of a knife in the same manner. Are the lines and shapes masculine or feminine? I often ask myself many questions when observing trees. Some look like old men with angular lines, others like young women with beautiful curves. Trees, just like streams, clouds, rocks or whatever else we see, seem to have certain attitudes. Use descriptive lines to express your observations of these attitudes. Allow these observations to lead you to design your canvases with strong forethought and conviction. Do your best to spot them and use them to express yourself clearly.

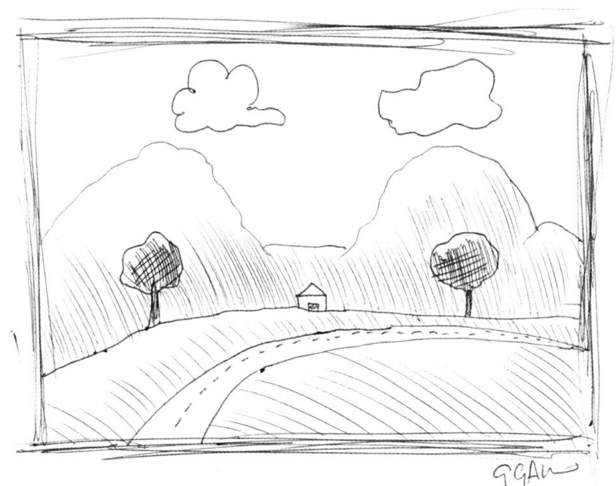

WEAK DIRECTIONAL LINES
You'll notice here most of the lines lead your eye out of the painting. The edges of the mountains slant downward at the edges of the sketch. The road also leads your eye out rather than in.

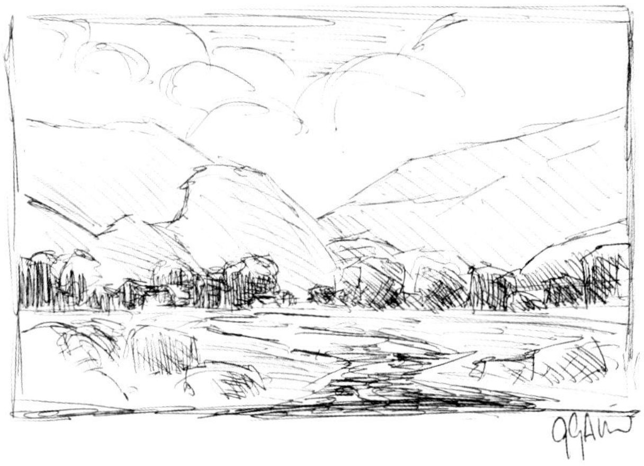

STRONG DIRECTIONAL LINES
In this sketch the lines lead into the painting. The mountains, clouds, stream and treeline all take you toward the center of the sketch.

VALUE

It is also a very good idea to see your overall design in black and white. Ask yourself where the big, dark masses are. Where are the light areas and masses? A good way to discern this is to squint at the landscape in front of you. Don't see objects as objects. Merely see them as abstract shapes, either falling into the light, mid-range or dark category. Find ways to connect the shapes. Imagine the mass of a tree and its shadow connecting to another large foreground shadow from a cloud overhead. These connective darks will unify the composition. The same thing goes for the light areas. Find ways to connect those areas, too, so that the design is cohesive and not spotty. Your eye will continue to move throughout the design.

Trees, just like streams, clouds, rocks or whatever we look at, seem to have certain attitudes. Look for them and allow these observations to lead you to design your canvases with strong forethought and conviction. Do your best to spot them and use them to express yourself clearly.

Part of making a strong design is figuring out where to place your lightest values. Values are how something would look if it were in black and white. Generally, you want to put your lightest value just off-center in your composition because this should also be the focal point, or main subject, of your painting. The viewer's eye will instantly be drawn to the lightest value on your canvas. If you can find a way to place your lightest value and darkest value alongside each other, that will create contrast and will hold the viewer's interest even longer.

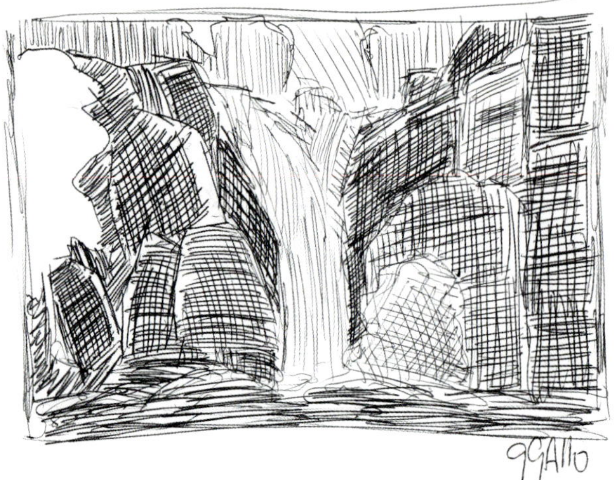

VALUES PLACED INCORRECTLY
The brightest thing in this quick crosshatched sketch of a waterfall is the mass that hugs the left side of the frame. In a painting this would be a mistake as it would draw your eye to the left edge rather than the center.

VALUES PLACED CORRECTLY
In this sketch your eye goes to the waterfall because it is the brightest thing in the sketch. This keeps the viewer's eye where it should be, which is on the center of interest.

COLOR

Another important element of design is the placement of color. I always think of big, abstract color spots when designing a canvas. To just see a canvas in terms of shape without color is not taking full advantage of a powerful aspect of design. A big, beautiful spring-green tree next to a wonderful broken-down red barn in orange afternoon light with purple shadows informs me of all kinds of great color design possibilities. It's essential to think of the interplay of your three secondary colors: green, purple and orange. Working all of this out ahead of time in terms of design ensures a greater rate of success.

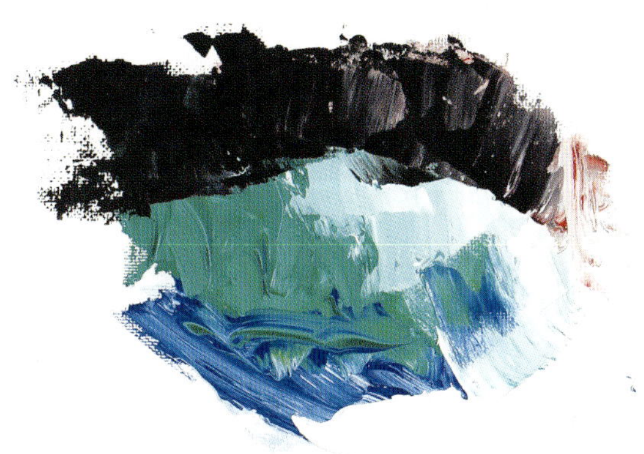

DULL COLOR COMBINATIONS
Although such combinations of colors are interesting, their interactions do not give the feeling of warms and cools. Painting a landscape with combinations such as these would lead to a dull affair.

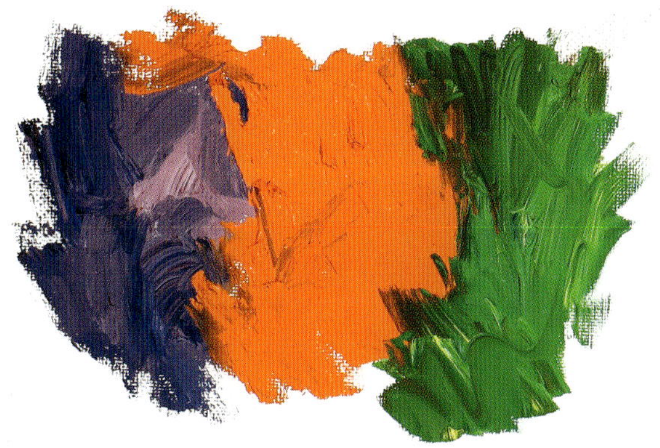

LIVELY COLOR COMBINATIONS
The three secondary colors—purple, orange and green—not only complement each other, they create a feeling of warms and cools. Using these colors together is essential to get your painting to vibrate.

Composition Notes

I suggest you get in the habit of designing things even when you're not painting. When you have free time, look at the things around you. Imagine them with many different design possibilities.

Get out your sketchbook and draw things you see in your backyard. Move them around in ways you find pleasing. You'll begin to see a pattern emerge, and as a result, you will develop your own personal sense of design.

Lastly, there are old axioms like, "Three objects are better than two" and "Five is better than four." Another one is "Don't paint things that have equal distance between them." For example, if you paint a group of trees that have equal distance between them, they will end up looking like telephone poles. I don't always bother with these so-called rules. The reason I don't is that some very inventive artists have come along and created some terrific, dynamic work by doing exactly what these rules say not to do. Look at the paintings you admire and study how their compositions work and flow. You'll be on your way to having a better understanding of good design.

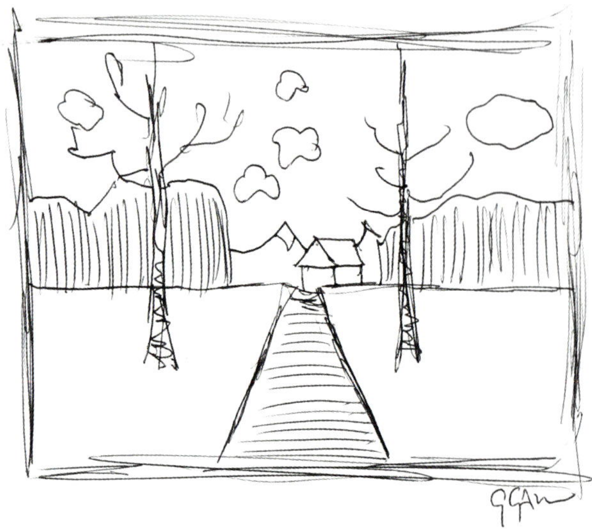

WEAK DESIGN

A road, a mountain, a house and two trees: This is the way a child might render these objects. Everything is centered and symmetrical. The trees on both sides are of equal shape and distance. The road moves up the center of the design and is also perfectly centered. The result is spotty and uninteresting.

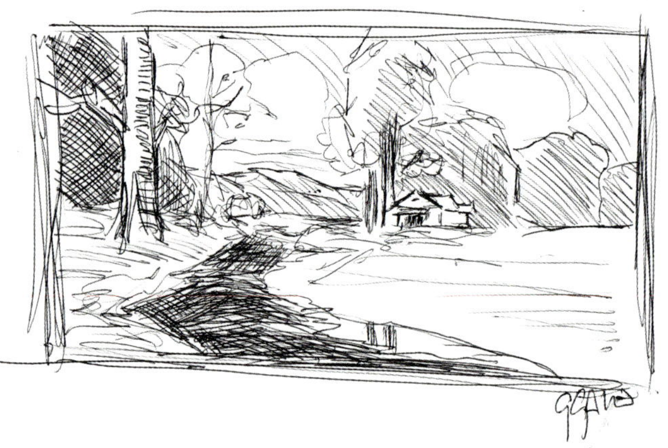

STRONG DESIGN

In this example everything is off center. The road curves into the design and vanishes in the distance. There's one strong tree on the left and a grouping of trees on the right. The tree lines are uneven, the way they would appear in real life. The house is off center. The lines in this piece are more interesting.

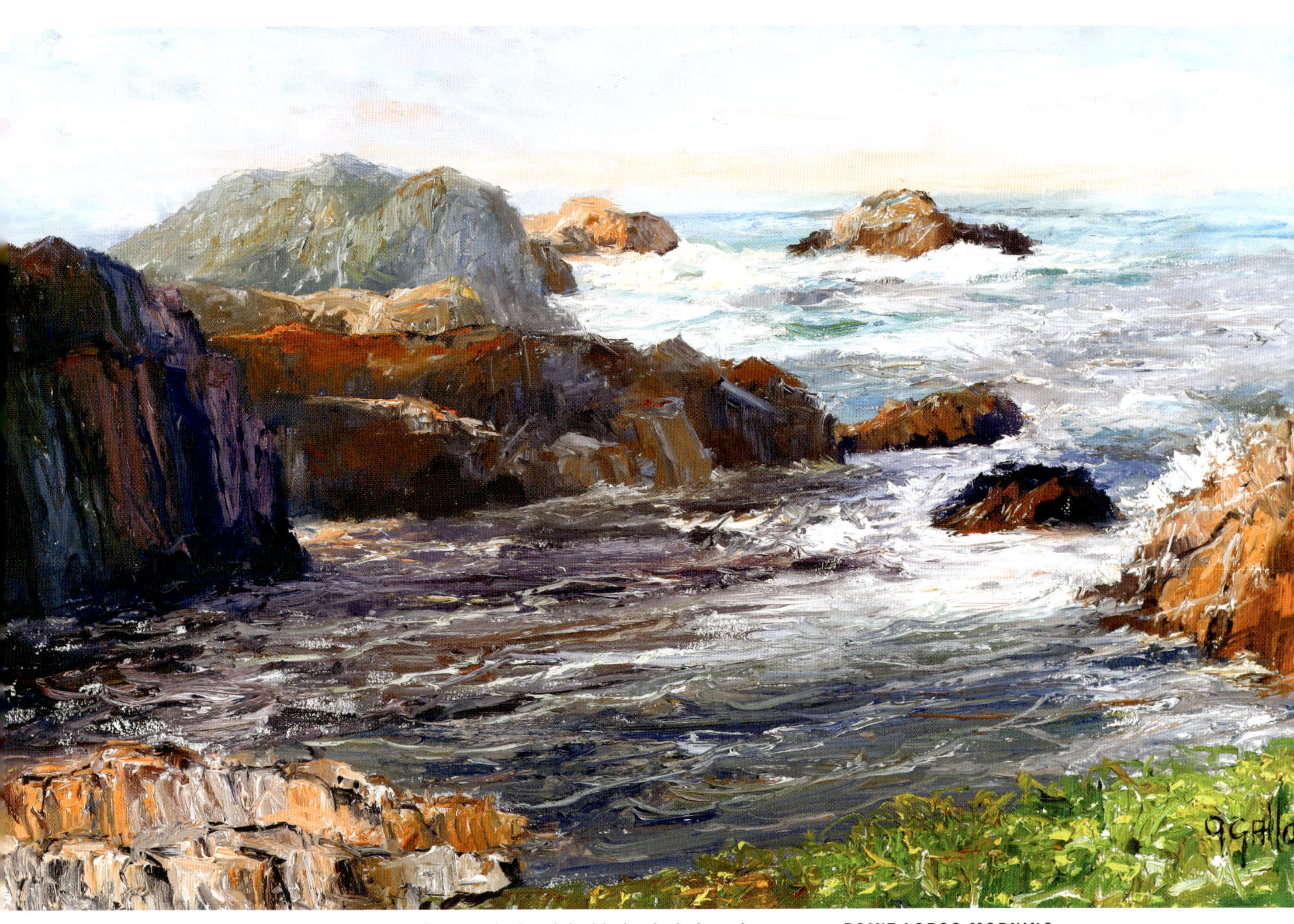

Point Lobos Morning is a good example of strong design. I decided to include a piece of foreground that features grass and wildflowers. I did it for two important reasons. If I didn't, the viewer would feel as if they were floating in space; the foreground element gives the viewer an understanding of where I was positioned. Equally important, I chose to add the foreground element to represent the yellow wildflowers growing everywhere because yellow is the first color to lose its vibrancy in regard to atmospheric perspective. Those few bright splashes of yellow instantly throw the rest of the painting into the background and create an illusion of distance between foreground and background.

POINT LOBOS MORNING
Oil on Canvas · 30" × 48" (76cm × 122cm)

In this painting I wanted to play up the height of the trees in the foreground. I created a design that not only uses the height of the canvas more than the width but also has the trees growing right out of the top of the composition. Had they just kissed the top of the canvas, you'd never get the feeling of their real height. Remember, everything in painting is relative in terms of design. The trees look tall compared to a background hillside, which is much lower. The trees tower over the mill, which is placed fairly low in the design. The horizon line is on the bottom quarter of the canvas, which helps further dramatize the height of the trees.

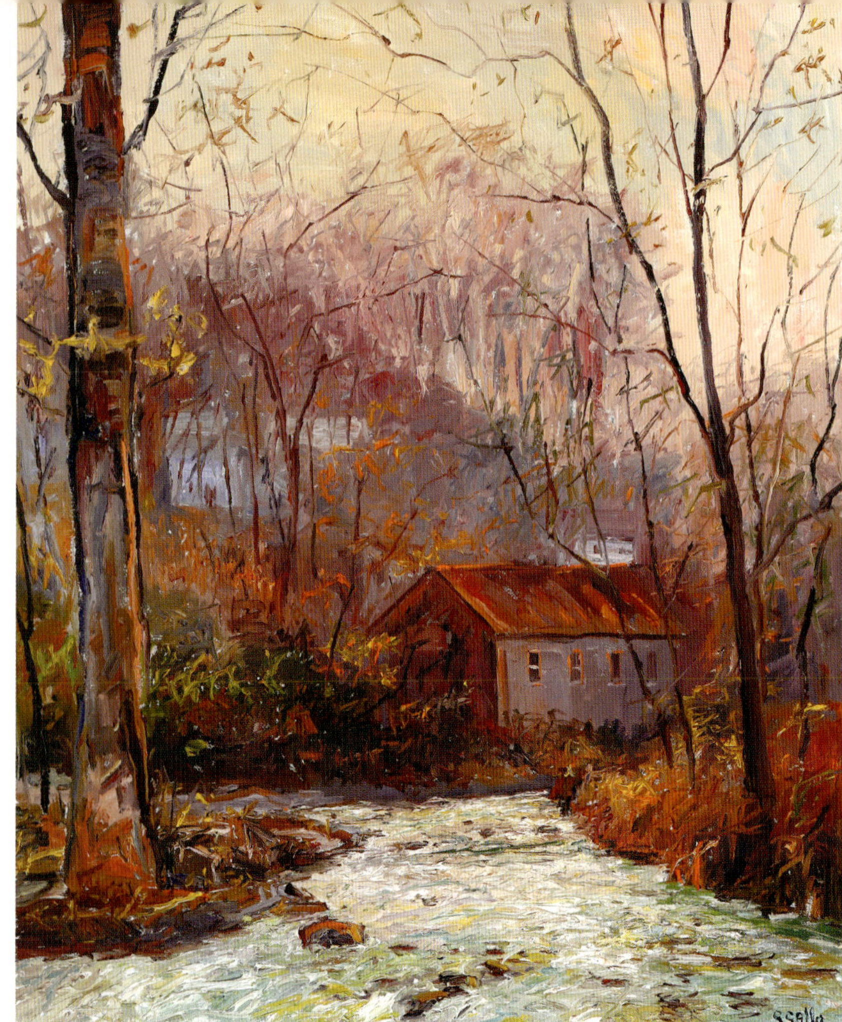

MILL STREAM · Oil on Canvas · 42" × 30" (107cm × 76cm)

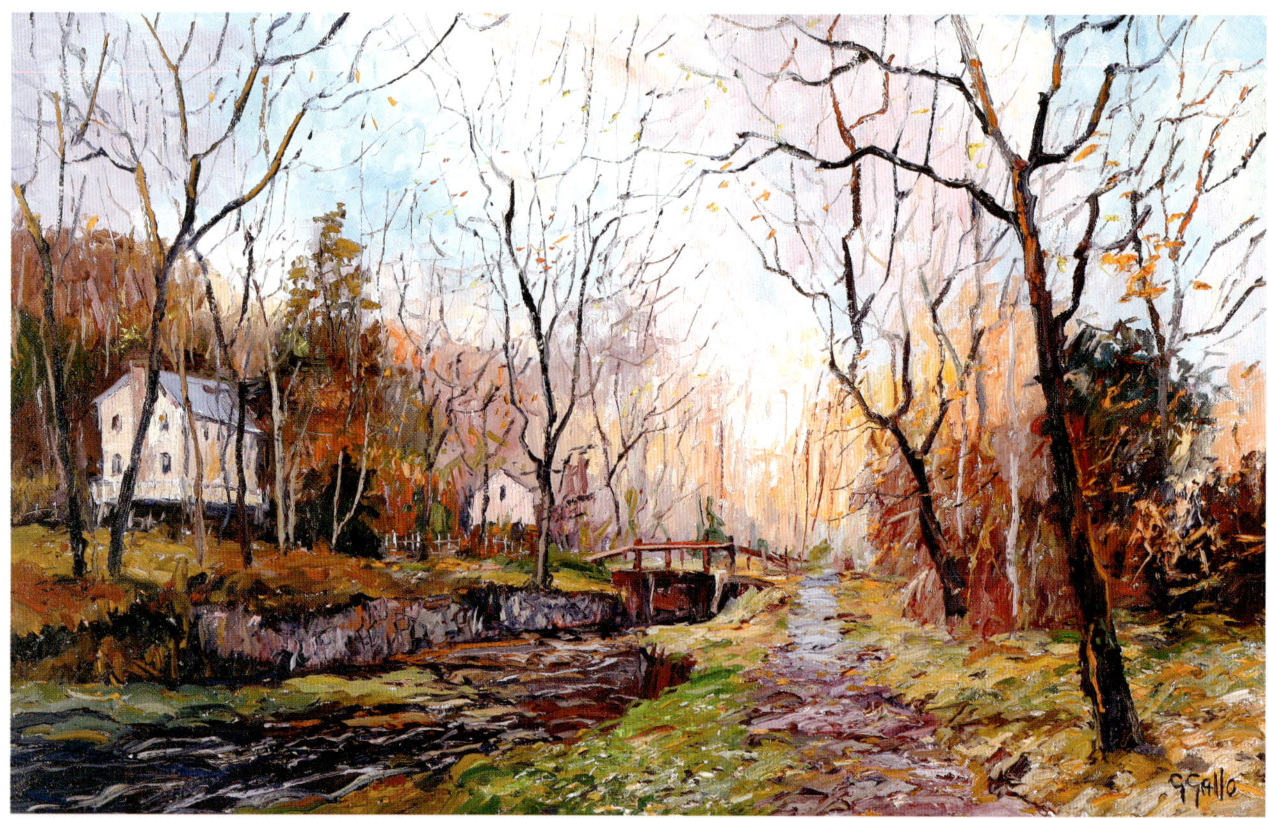

EARLY EVENING BUCKS COUNTY · Oil on Canvas · 30" × 48" (76cm × 122cm)

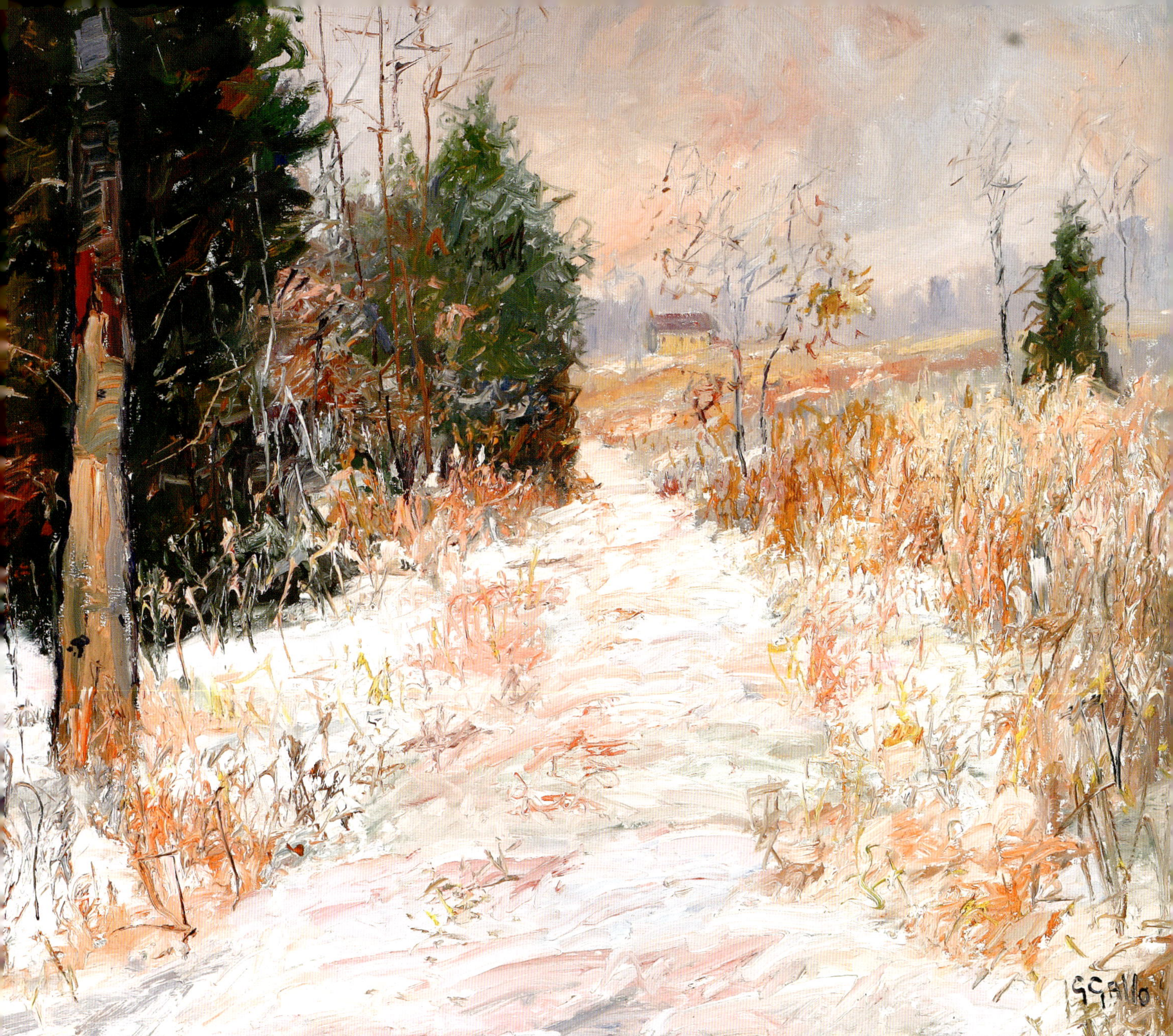

WINTER PATH · Oil on Canvas · 30" × 36" (76cm × 91cm)

Because of the subject matter, this is a gentler composition. I widened the road at the bottom of the canvas to help pull the viewer's eye in. I then raised the road higher than it was in reality to create a feeling of moving uphill. The road vanishes around a corner, creating a sense of mystery. In an abstract sense, the design of the piece is about repeating patterns of triangles. The shape of the road echoes the shape of the evergreen trees. The small V-shaped tree in the middle distance is practically an inverted triangle.

◄ Here, even though I used a more horizontal canvas than in *Mill Stream*, the design is similar. Your eye wanders up the path to the bridge and then back down the bank and stream. The trees appear massive compared to the houses, and the viewer instantly has references for comparison. Once again the trees grow right out of the top of the painting, playing up their immense size.

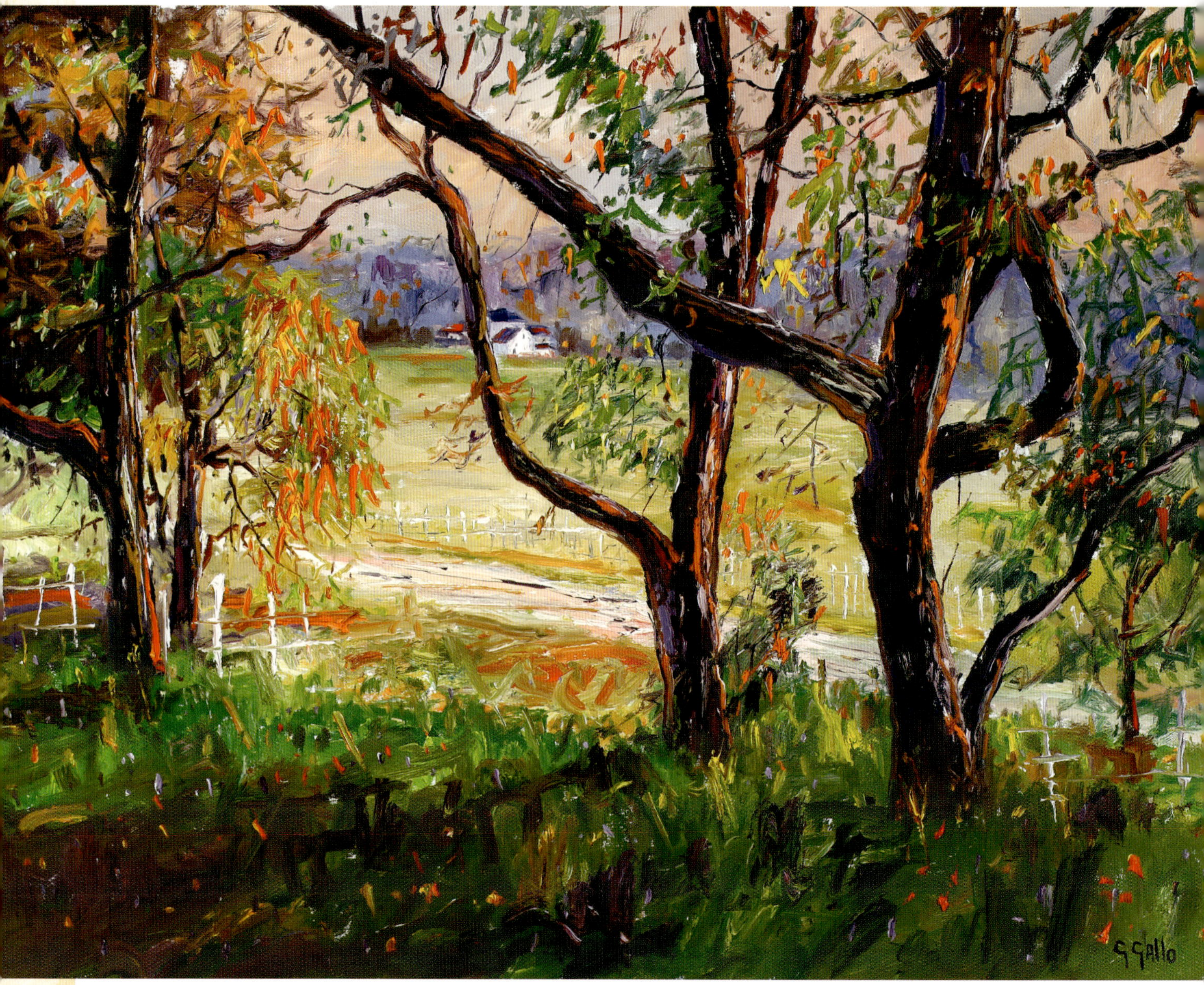

This painting is a study of horizontal and vertical lines. The trees are strong dark verticals against the gentler horizontal lines of the distant hillside, horizon and road. I added a slope to the hillside so the horizontal lines weren't too redundant and the slope would echo the curves of the main branches of the trees on the right. I grouped the trees on the left together to make them play as a unit. Had I not created that unit, the design would have fallen apart by becoming too even and spotty. I took the liberty of adding distant farmhouses to the design. In reality, they were much farther to my left, but I felt the background needed a place of interest.

SONOMA COUNTY TREES
Oil on Canvas · 36" × 48" (91cm × 122cm)

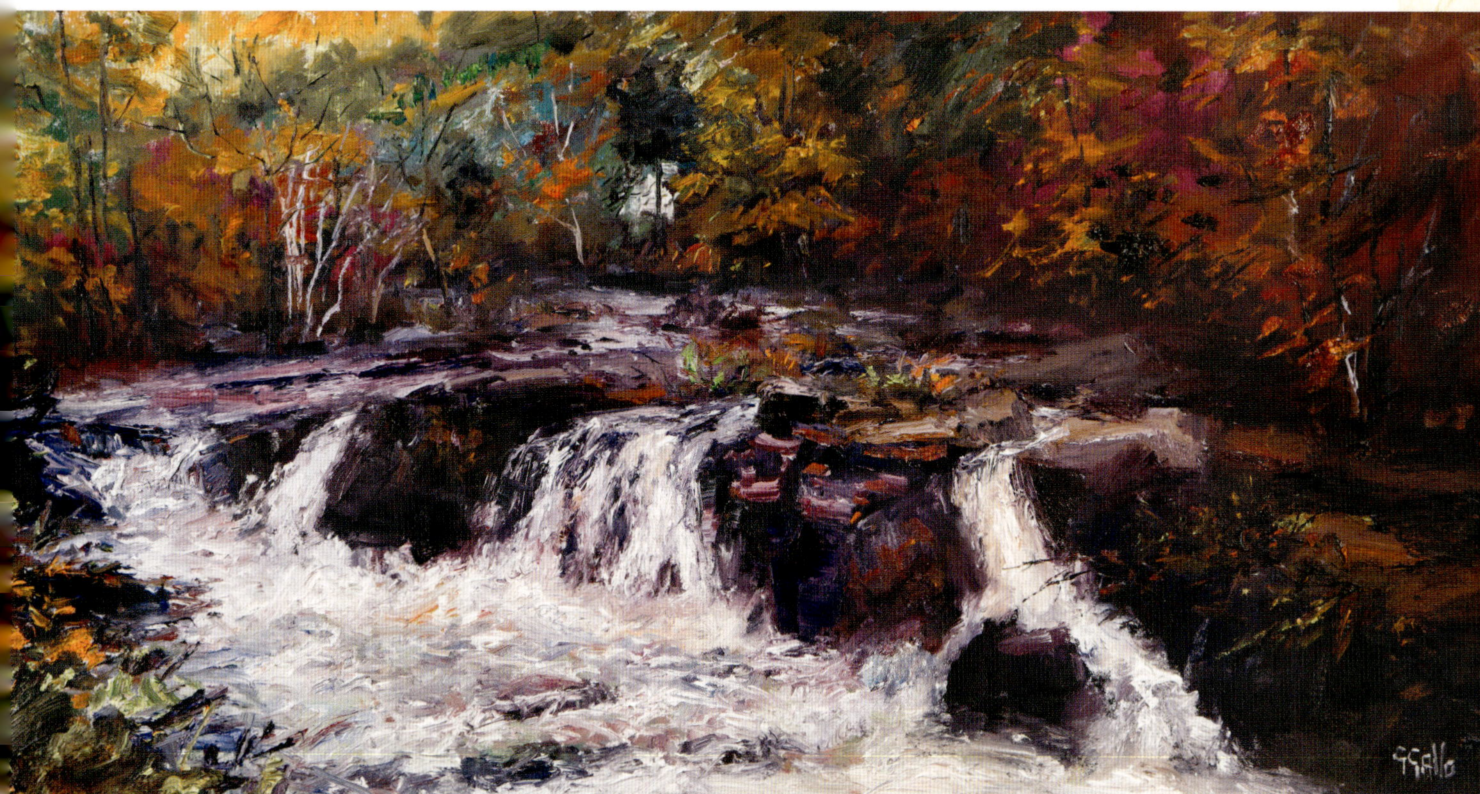

Design is not just about the placement of objects. It is also about the placement of lights and darks. In this painting the dark rocks move downward, from left to right. They connect to a dark mass on the right and back through the top third of the painting with another dark mass. I simplified these masses to keep the design unified. The lights (water) and darks (rocks and shadows) all connect to create a pleasing design of darks and lights that are interconnected. Had I not done that, the painting would have become spotty, and your eye wouldn't know what to look at. Here your eye moves gracefully through the piece because of all the connections.

UPSTATE FALLS · Oil on Canvas · 20" × 40" (51cm × 102cm)

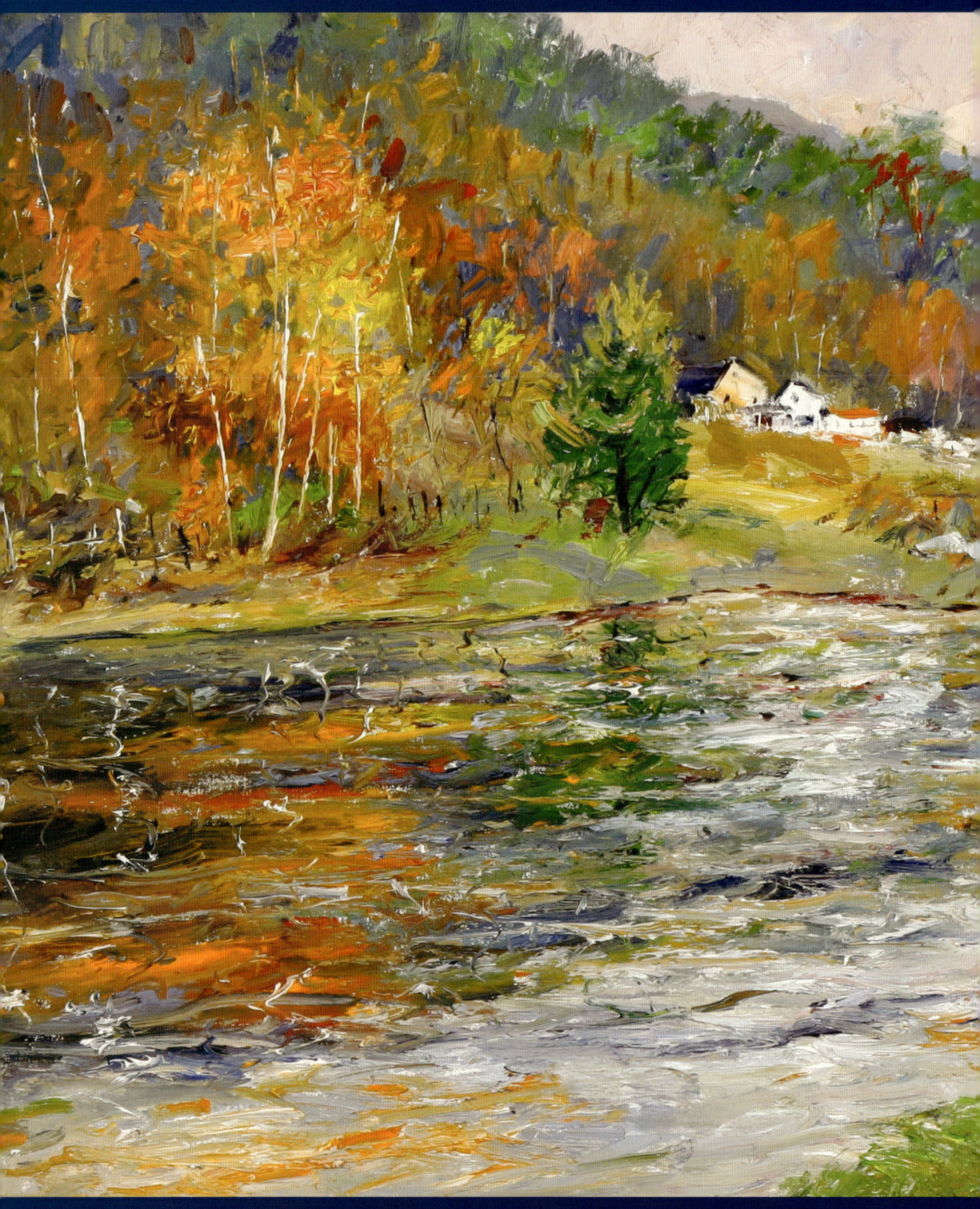

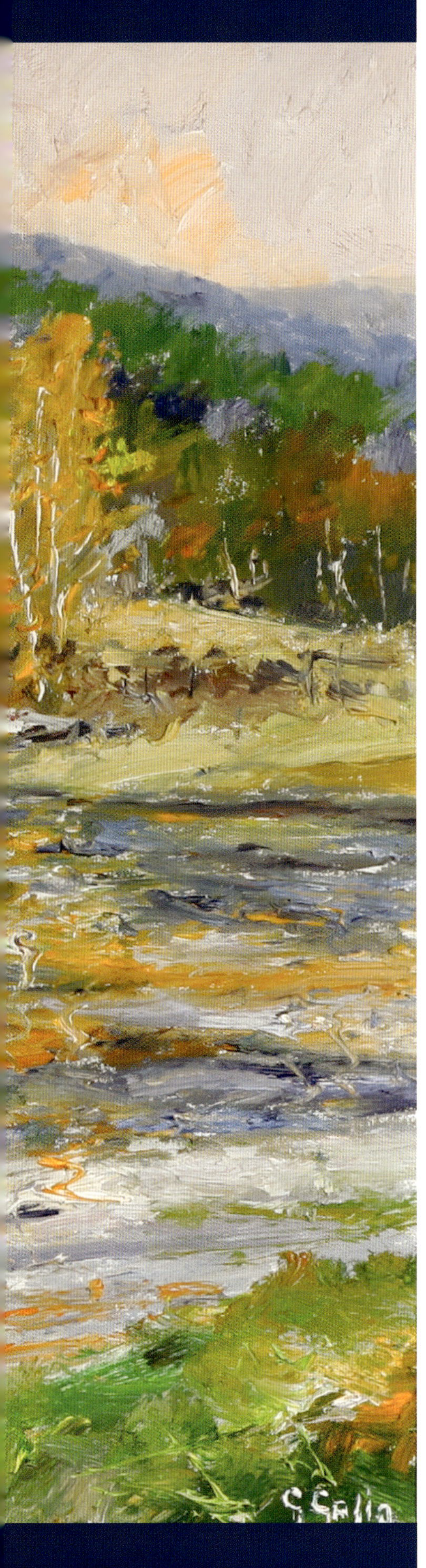

CHAPTER 3
VALUE AND COLOR

As much as I am a lover of great color, the first thing I ask myself when I observe something to paint is *What is its value*? Colors are wonderful, but if they are not the correct value or color temperature, then they are truly not beautiful at all in the context of painting. It is the truthful and harmonious relationship of colors that creates beauty, and the way to get to that beauty is to correctly gauge the value of the colors. Don't assume anything when painting. Don't assume the sky is blue, the clouds white or the grass green. Forget everything you think you know about the color of things. Look at each object in front of you as if you were seeing it for the first time. Then, and only then, using fresh powers of observation, will you see true values and colors.

Many times we make the mistake of thinking something is lighter in value just because it is warm. The same is true of shadows. Sometimes because they are cooler, we mistakenly see them as darker. That is not always the case. Again, don't assume anything. Gauge your values and colors by comparing them to what is alongside them. Get your values right, your color temperatures right, and I promise you you'll be well on your way to doing beautiful work.

CONNECTICUT YANKEE AUTUMN · Oil on Canvas · 24" × 30" (61cm × 76cm)

Value

Value is the second most important thing to get right when painting. Some people think color is more important, but that is a fallacy. People respond to colorful paintings only if the values are correct and interplaying beautifully together. Put too much intense color in a painting and watch how people cringe. So for this reason alone, remember, values are more important.

WHAT ARE VALUES?

Values are how things would look if everything were in black and white. Although there are countless values in nature, we don't need to work with more than nine. There are great artists, like John Singer Sargent, who worked with only five. Values can be daunting to grasp, especially for students, but you must grasp them and master them if you wish to do convincing work.

HOW VALUES WORK

Values happen outdoors for three basic reasons:

- The type of day it is. Is it cloudy or sunny? The sun creates strong contrasts and therefore a wide variety of values. A gray day, as a general rule, narrows the value range.
- Are the objects before you in light or shadow? This is perhaps the most important question you can ask yourself when determining value.
- Is the object close to you or far away? Things have a tendency to lighten as they recede. In terms of color, they also have a tendency to cool and gray as they get farther away.

HOW TO SEE VALUES

At first it's not easy to see values. We are so conditioned to being distracted by all the details we see in front of us that we almost refuse to eliminate them. But we must eliminate the details we see at first in order to properly gauge the values before us.

DON'T WORRY

A great tip to help you understand values, especially when working outdoors, is to squint. Look at the scene before you and close your eyes just a little. Figure out what is the darkest dark and also the lightest light. As you squint some more, you'll be able to see less and less. As you almost close your eyes completely, you will see only the brightest value left. Once you've established this, you can start to go to work.

None of the elements of painting—design, value and color—are mutually exclusive. They all work hand in hand. But it is important to separate them in your mind in order to combine them when you need to. Once you figure out what the values in your painting are, use them in your design.

Learn to See in the Abstract

Much of painting is learning to see things in the abstract. This means that you shouldn't see the things before you as objects but simply as masses of shapes with value, color and line. Once you can do this it'll be much easier to correctly gauge one value versus another. After you've established the value of an object, the next consideration is figuring out what its color temperature is. Is it warm or cool? Many times something can be the same value but one value could be warm and another cool. We'll get more into this when we deal with color.

Students respond to loosely painted paintings because of the confidence of bravura brushwork. They want to know the secret of painting in a painterly way. This is thinking backwards. It's very easy to paint in a painterly manner once you've forgotten that you are looking at trees, rocks, clouds and streams.

Everything before you is nothing more than shapes of value and color. Once you've eliminated the desire to paint every leaf and instead squint at an object to ascertain its shape, value and color, it will be much easier to put down paint simply and in a painterly manner. The viewer will see that you've painted a tree or stream because you've suggested it with such simplicity and accuracy by getting the shapes, values and colors correct. Once you begin to master values, your work will look more beautiful and will have more mood and atmosphere.

KNOWING VALUES KEEPS IT PAINTERLY
This is one of the many landscapes I did in Southern California. You'll notice that a lot of the values are close. Although the subject matter consists of a mountain, groupings of trees, a field and a path, I saw everything as shapes of value and color, and therefore I could render everything in a painterly manner.

VALUES CREATE MOOD
This is an example of an atmospheric painting in which many of the values are close, especially in the bottom half of the composition. Special care must be taken not only to get the values right but also to define them by their warmness or coolness. Without rendering these subtleties truthfully, these darker passages would be nothing more than mud.

CUTTALOSSA FARMHOUSE
Oil on Canvas · 36" × 48" (91cm × 122cm)

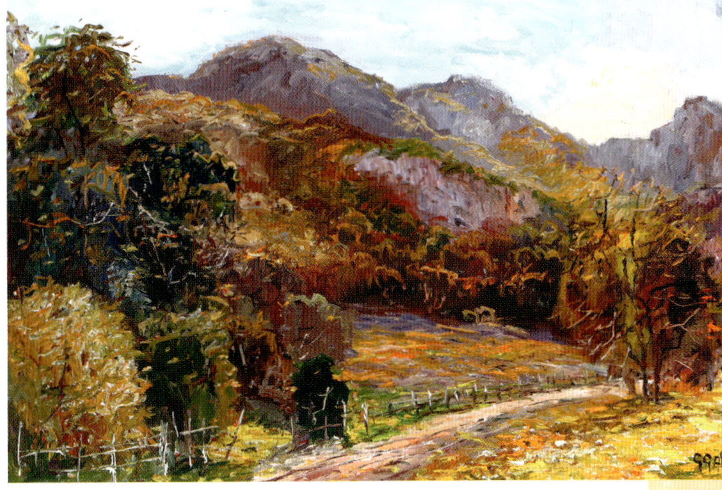

MALIBU CANYON
Oil on Canvas · 30" × 48" (76cm × 122cm)

Many Values Are Closer Than You Think

One issue students have is worrying that they're not seeing subtle differences in values because they are seeing them as too close to one another. They are actually seeing the values correctly. I paint outdoors almost exclusively and am always astonished at how close most values really are. The extreme darks and lights are easy to gauge, but students tend to stress about the ones in between. Many values in nature are nearly identical side by side. Sometimes they can only be separated by color temperature. Color temperature refers to whether a color is warm or cool. This brings color into the discussion.

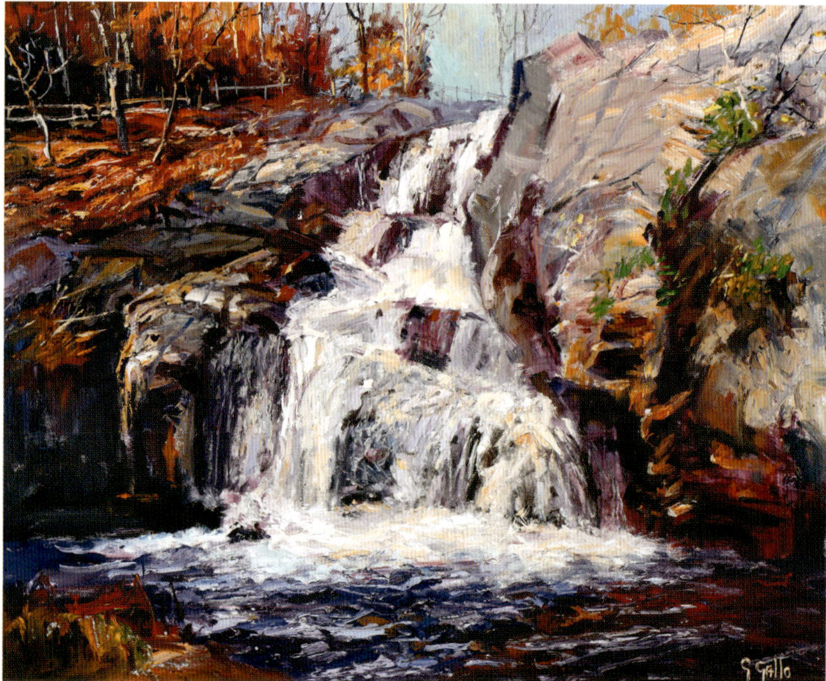

USING VALUES TO CREATE STRONG DESIGN

In this painting careful attention is given to not only the waterfall (the main subject) but also the surrounding areas. First of all, the waterfall is not just white. There are three value shifts and several color temperature changes inside the movement of the water. I also made sure to lessen some of the values surrounding the falls so they do not compete with the main subject.

CONNECTICUT FALLS
Oil on Canvas • 30" × 36" (76cm × 91cm)

SIMPLE IS BEST

This painting was rendered on a day with high overcast light. Many of the values were very close and the largely undefined edges made the piece even more fun to execute. Sometimes it's a good idea to fight the urge to add more in terms of values. The closer your values are, the more poetic the painting can become.

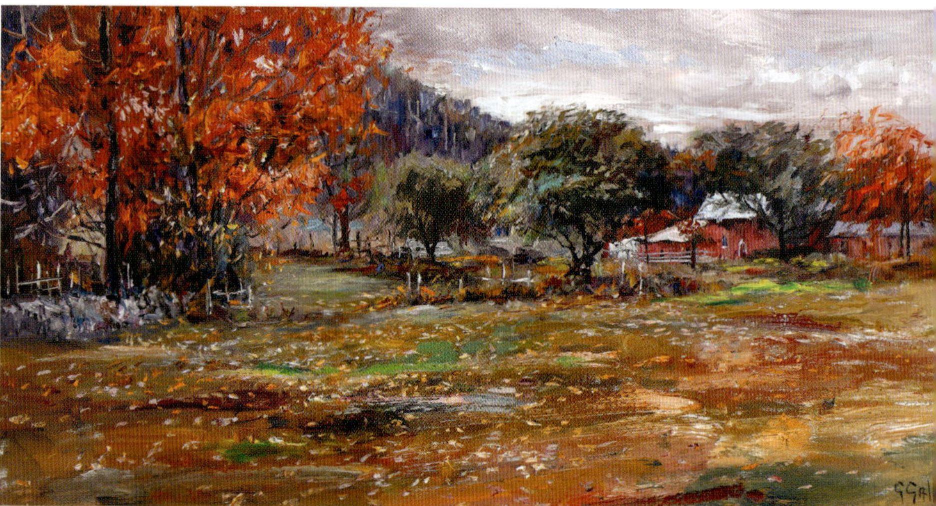

FARMHOUSES, ARLINGTON, VERMONT
Oil on Canvas • 24" × 48" (61cm × 122cm)

Comparisons and Patterns

Finding the values in nature as you work outdoors can be a lot of fun. Think of it as a challenging puzzle. It's really a lot easier than you might think, and once you grasp it, you'll love it. Whenever you're outdoors, just look at what's going on around you. You don't even have to be painting. It's a good idea and a terrific exercise to do this whenever you have free time. Pick out the darkest object or mass in your field of vision. Then figure out what is the lightest. All the other values fall in between. If you master values, the quality of your work will grow to new heights.

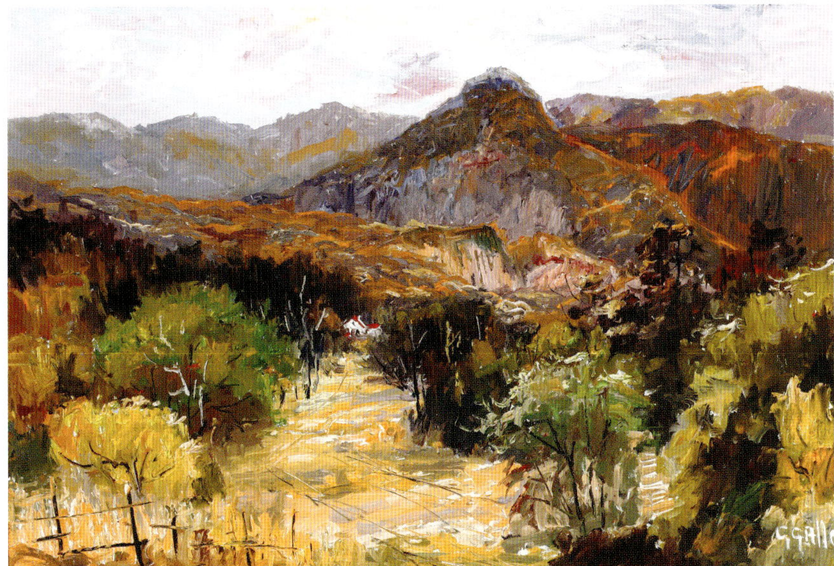

USING VALUES TO CONNECT PATTERNS
You can use values to create patterns. Here the dark tree line in the middle ground holds the entire painting together. It moves from left to right and past the midsection where it frames the lightest value in the painting, which is the small, white farmhouse. The dark patterns continue, a bit more broken up, on the right. This painting is as much about the patterns as it is about the subject matter.

MALIBU CANYON, AFTERNOON
Oil on Canvas · 24" × 36" (61cm × 91cm)

DECORATIVE USES FOR VALUES
The lighter and darker values in this painting create a wonderful abstract pattern of shapes in the houses tucked into the hillside. The even darker masses of bushes and trees also create a fun pattern against the hillside and join all of the elements together.

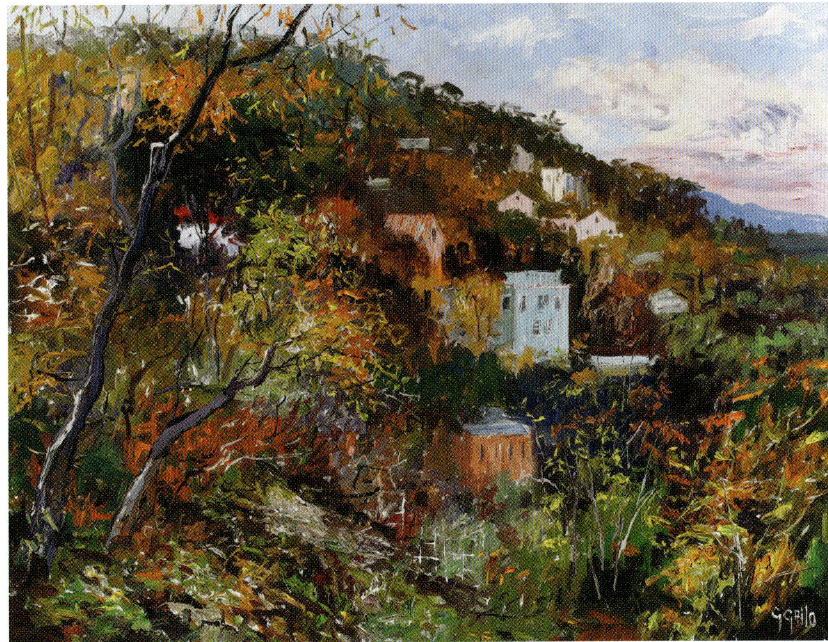

HOLLYWOOD HILLS · Oil on Canvas · 36" × 48" (91cm × 122cm)

Using Light and Dark Masses

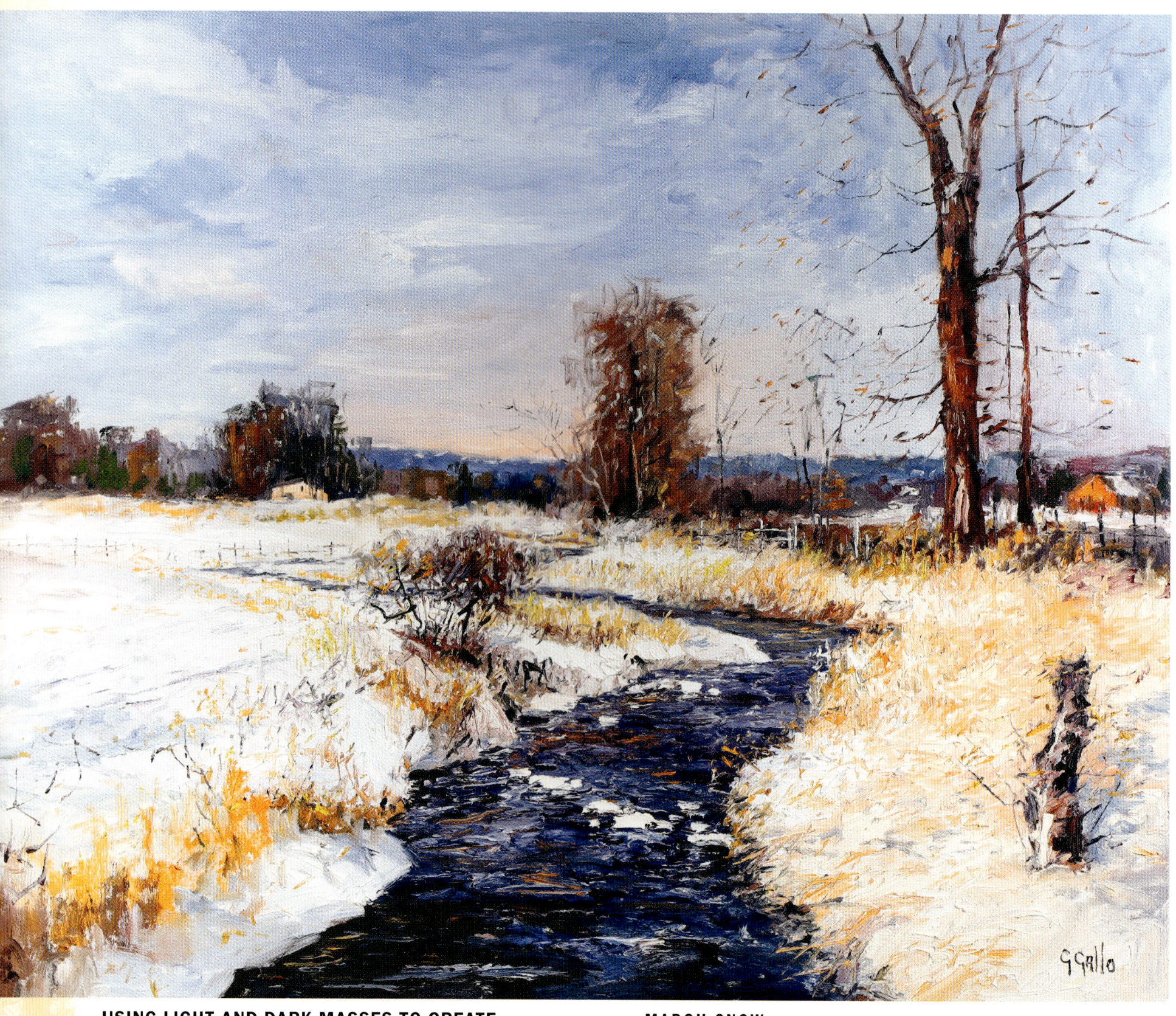

USING LIGHT AND DARK MASSES TO CREATE YOUR DESIGN

Can you see here how the dark value of the creek holds much of the composition together? The distant hillside and trees that run across the horizon line connect the center of the painting. I purposely kept the sky uncomplicated in terms of value and color temperature. If I had added more shifts, the sky values would compete with the other values in the painting instead of complement them.

MARCH SNOW
Oil on Canvas · 48" × 60" (122cm × 152cm)

Creating Atmospheric Perspective

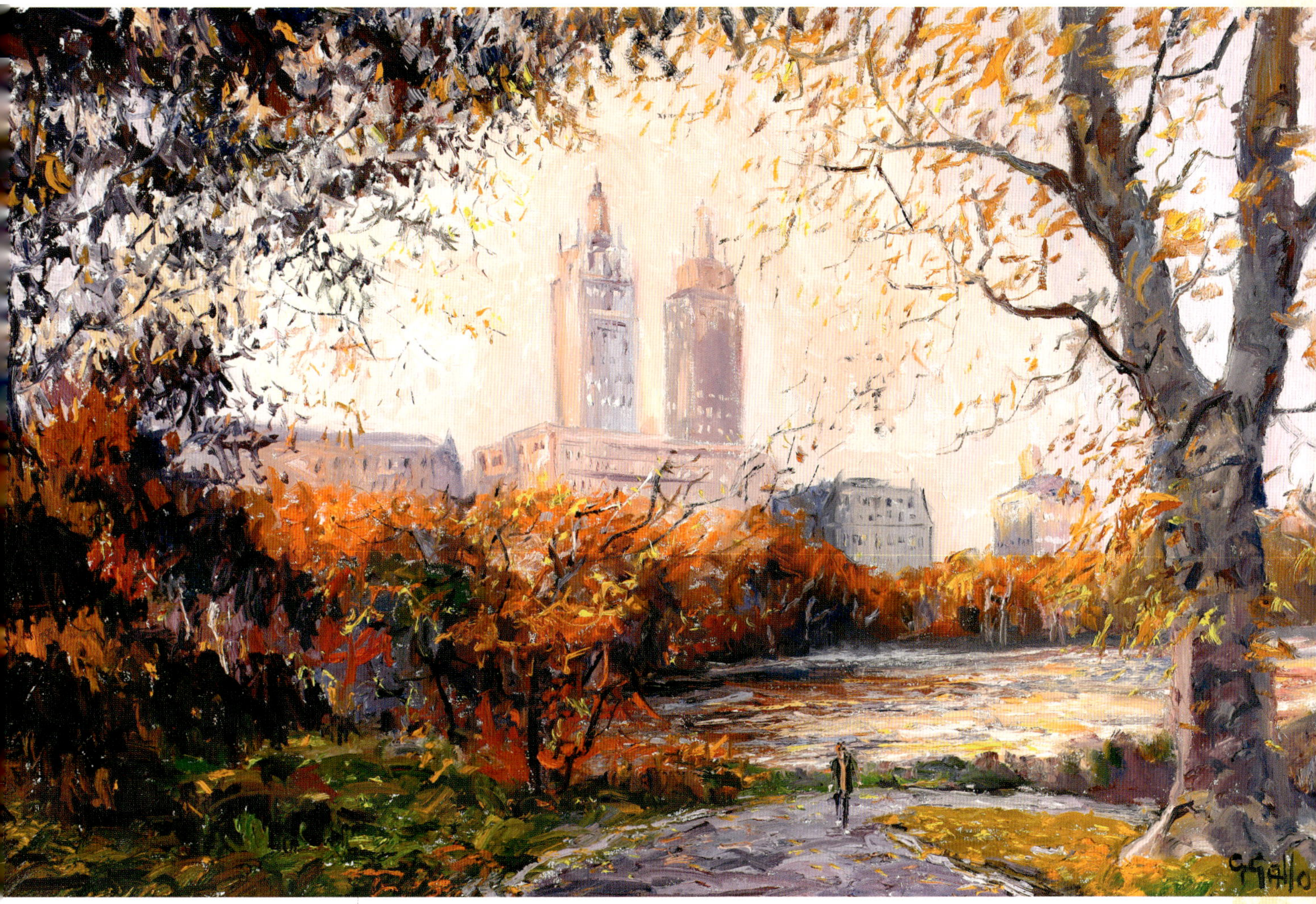

CREATING ATMOSPHERIC PERSPECTIVE WITH VALUES

I exaggerated the values of the buildings—making them lighter than they actually were—to make them feel distant. Therefore, the darker values of the foreground feel really close. Also, notice how the darks of the painting are all connected. The tree on the right acts as an anchor connecting the entire painting from bottom to top.

AUTUMN SOLITUDE, CENTRAL PARK
Oil on Canvas · 30" × 48" (76cm × 122cm)

Seeing Naturally

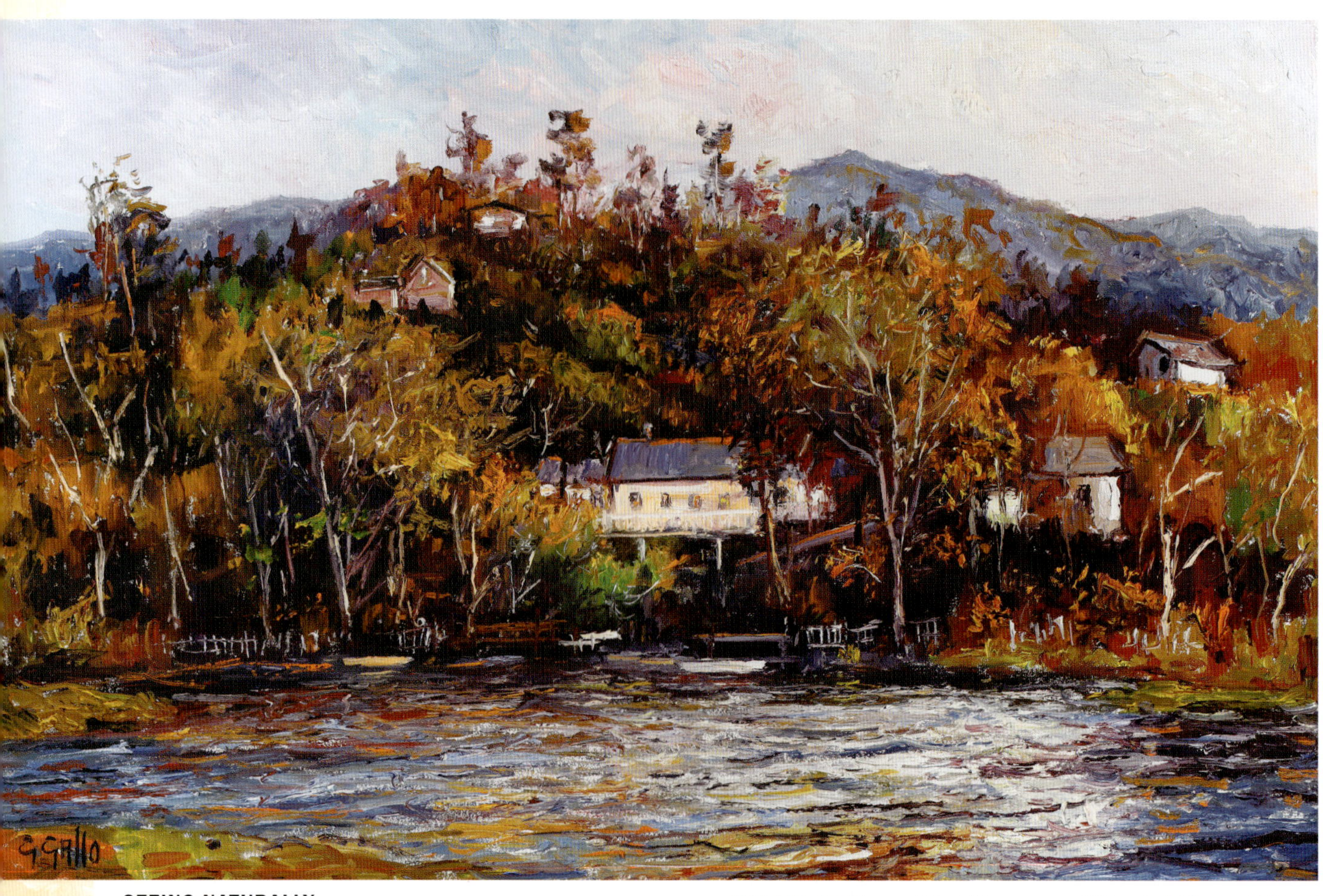

SEEING NATURALLY

You don't always have to paint exactly what you think you see. Our eyes can play tricks on us. If you stare at something long enough, it has a tendency to gray out. To see colors properly, continue moving your eyes all over the scene. This way the eye doesn't become "tired." If you want to see how red something is, turn away from it and look at something green for a few seconds. Then turn back and look at the red object, and you'll see how red it really is.

MALIBU LAKE · Oil on Canvas · 30" × 48" (76cm × 122cm)

Local Color

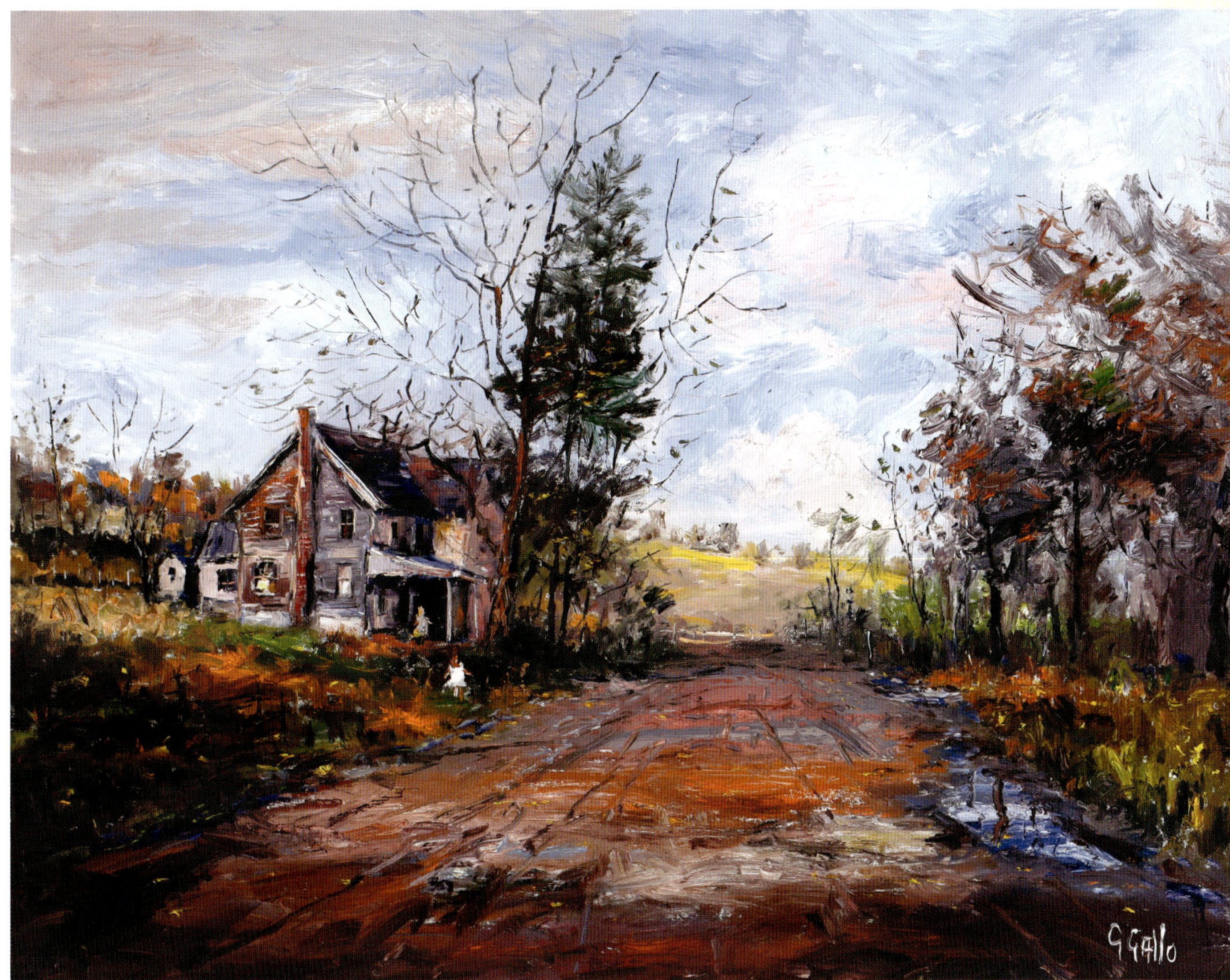

LOCAL COLOR

Local color is a term for the natural color of objects, for instance, a white house, red car or black cat. Too often students will see only the local color of an object and not consider everything else that is going on around it. The objects in front of us are profoundly affected by both light and shadow. For instance, a white house hit with sunlight will take on a yellow or orange tone. The shaded parts of that same white house fall into the blue or purple category. And remember, things tend to cool as they recede into the distance. A white house that is fifty feet away from us has a lot more intense color than that same white house seen on a distant hillside.

The gray house in *Home Sweet Home* takes on not only the warmth of the sun, making it a burnt orange, but also the cools of the sky making other parts purple.

HOME SWEET HOME
Oil on Canvas · 30" × 40" (76cm × 102cm)

Color and the Palette

Color is probably one of the major reasons we are drawn to becoming artists. After all my years of painting, talking to other artists and reading endless books on art, I know that theories of color vary from artist to artist. Color choices are as personal to a painter as seasoning food is to a chef.

WHERE MANY STUDENTS GO WRONG

Many times students suffer when it comes to learning about color. Don't be afraid of color. It's probably the greatest joy of being a painter. It's not that students can't grasp color as much as they have trouble learning to see color. What we do as artists is very unnatural in terms of staring at objects for long periods of time. The longer we stare at something, the more our eyes tire of what we're seeing, and the objects in front of us tend to gray out. This is the wrong way to gauge the color of something. You must learn to see naturally. (More on this later.)

COLOR THEORIES

There are a lot of wacky color theories out there. I've read about and even experimented with some of them over the years. Some involve creating color charts. For example, to ensure harmony, you might predetermine the colors you'll work with before you start painting. Others involve adding a "mother color" to every mix to achieve harmony. Both of these methods have been used successfully by some great painters, but these approaches are a bit too technical for my liking. I also find that they are of little use for the outdoor painter, whose mission is to quickly record what he sees before him.

THE PALETTE

My ideas about color have been forged through a great deal of trial and error. I've experimented with several palettes. Some were elaborate. Others weren't. I have found that simple is best, especially for painting outdoors.

My approach to color is based on the color discoveries arrived at around the turn of the twentieth century. Many terrific artists were working out color theories and ideas for how to apply color to painting. Some painted landscapes without earth tones. Emile Gruppe, a brilliant colorist who learned about color from Charles Hawthorne, fully adopted this idea. I have embraced this idea for several reasons. I believe mastering this palette will help you create paintings that are not only wonderfully vivid but also illustrate color harmony because the colors are already inherently harmonious. Although some painters may argue that there are no colors that harmonize naturally, this is simply untrue. Look at the color wheel. There are colors called "complements." They are called this for a reason. The palette is based on the simple understanding of how the color wheel works and how the various colors all interact.

My palette is as follows:

- Ivory Black
- Ultramarine Blue
- Alizarin Crimson
- Cadmium Red Deep
- Cadmium Orange
- Cadmium Yellow Deep
- Cadmium Lemon Yellow
- Phthalo Blue
- Titanium White

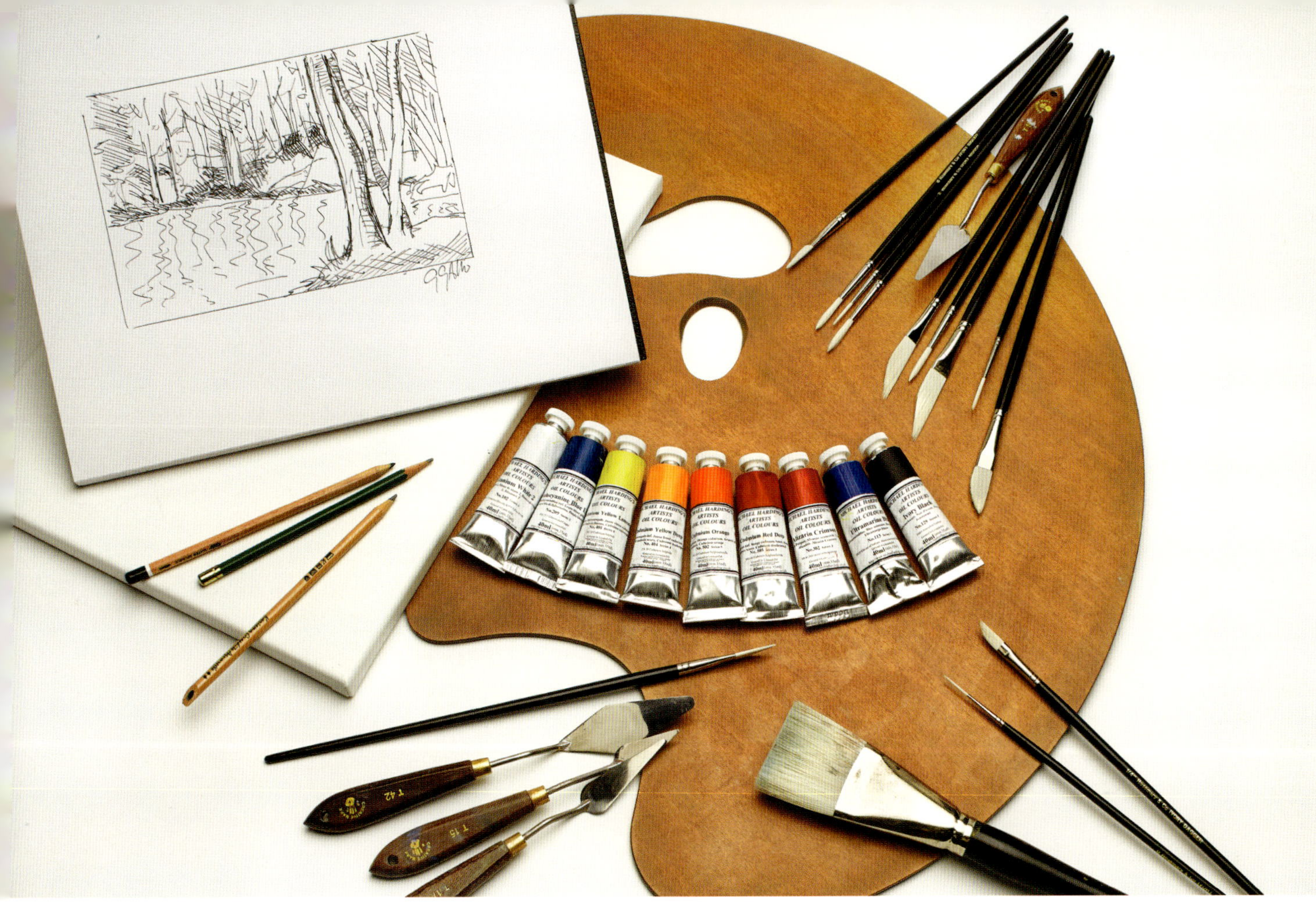

You'll notice there are no earth colors in my palette. You don't need them. They can be mixed easily by cutting complements into one another. That's also how you can control the color temperatures of your neutral tones.

You have two yellows, two reds and two blues. All three primaries: a warm and a cool of each. With the exception of black and white, I paint with pure color.

Ultramarine Blue is a blue with red in it. Alizarin Crimson is a red with blue in it. These two colors combined give you your purest purple.

Cadmium Red Deep is a red with yellow in it. Cadmium Orange is for the center of the palette. It's a combination of red and yellow. It acts not only as an orange but as a modifier to create all neutrals by mixing them with the purples. Imagine a stone wall that is in both light and shadow. As a result it is both warm and cool. This can easily be rendered by going back and forth between the warm and cool mixtures of your purples and oranges. What's best about this is that these colors harmonize naturally as opposed to earth tones, which vibrate much differently than the Cadmium colors.

Cadmium Yellow Deep is a yellow with red in it. With Phthalo Blue, it's great for mixing deep, warm greens. The red in Cadmium Yellow Deep not only creates rich greens, but also re-creates what happens in nature when greens darken and take on their complementary color, red.

Cadmium Yellow Lemon is the brightest of all yellows. It also has a touch of blue. It works to create the brightest of greens when mixed with Phthalo Blue.

Phthalo Blue is a blue with yellow in it. This is why it creates such beautiful greens; there is no modifier of red.

You could leave black out of your palette if you wanted to. I did for years. In fact, for students it might be a good idea to skip it so you aren't tempted to use it to make gray. Gray in nature is never merely gray; it's a combination of complementary colors with a particular color temperature. I use black on occasion to help gray down a color, especially when working outdoors on a winter day. But black should be used with caution.

Hopefully you will discover how ideal this simple palette is. You can mix whatever you need with it while painting outdoors. Because it is so logically constructed, it should help you create great color mixtures quickly. None of this is arbitrary; each color is there for a very specific purpose and works well with the color next to it. Master this palette and you'll understand how color interacts as well as how it relates to what is going on in nature. You'll be well on your way to creating wonderful Impressionistic paintings.

More About Color

ACCENTUATING COLOR

Everything in color, just like values, is about comparisons. Green only looks very green because of the complement of red next to it. Take away that red and the green loses its bite. The same is true of all complementary colors. If you want a blue to read strongly, put its complement, orange, next to it. It's essential to get these complementary colors working together in your composition in order to create paintings that pop. An autumn scene with reds and oranges needs blues and greens to complement these colors. This isn't a trick. It's how nature works, and how our eyes work, too. A painting with lots of green *needs* the complement red. Have you ever noticed how white clouds have a touch of pink in them on a very green summer day? That is because the human eye needs that complement.

WARM AND COOL

One of the greatest discoveries you make as a painter is discerning whether objects are warm or cool. This is really the basis for all painting. It is the only way to get the feeling of light and shadow in your work. But a word of caution: Once you make this discovery, you may be inclined to overdo it. If you can keep your temperature shifts subtle and pay close attention to values, your work will appear masterful.

ATMOSPHERIC PERSPECTIVE AND COLOR

Things lighten in terms of value as they recede. Things also have a tendency to cool as they recede. This is all because of the particles in the air. On a clear day with a blue sky, things appear more blue as they recede into the distance.

CREATING HARMONY

I sometimes paint my skies first. Once you have properly painted the sky, the rest of the painting will be much easier to gauge, especially since the warm and cool notes of the sky will appear in some way in everything else. In many ways the sky is the father of the picture. Imagine a blue sky with beautiful warm clouds over a river. If you've laid in the sky properly in terms of color and value, logic will tell you that it gets easier to gauge the colors and values in the stream and its surroundings. But if you then make a color mistake, it will jump out at you. Keep in mind that everything in nature reflects everything else around it. Some painters start out by toning the canvas to develop a particular color key; others mix a little sky color into their other mixtures. Both approaches aim for the same goal, which is to create unity and harmony. This is how nature behaves.

Reflected Light

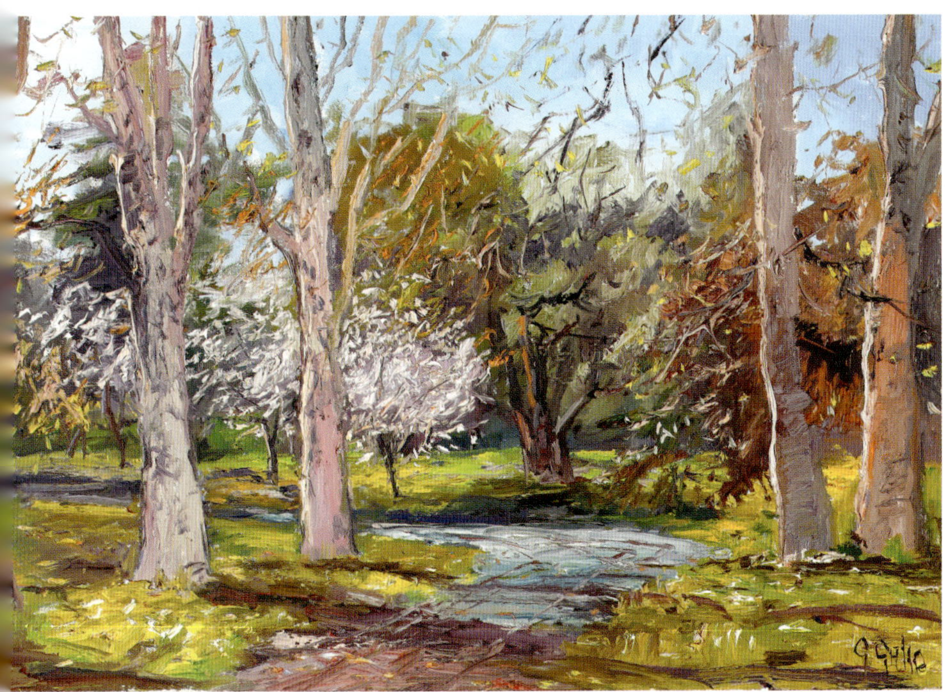

REFLECTED LIGHT, AFTERNOON
I painted this picture late in the day. One reason it feels so filled with light is the careful attention I gave to getting the quality of the reflected light right. Notice how light the barks of the trees are. This is because the sunlight is bouncing off the grass and throwing light back into the shadowed areas of the trees. Had I painted them darker, you would never get the feeling of warm, intense light.

GILLETTE RANCH
Oil on Canvas   ·   20" × 30" (51cm × 76cm)

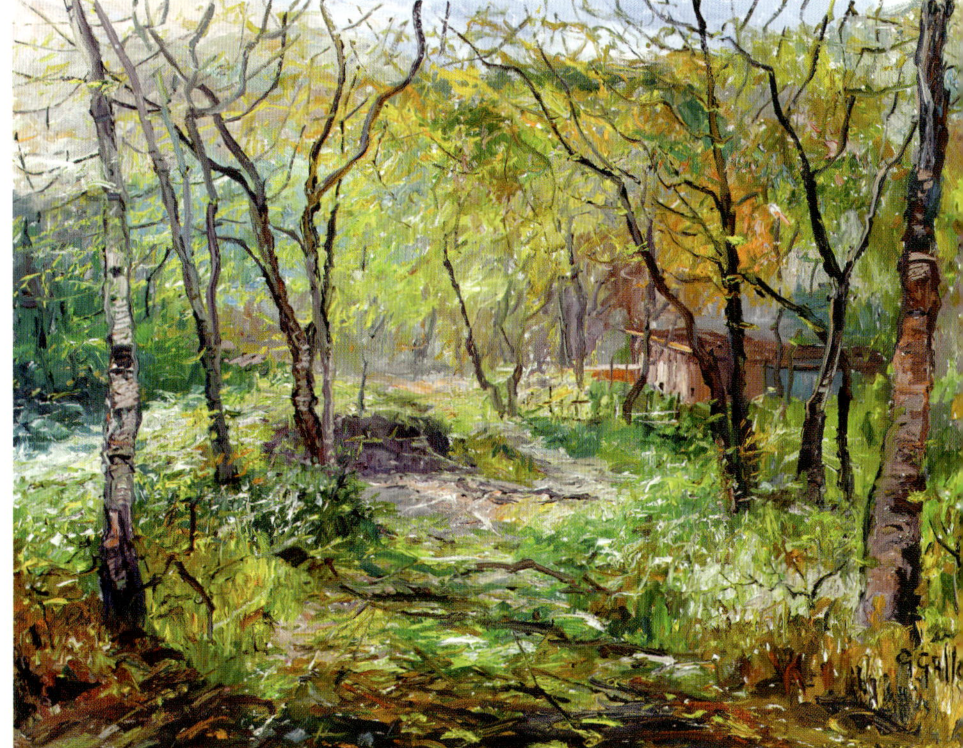

REFLECTED LIGHT, MORNING
This was painted in early morning light. Normally, light as intense as this would turn the trees into silhouettes. But here the light is so strong it bounces off the earth and grass and into the shadows, creating wonderful, warm complementary colors.

GARRAPATA MORNING   ·   Oil on Canvas   ·   36" × 48" (91cm × 122cm)

Early Morning Light

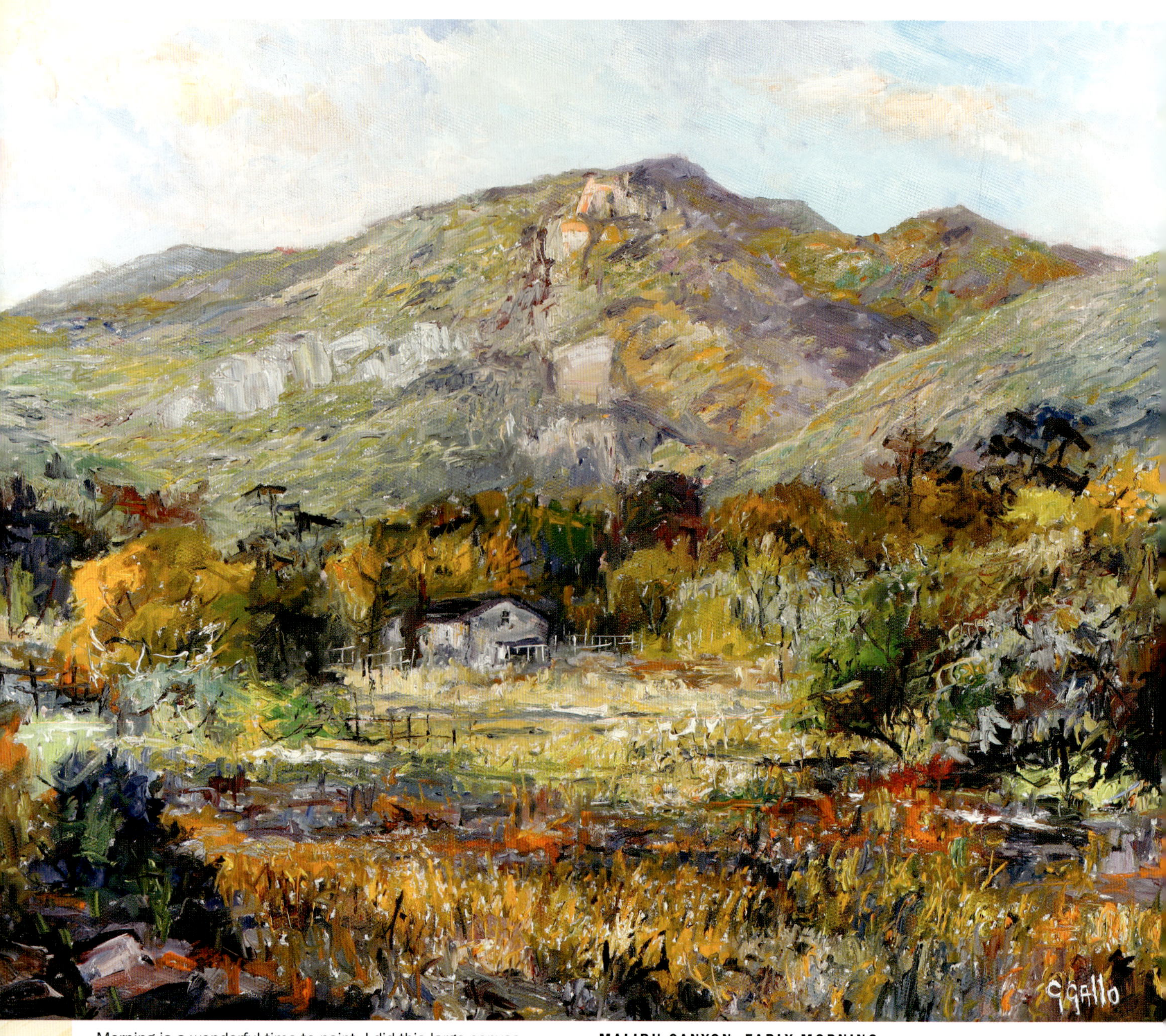

Morning is a wonderful time to paint. I did this large canvas entirely en plein air. The morning light created a series of warm and cool notes with values that were very close in both the sky and the mountain. Below, the other masses such as the land, trees and structures were either lighter or darker in value. In addition to the local color, they have to have some version of either the warms or cools that come directly down from the sky.

MALIBU CANYON, EARLY MORNING
Oil on Canvas · 48" × 60" (122cm × 152cm)

Afternoon Light

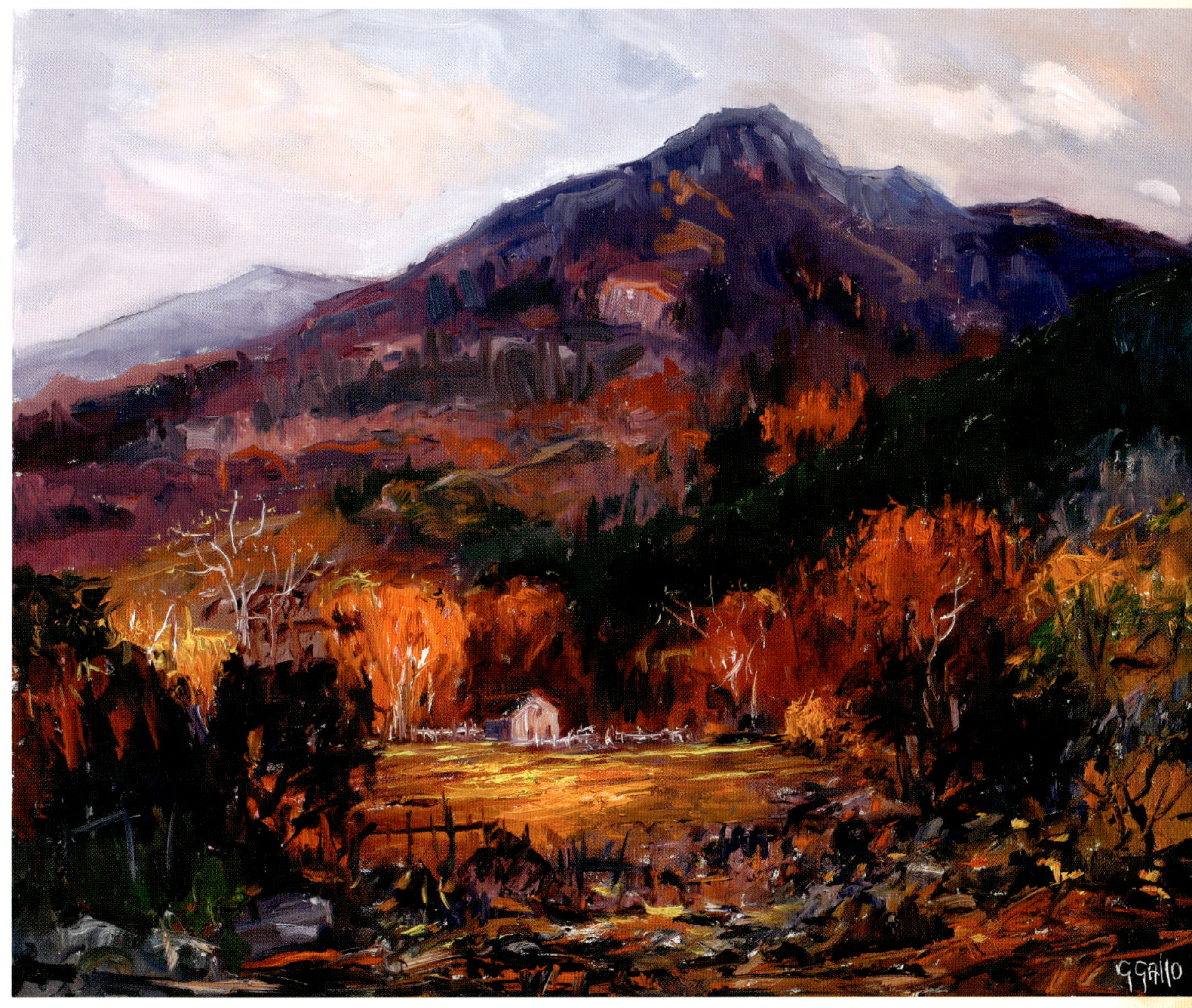

MALIBU CANYON, LATE AFTERNOON
Oil on Canvas · 24" × 30" (61cm × 76cm)

Late afternoon is my favorite time to paint. It's as if nature gives
you her best light before bidding farewell. In this painting the
darker values are close, so they need to be clearly defined by
warm or cool color temperatures. The house in the distance,
although white, appears to be nothing more than a warm gray. I
mixed the color with my purple and orange mixture and a touch
of white. I added a speck of Cadmium Yellow Lemon to give the
feeling of the cooler end of the spectrum. Whenever you can get
purple, green and orange working together within a strong design,
chances are you've got a winner.

Autumn Scene

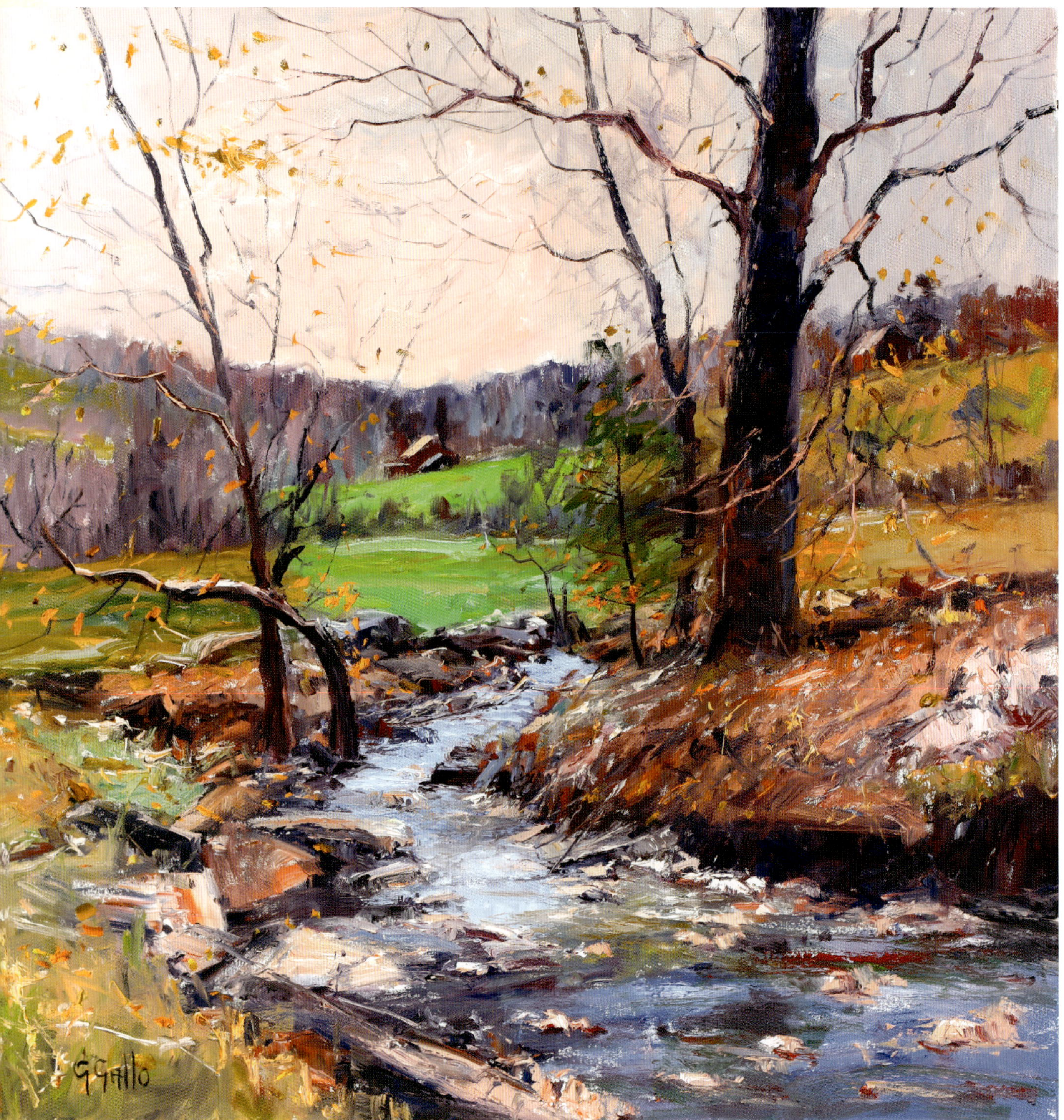

This composition looks directly into the sunlight—notice the lack of blue in the sky as a result. Notice how warm the green is at the center of the painting and how it loses its intensity at the sides. The top light creates strong highlights on everything that slants toward the sun. These observations help bring truth to the painting.

TONY'S CREEK, FALL
Oil on Canvas · 36" × 36" (91cm × 91cm)

Winter Scene

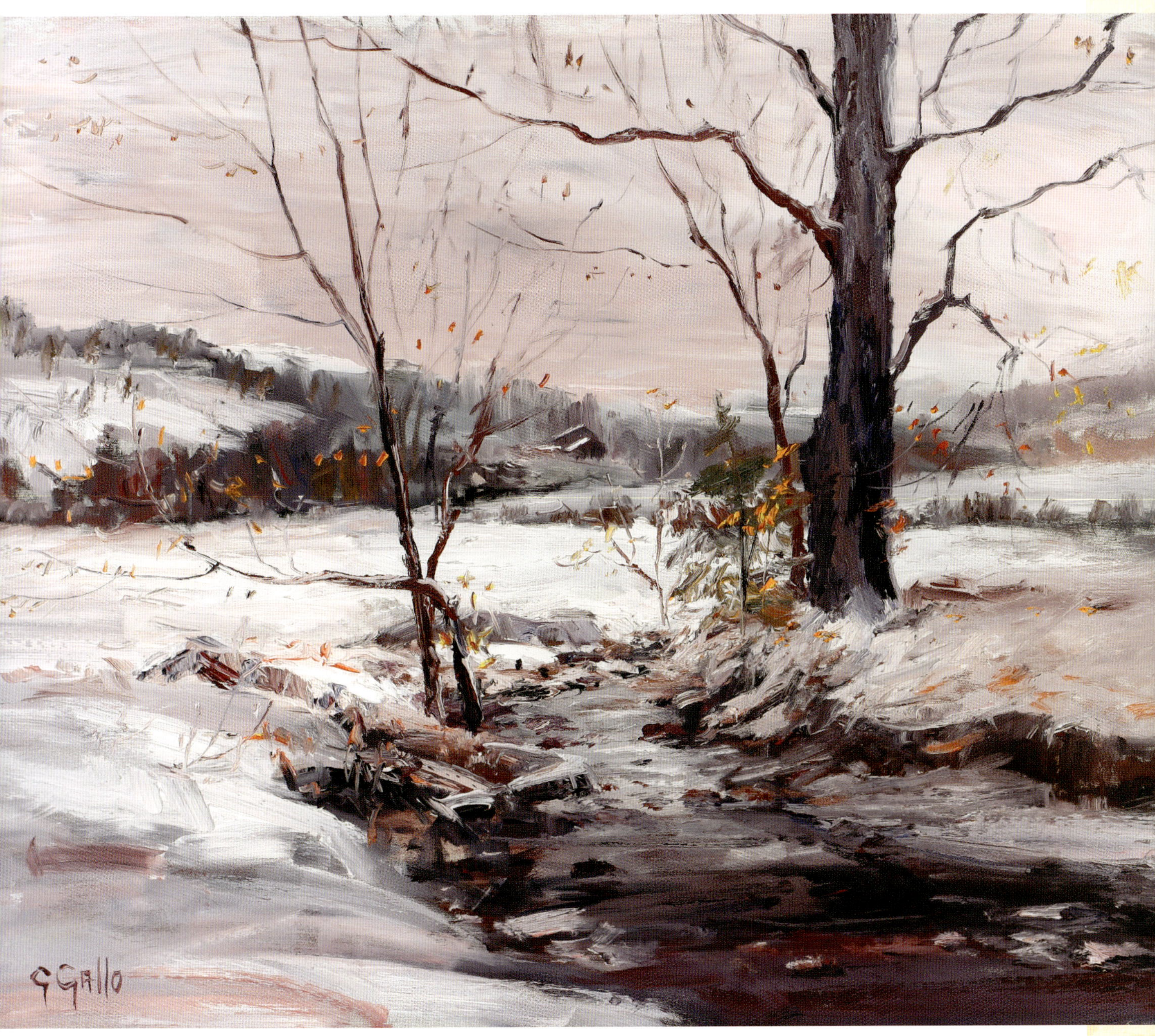

The light in this painting comes from a gray day mixed with intermittent high overcast. Therefore, the light is cold and the shadows have some warmth. Extremely close observation is needed to capture the scene faithfully, to discern where the subtle warm and cools are. Otherwise this picture could easily look like a black-and-white photo.

TONY'S CREEK, WINTER
Oil on Canvas · 24" × 30" (61cm × 76cm)

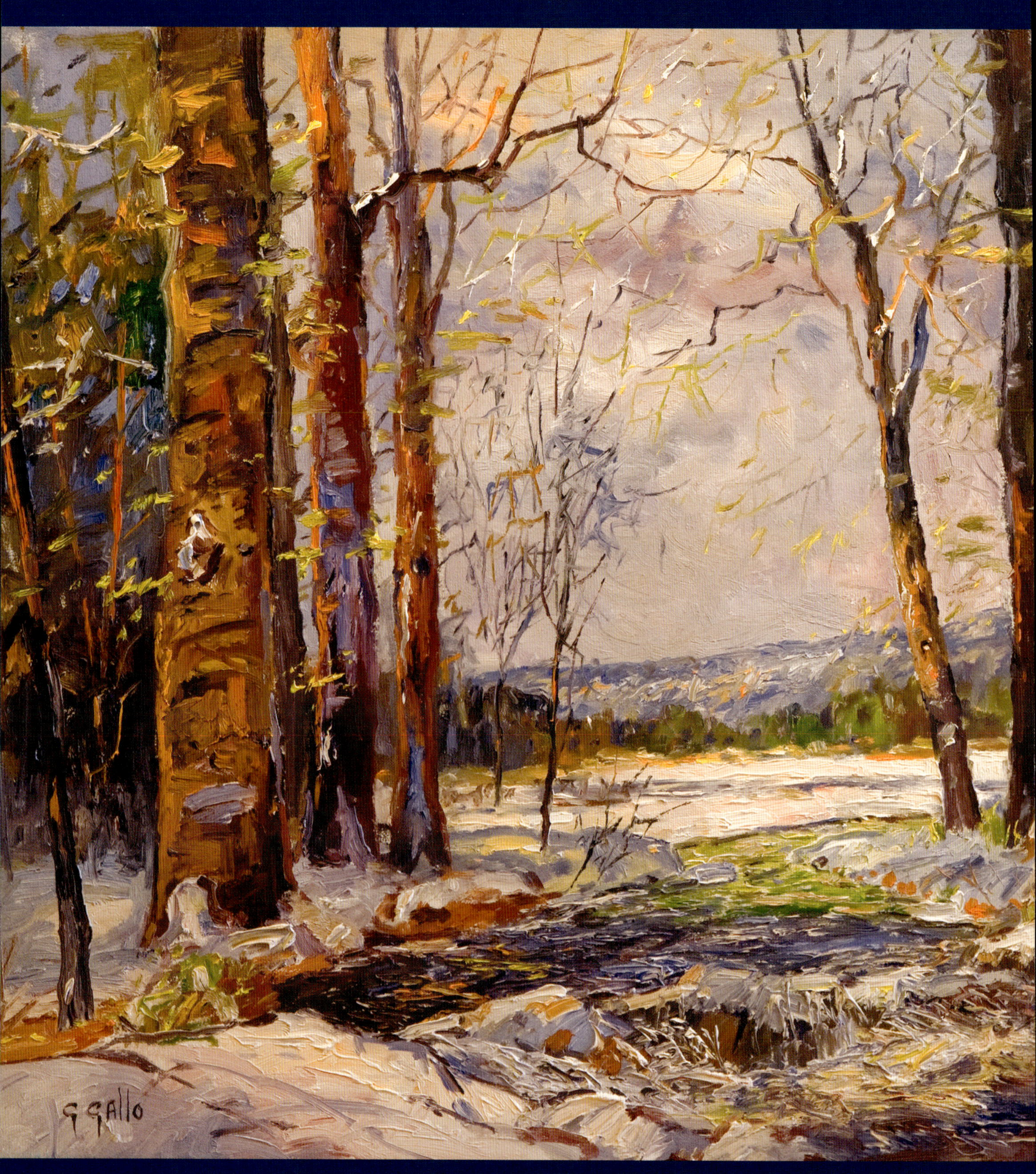
G GALLO

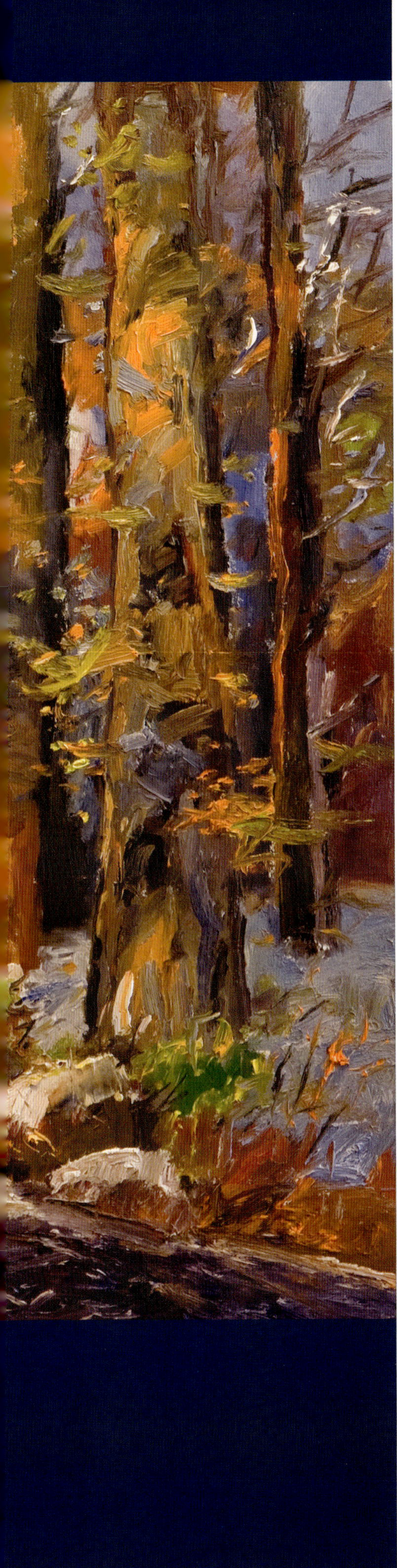

CHAPTER 4

THE COLORIST APPROACH

I've heard the word *colorist* used for much of my life. I assume it means an artist who *pushes* color, making it more dynamic than reality. If that's the case, I guess I'm a colorist. A lot of painters have been colorists since the Impressionists began using color alone to express themselves. We all seem to agree what a color is when we look at it. Yet we also seem to have our own unique ways of interpreting these colors when we paint. Several artists can paint the same scene using different colors. Each of their paintings can appear to be accurate.

WHAT IS ACCURATE COLOR?

Many painters today seem to be obsessed with painting accurate color. But people don't all see everything, every color, exactly the same. Accurate color and accurate value are relative. The color relationships need to be accurate. Make sure that what you are painting is harmonious. Color harmony is all about understanding color relationships. Van Gogh pushed color to its limits, but somehow his work still appears believable in the context of the world he is creating because he understood color relationships. Pushing colors, making things more colorful than they actually are, can be fun. But one must use some restraint when doing this. The secret is to understand how *light and color* work together.

COLOR VIBRATIONS

What fascinates me most about painting with pure color are the wonderful vibrations we can describe by understanding the interaction of our three secondary colors. The Impressionists knew this inside and out. When we are standing under a canopy of maple trees in autumn and sunlight is blasting into the leaves before us, if the leaves are bright yellow, the shadowed sides of the leaves will invariably be some form of violet. As an experiment, paint a bunch of yellow dabs and leave a little bit of space between them. At this point they will look like little more than yellow spots. Add a few dabs of violet in the empty spaces and watch how the yellow jumps. It's because the two complements cause one another to vibrate.

WOODSTOCK IN WINTER · Oil on Canvas · 38" × 50" (122cm × 152cm)

Your Subject Is Always the Light

MAKE COLOR YOUR BEST FRIEND

Knowing your palette and the color wheel is essential to creating colorful works that vibrate. You must learn the color wheel the same way a musician learns where all the keys on his instrument are. Using color isn't arbitrary. It comes from knowledge. A red barn illuminated with sunlight will warm up. That means a touch of orange. Where the barn falls into shadow, the color cools. Generally this is illustrated (on our palette) with a cool blue like Ultramarine, which leans toward purple. If green grass below the barn catches sunlight, a bit of that green will reflect into the eaves of the barn. What I just described happens in nature. Knowing that means you can add these color notes to your painting. They don't always occur in that exact fashion, but understanding these effects will help you create colorist work. Using the interaction of your three secondaries always creates something that is both truthful and pleasing to the eye.

YOU CAN'T HAVE IT BOTH WAYS

As I stated earlier you have to make up your mind as to the story you wish to tell. If your painting is about the light, make sure your dark or cooler elements don't fight for equal interest. Don't fill up your secondary passages with unnecessary details.

If the main subject of your painting is the lighter passages, then the shadowy areas of the piece have to support that original idea. When looking at your subject, your eye cannot focus on both the light and shadowed areas at the same time. Therefore you should only paint one or the other in great detail. If you paint both in great detail your painting will have too much information. It will be confusing to the viewer because you didn't make up your mind as to what to feature. Make a strong choice. Feature the light or the dark but not both.

QUALITY OF LIGHT

I prefer to paint in afternoon light. In fact, many times the later in the day, the better. I also like painting early in the morning. Early and late in the day, the light is much warmer and at a lower angle. This creates beautiful light, dark patterns, and warm and cool colors. In fact, you will always see your three complementary colors jump out at you at these times of day.

SUNNY DAY

Painting on a sunny day is a joy. You have to move quickly because the light is rapidly changing, but the interplay between warm light and cool shadows is intoxicating. Learning to capture the effects of light is one of the toughest—but ultimately most enjoyable—tasks of a plein air painter. Understanding complementary colors and their interactions is a surefire way to capture the feeling of sunlight.

GRAY DAY

A gray day can be a colorist's dream. This may sound like a contradiction, but the better we get at painting, the more we can see and control the subtleties of color. Too much color can be like too much loud music. Learn to see grays as either warm or cool. Are they leaning toward yellow or orange? Or are they leaning toward blue, purple or blue-green? The subtle interactions of grays can create incredibly dynamic work.

COLOR TEMPERATURE

When paintings start to go wrong in terms of color, the problem is usually an issue of color temperature. Here is a hard and fast rule to remember when you're getting into trouble:

> Warm light creates cool shadows.
> Cool light creates warm shadows.

Remember this and you will avoid paintings that become muddy. A muddy paint mixture always means that your color temperatures are off. Whistler once said that muddy paint was a great color in the wrong place.

GET YOUR COMPLEMENTS WORKING

Many times I plan my paintings as interactions of purple, green and orange no matter how subtle the interaction might be. For instance, if I am painting a seascape in afternoon light and I see green foam, warm rocks that have an orange glow and shadows that fall into deep purples, then I know the painting shouldn't fall apart because of boring color choices. If I establish a strong design and pay close attention to both color and values, the painting should work in a dynamic sense.

WHY NOT JUST PAINT WHAT YOU SEE?

One can make the argument that if you just paint what is in front of you, your painting should work because you're capturing the truth before you. Truth, yes, but stop for a moment and ask yourself this question: "Do I want truth or something that is dynamic and interesting?" I want my paintings to have a lot of impact. As you continue growing as a painter you must break away from just painting what you see and try to say something more personal.

THE SOLUTION

The best course of action is to find the smartest way to get your three secondary colors working. A winter evening with an orange sky will invariably produce purple shadows. If there's a creek, it will most likely turn an emerald green. These color combinations plus good design and drawing should produce exciting work.

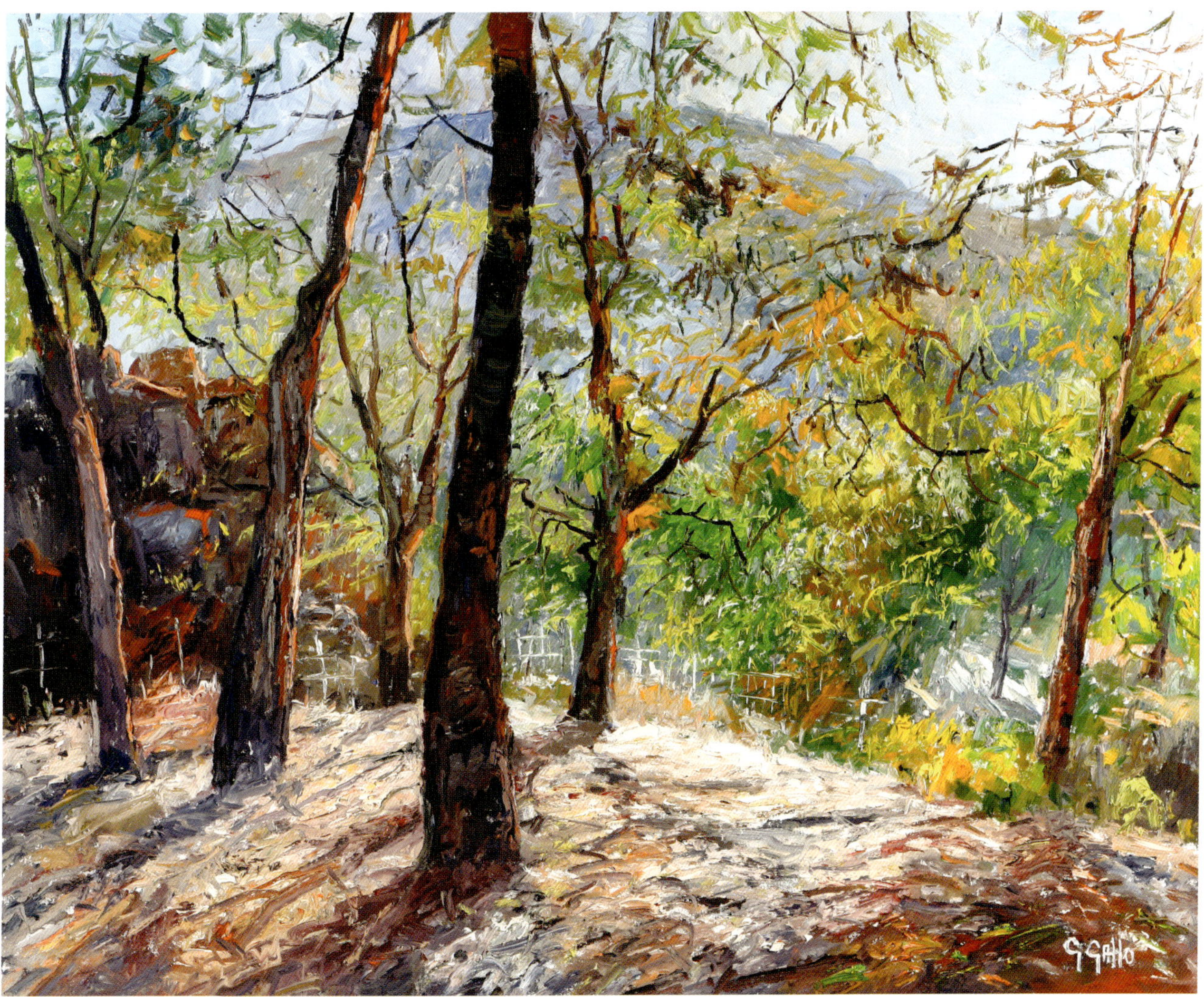

EDGE OF THE FOREST · Oil on Canvas · 48" × 60" (122cm × 152cm)

Color Mixing

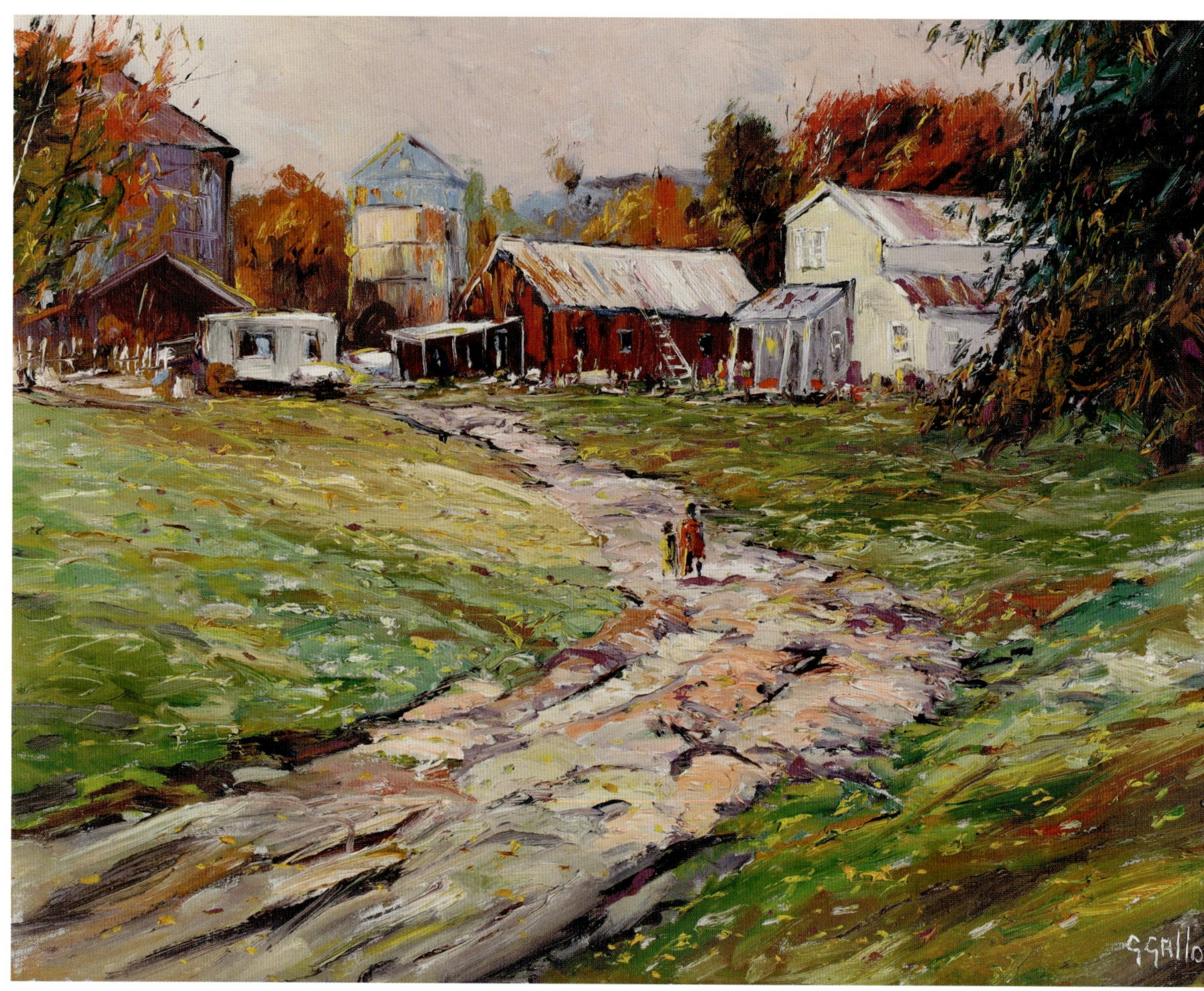

This painting is a study in complements. There are plenty of greens, both warm and cool. But they don't overwhelm because the introduction of red via the barn, trees and figure offers the eye relief. The road is a neutral color that also has some red in it. Even the gray/blue sky has a touch of red. The shadowed areas contain purple, completing the secondary color triad.

ALMOST HOME, SANDGATE, VT
Oil on Canvas · 30" × 40" (76cm × 102cm)

Look for These Complements as Subject Matter

The more we paint, our ability to spot what will make a good painting increases. As you search for your subjects, look for these colors in nature. They are always there, even if muted. Some painters dislike summer because of the overpowering green everywhere. But there are many shades of green, especially in morning and evening light. Look for the warmer greens that lean toward orange. Look for the colors of stones and rocks on days with lots of green, and you'll see the opposite color of red in them. Look for the complements and you'll not only see them, you'll create better paintings full of life. Again, this is not a secret or trick; it is how our eyes work and what occurs in nature. If these color ideas were good enough for Claude Monet and his pals, they should be good enough for us.

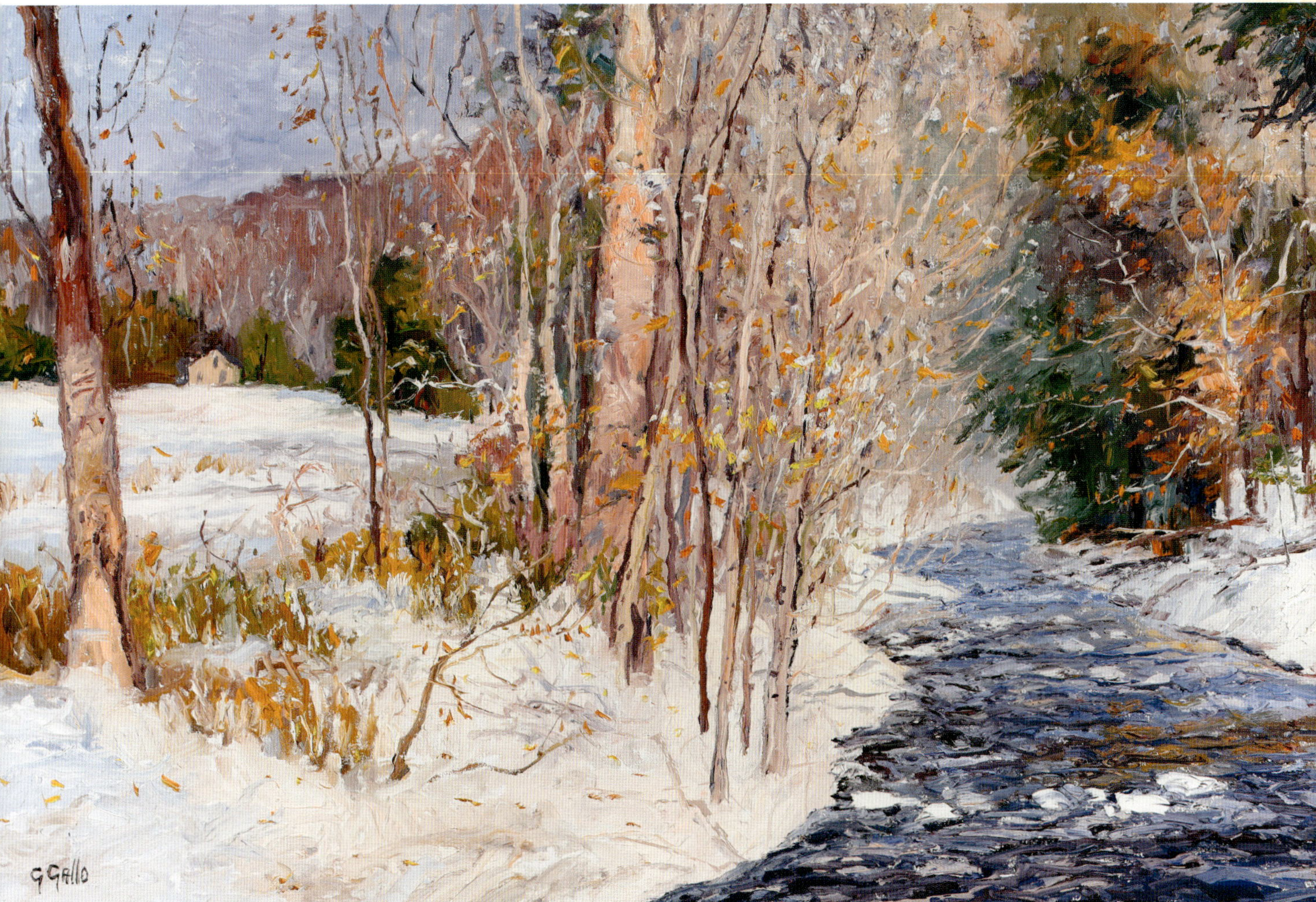

Because there are a lot of neutral browns in this painting, using pure earth colors could make it a pretty dull affair. Mixing your neutrals and allowing them to interplay from warm to cool inside the masses creates a wonderful, dynamic Impressionist approach and a much more lively painting.

CONNECTICUT WINTER
Oil on Canvas · 30" × 48" (76cm × 122cm)

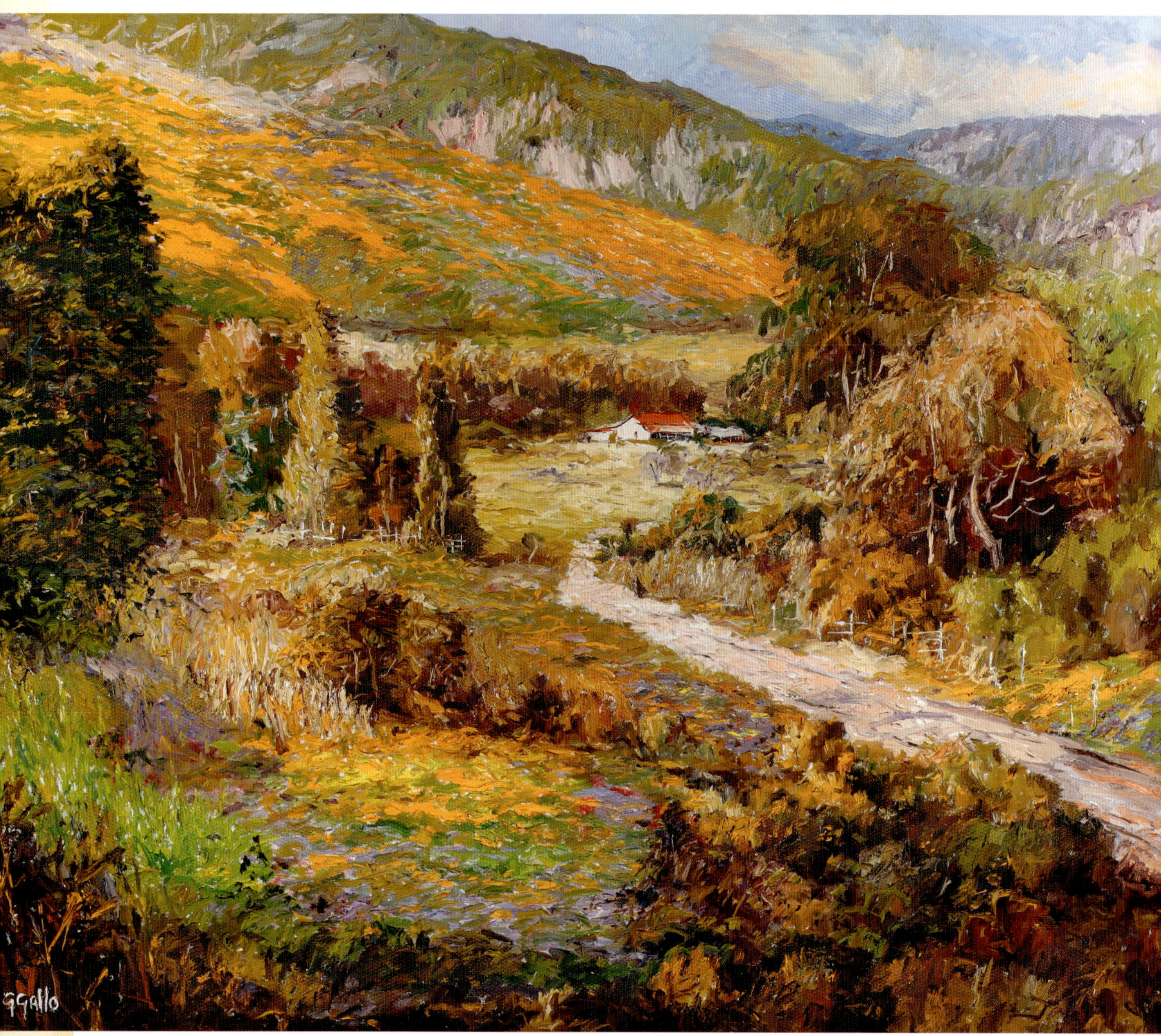

The composition of this painting of a poppy farm just north of Santa Barbara is loaded with yellows and violets, which of course are complements. There is also a lot of green in the painting. The way to get your eye to go to the farmhouse is to make the roof an orangey red, the opposite of green. I was lucky. Whoever built the farm added a red roof. If they hadn't, I probably would have painted it red anyway.

CALIFORNIA POPPIES
Oil on Canvas · 48" × 60" (122cm × 152cm)

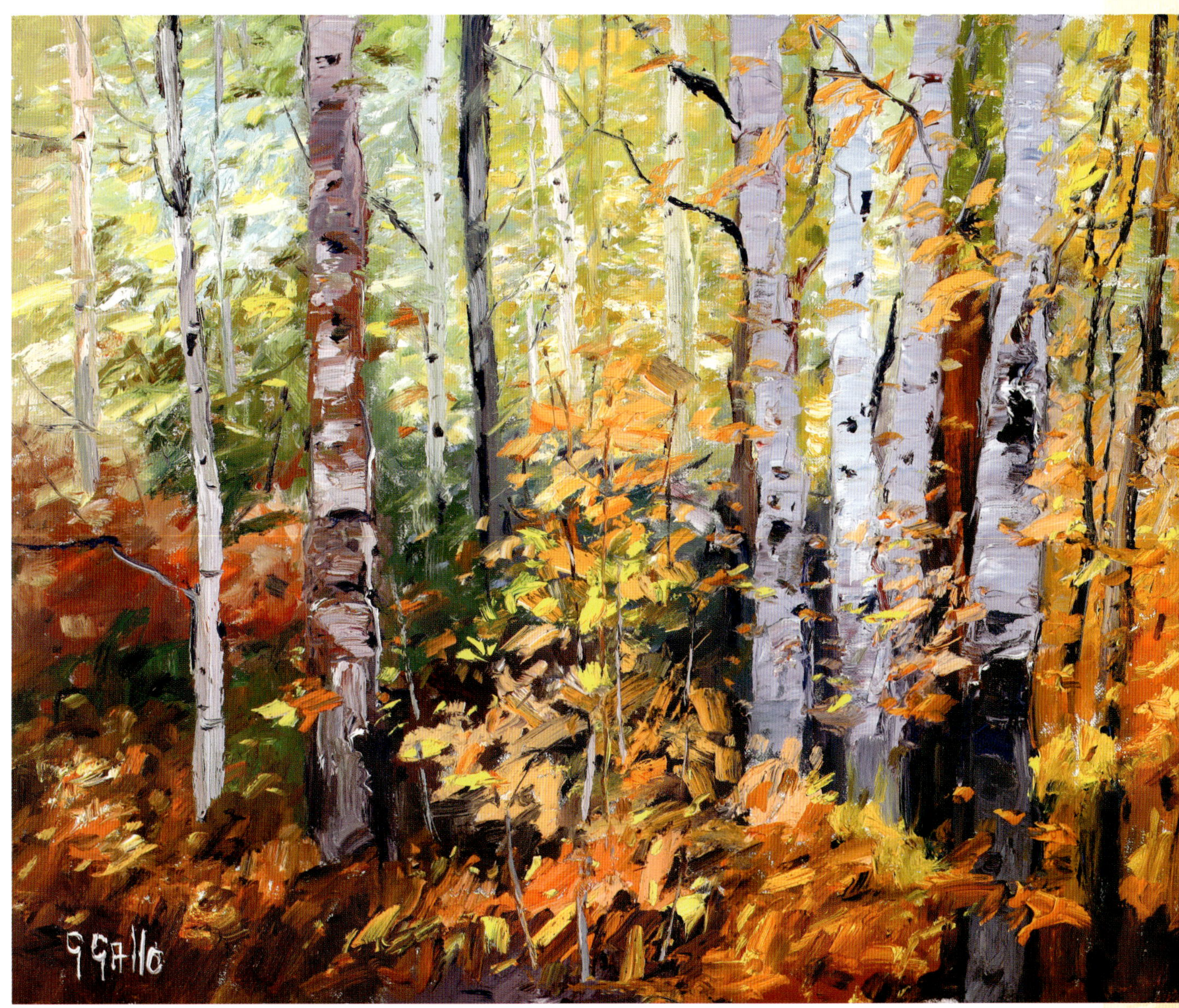

This painting is all about complementary colors and how they interact. The cool violets of the aspens make the yellow-oranges of the leaves vibrate. The darker orangey reds cause the lighter shades of green to vibrate as well. There are also many grays that I created by merely laying complements side by side. From a distance they read as a neutral. Upon closer examination of the painting, you can see that the mixing was actually done in the viewer's eye.

ASPENS · Oil on Canvas · 24" × 30" (61cm × 76cm)

Pushing Complementary Colors

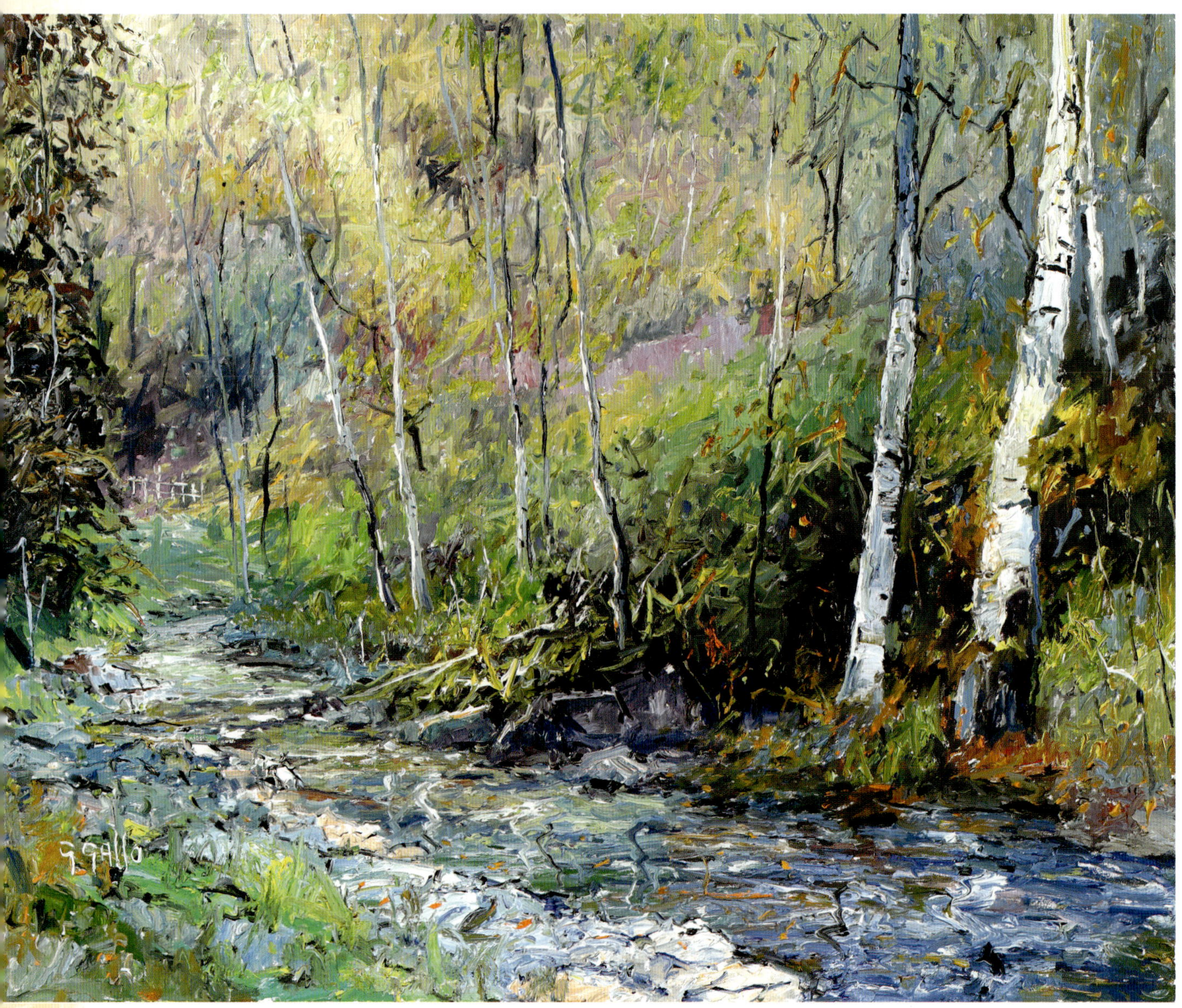

This painting could have been overwhelmingly dull if I hadn't pushed the complements. To counteract all of the various green shades, I added a speck of Alizarin Crimson to the white rocks and stones along the foreground and in the stream. The blue-violet sky overhead caused the shadowed sides of the aspens to go a touch purple. This helped me justify pushing the orange and yellow highlights a bit. I used Cadmium Yellow Lemon, white and a touch of Phthalo Blue to get the feeling of extreme sunlight. I used Cadmium Yellow Deep for a few of the darker highlights. Although perhaps more subtle, this painting is still very much about the interaction of complementary colors.

SUMMER CREEK
Oil on Canvas · 40" × 50" (102cm × 127cm)

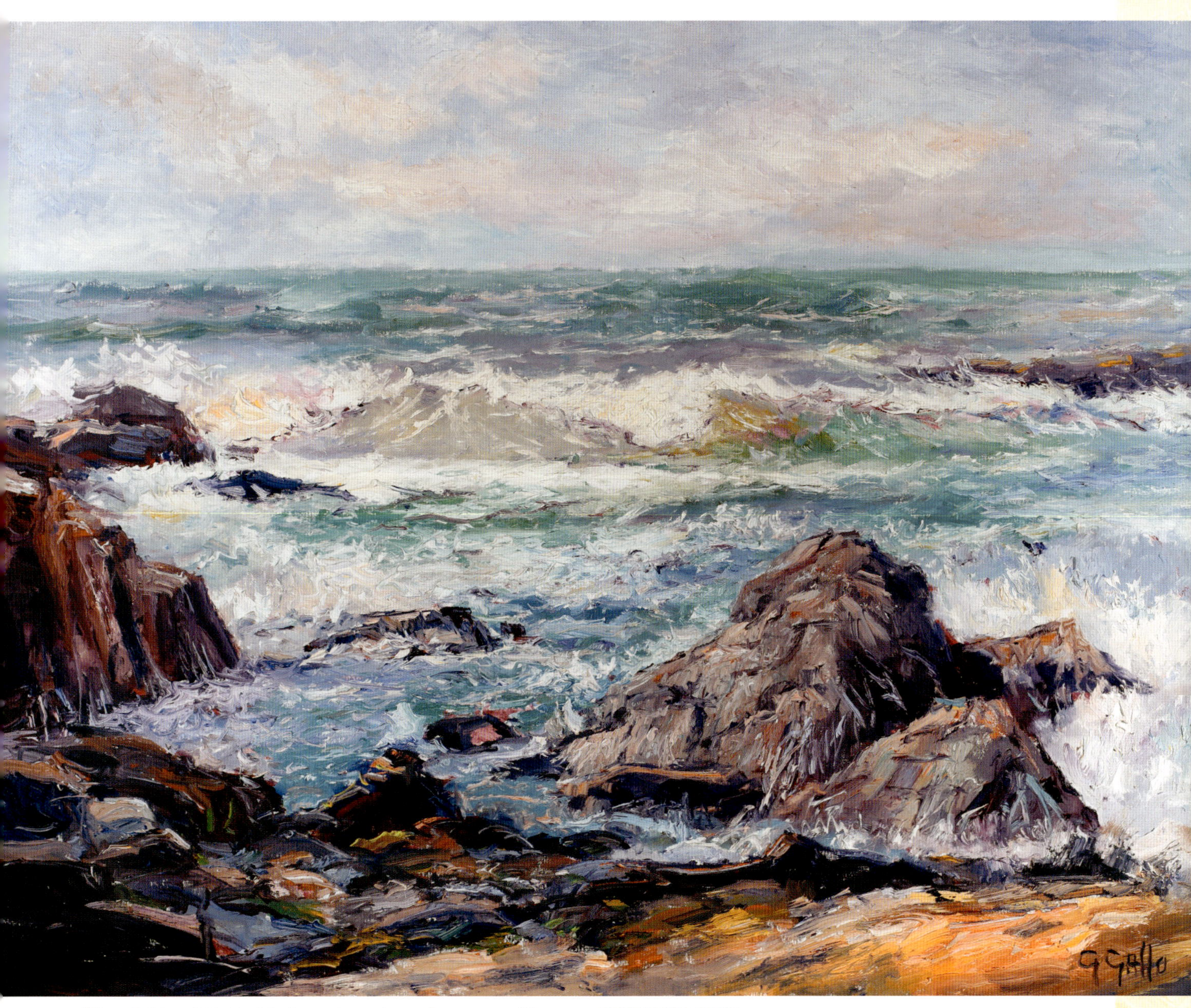

Although this painting is full of complementary colors, some of them are subtle and could almost read as warm or cool grays. Knowing your complements and how they'll interact is a great way to get grays that have impact. I painted the breakers with both pink and green tones, which caused them to go gray yet remain vibrant. Both the warm and cool notes of the sky are repeated in either the highlights or the shadows throughout the painting. This is how color harmony is achieved. See the entire painting as one unit of interacting color and not all its separate parts.

MONTEREY SURF
Oil on Canvas · 36" × 48" (91cm × 122cm)

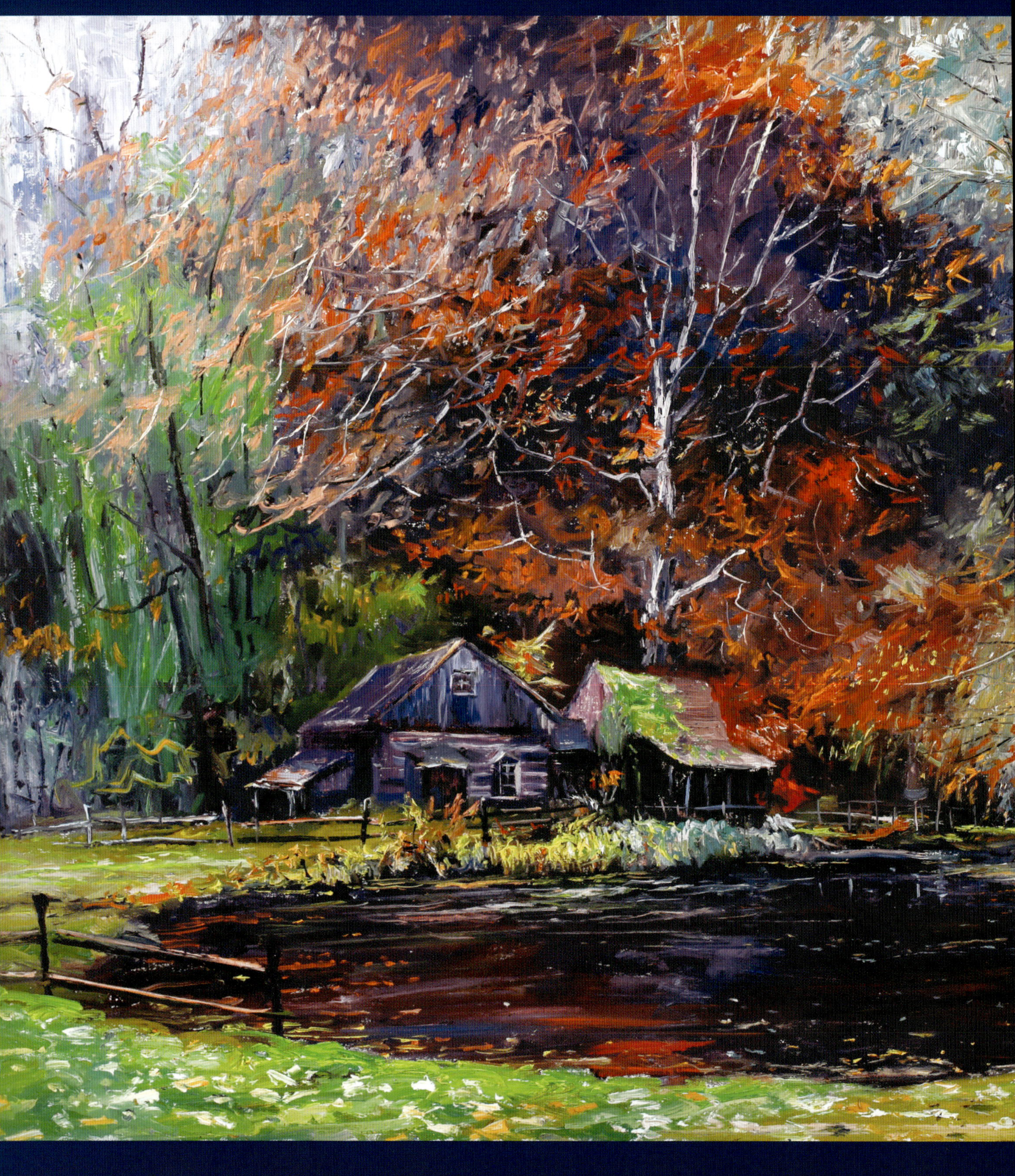

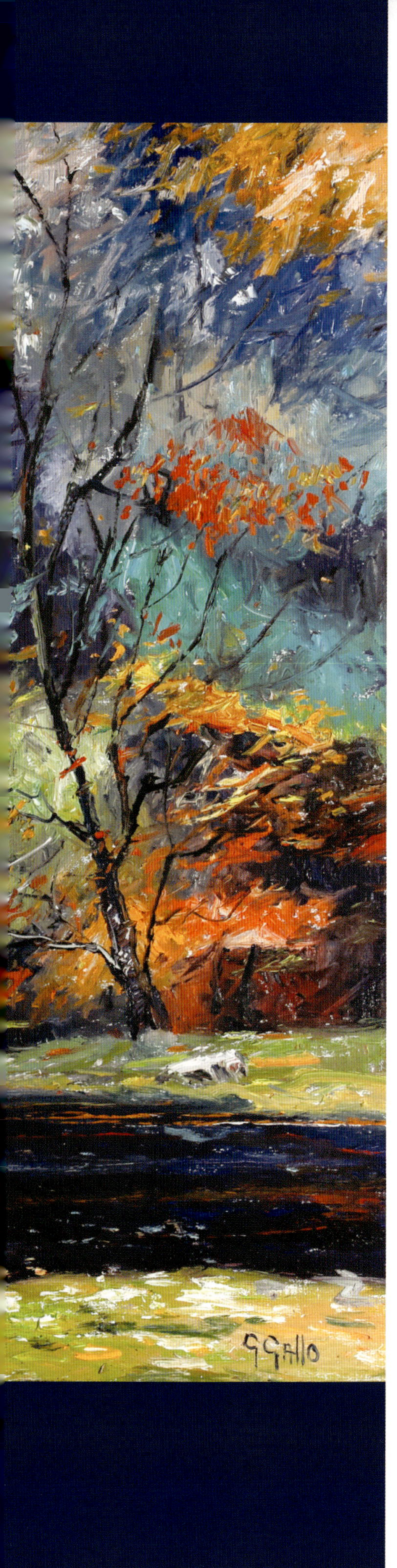

CHAPTER 5
EXPRESSIVE BRUSHWORK

I have always enjoyed the look of big, descriptive, juicy brushstrokes. When I was seventeen years old, I went to Grand Central Art Galleries in New York City. The first time I stood in front of a 50" × 56" (127cm × 142cm) Edward Redfield painting, my heart started to pound. I couldn't believe how descriptive his brushstrokes were! This can only be achieved using oils. The reason I'm so excited by brushstrokes is that they are the closest the viewer gets to chatting with the artist. You get to see and feel the artist's thought process and how he chose to describe what he saw. The brushstrokes the artist uses are the words of the painting. It's your chance as an artist to really cut loose and enjoy the sensual aspects of the paint itself. You're using your brush to describe everything you see. Clouds. Leaves. Moving water. Sharp-edged rocks. The bark of trees. It's a chance to use contrasts. Horizontal strokes to describe one thing. A vertical stroke alongside it to describe another. Choppy strokes for water and foam. Long sensuous strokes to describe grass. Palette knife strokes to describe the sides of buildings and barns. And on and on. The options are as endless as your imagination allows.

My favorite artists use the texture of paint as one of their most descriptive tools. I notice most students are too timid about laying out their paint. George Cherepov, one of my teachers, once saw me laying out pea-sized piles of paint. He grabbed one of my tubes and emptied it out onto my palette. He said, "If it's not on your palette, it never gets to your painting." It was a lesson that stuck with me: You won't get the texture you want on the canvas if you don't put it on your palette first.

CUTTALOSSA POND AND FARMHOUSE · Oil on Canvas · 36" × 48" (91cm × 122cm)

How the Old Masters Did It

Part of the reason the Old Masters live on in our memories is that they were fearless and brilliant. They flew in the face of the conventions of their day. They were free thinkers with paint and had amazing skills. Another reason they pushed the bar forward is that the world they lived in was ready for change. Great art, literature, music and industrial growth all seem to advance at once, as if there is a human awakening, from century to century. These awakenings are easier to spot in retrospect than they are in the moment. Although the Impressionists knew they were onto something, I doubt they knew they were on the verge of changing forever the way mankind looked at painting. Their accomplishments are still rippling through everything artists do today.

We can raise the bar in our own time by looking to those who did so before us. Look at the Impressionists and get to know their work inside and out. Something in their painting has been lost in the representational work of today: a sense of uniqueness. I'm sure the Impressionists wanted to sell their work like everybody else, but sales weren't their first concern. I suggest you work at doing your best to be not only good but unique as well, before you worry about making art your way to pay the bills. It might take you longer to get there, but you will own your success and your work will be uniquely yours.

The Impressionists painted outside. They didn't sit in a warm, cozy studio and paint while eating teacakes. They went to their subjects and found out how to paint them in far from perfect circumstances. They were bronzed by the sun and drenched by the rain. They weren't so obsessed with getting everything perfect in terms of control and drawing. They were chasing a different kind of perfection, which could be better described as searching for visual, universal truths. They were reaching beyond their means in an attempt to synthesize the beauty of nature and the human heart. This can only be done with struggle. You must go into the field like they did and capture what *you* see to the best of your ability. Only here will you grow and truly define yourself as an artist.

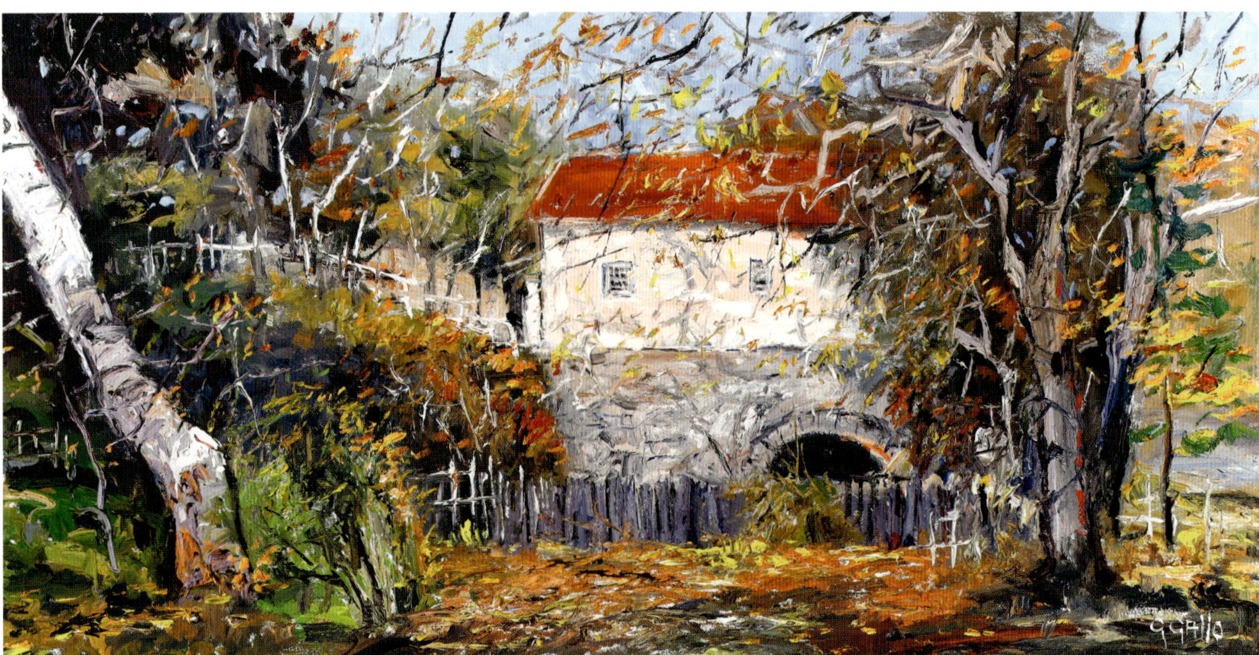

When you speak you don't use random words. If you want to make a point, you need to be clear. That's how you need to think about brushstrokes. Ask yourself, "What do I want to say?" Then say it loud and clear. Brushstrokes will become your personal handwriting and your unique way of telling a story the way you and only you see it and can describe it.

CARETAKER'S PLACE
Oil on Canvas · 24" × 48" (61cm × 122cm)

Juxtaposition of Painterly Brushstrokes

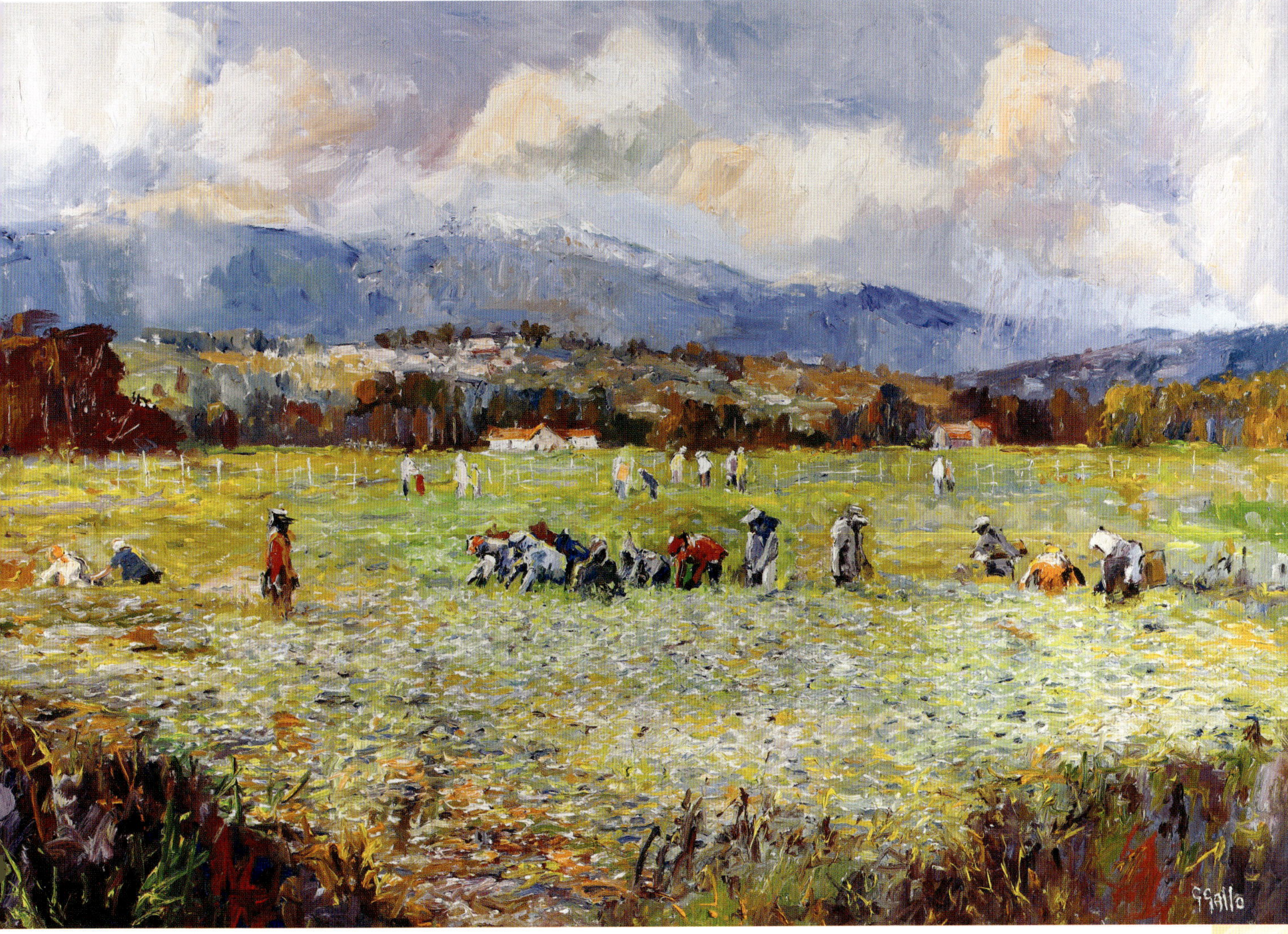

SIMI VALLEY PICKERS
Oil on Canvas · 40" × 60" (102cm × 152cm)

This painting is a study in the juxtaposition of painterly brushstrokes. I used blocky strokes for the sky and swirling strokes for the clouds. I dragged my brush over the wet paint to suggest rain in the distance. The mountains were done with angular strokes. I used spotty, staccato-like strokes to suggest architecture on the hillside. I used countless Impressionistic dabs to suggest the field, followed by direct strokes to define the attitudes of the figures. Painting in this manner is one of the joys of being an oil painter.

Juxtaposition of Impressionistic Brushstrokes

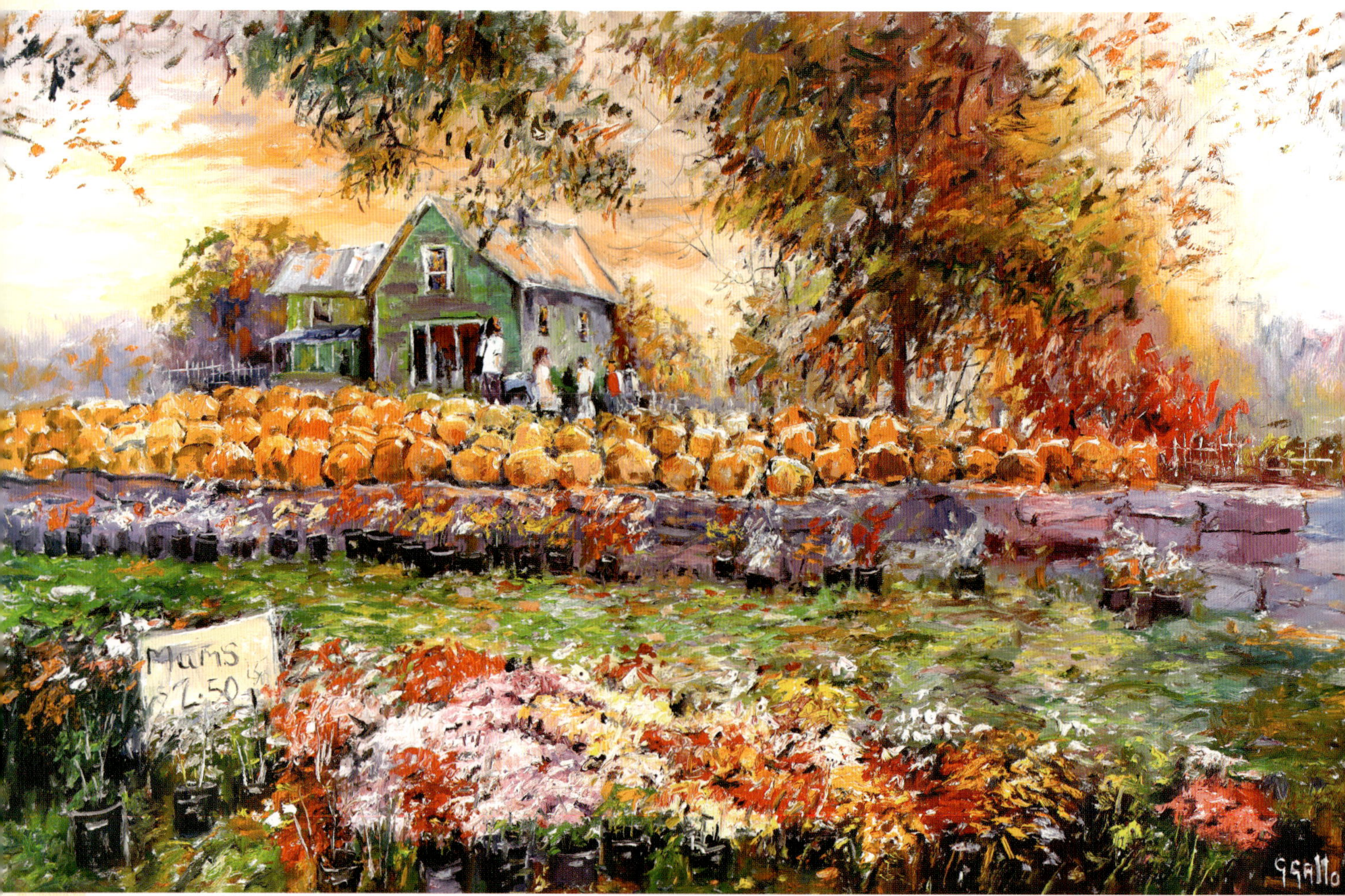

Much of this painting is Impressionistic in terms of brushstrokes. Choppy, short stitch-like strokes are everywhere in this piece. The trees are rendered in this way, with bits of both local color and sky color applied in an alternating manner and creating a wonderful, scintillating effect. The grass and endless petals of mums are also applied in the same manner. The figures and structure are painted more broadly to define their masses. These juxtapositions of alternate brushstroke approaches will create wonderful variety in your paintings.

PUMPKINS AND MUMS
Oil on Canvas · 40" × 60" (102cm × 152cm)

Using Brushstrokes to Indicate Direction

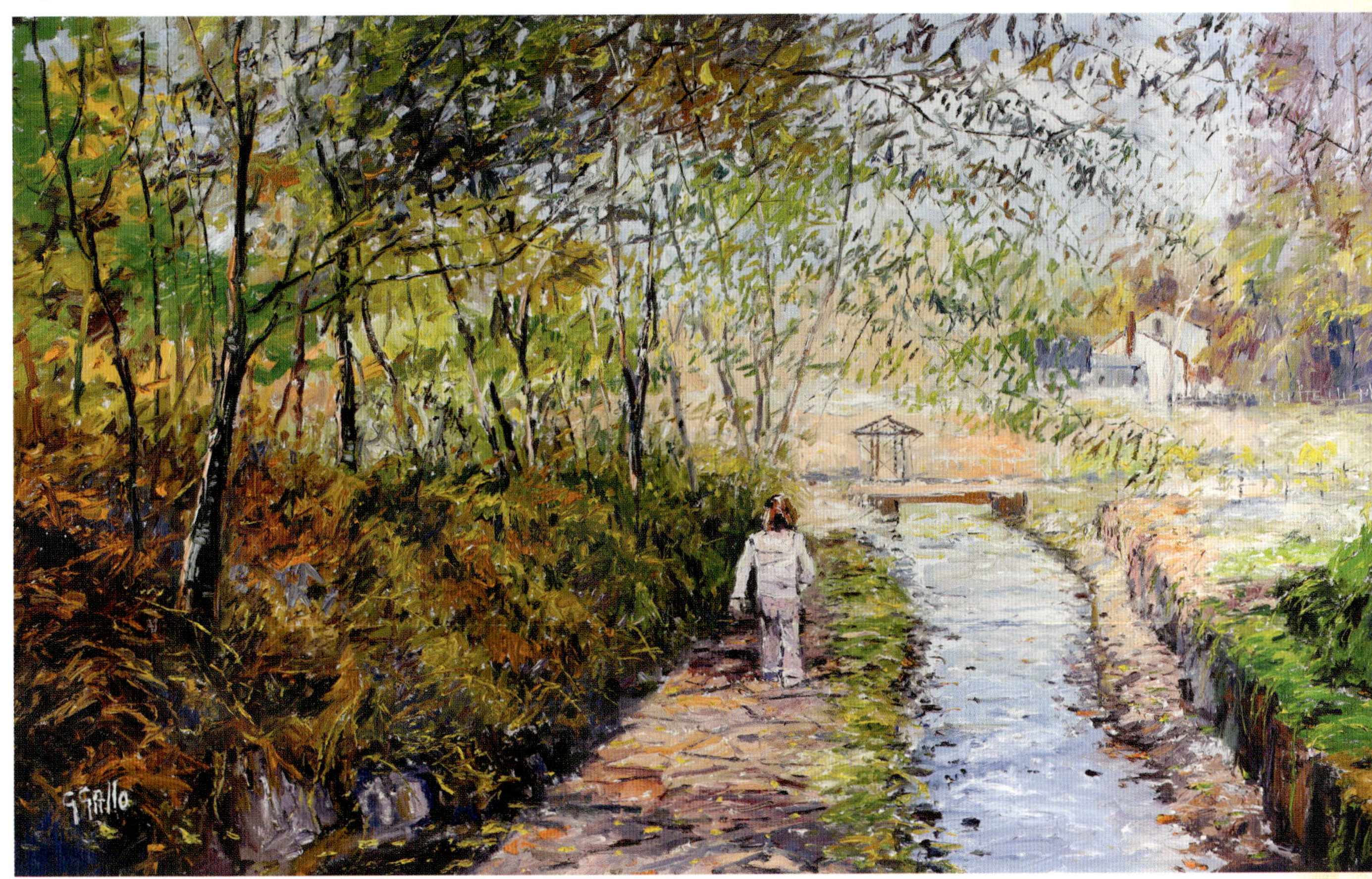

Here I not only applied Impressionistic brushstrokes to describe the endless tangle of leaves and bushes, I also used them as a directional device to lead the eye around the painting. You'll notice that a lot of the leaves above the figure lead your eye toward the figure. The direction of the strokes along with other compositional choices takes your eye around in a classic circle pattern, always leading back to the focal point.

HEADING HOME
Oil on Canvas · 40" × 60" (102cm × 152cm)

Go Big and Go Outside

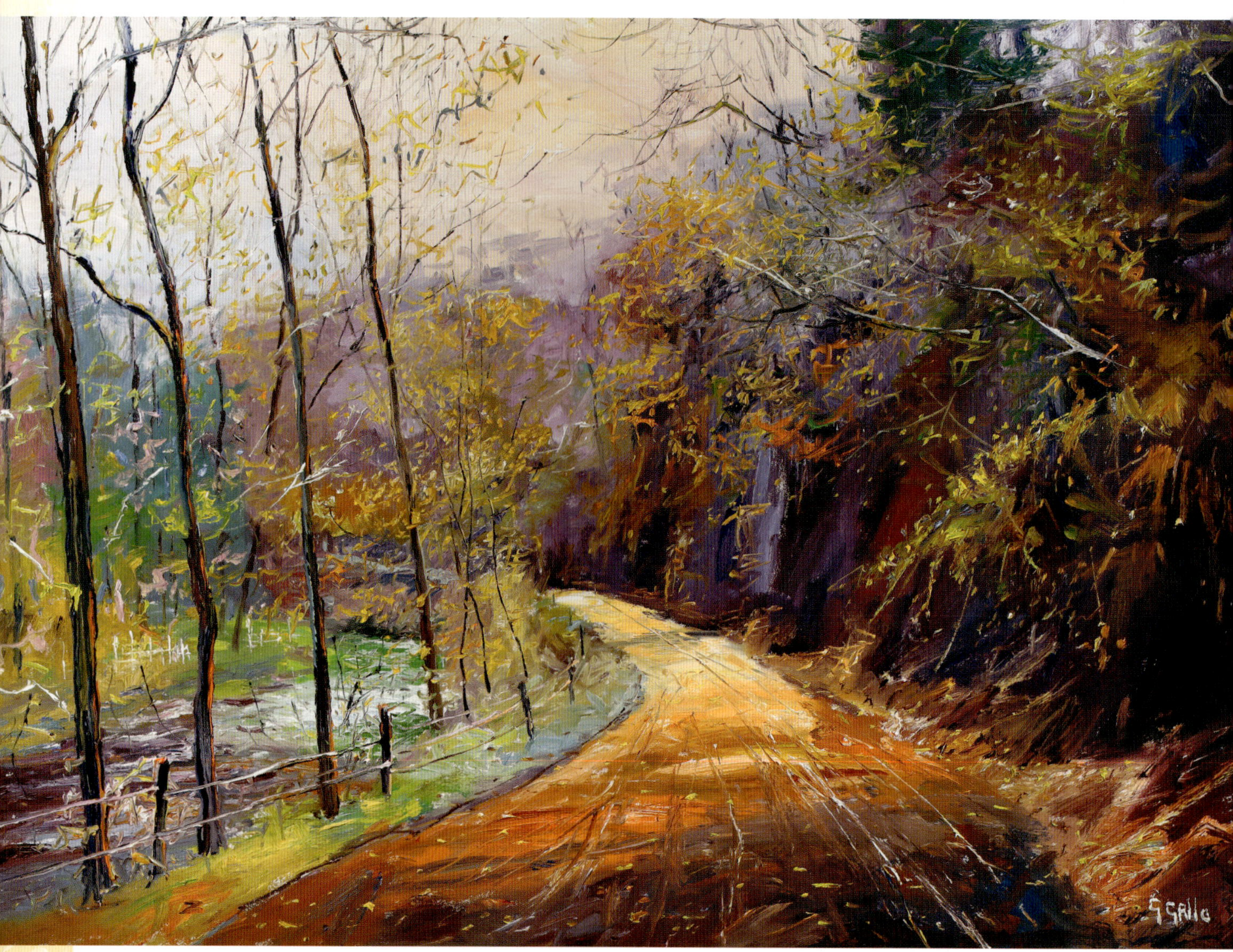

I feel it is virtually impossible to develop as an artist and find your own style if you don't paint larger canvases. It is a great way to discover who you are as a painter. Using brushstrokes on larger canvases is one of the great thrills of painting outdoors. Don't be afraid to load up your brush with paint and go for it! Swirl it around! Express yourself! Use the paint to describe not only what you're seeing but how you feel about it. Paint with your whole body and not just your wrist.

RIVER ROAD · Oil on Canvas · 50" × 70" (127cm × 178cm)

Go for It!

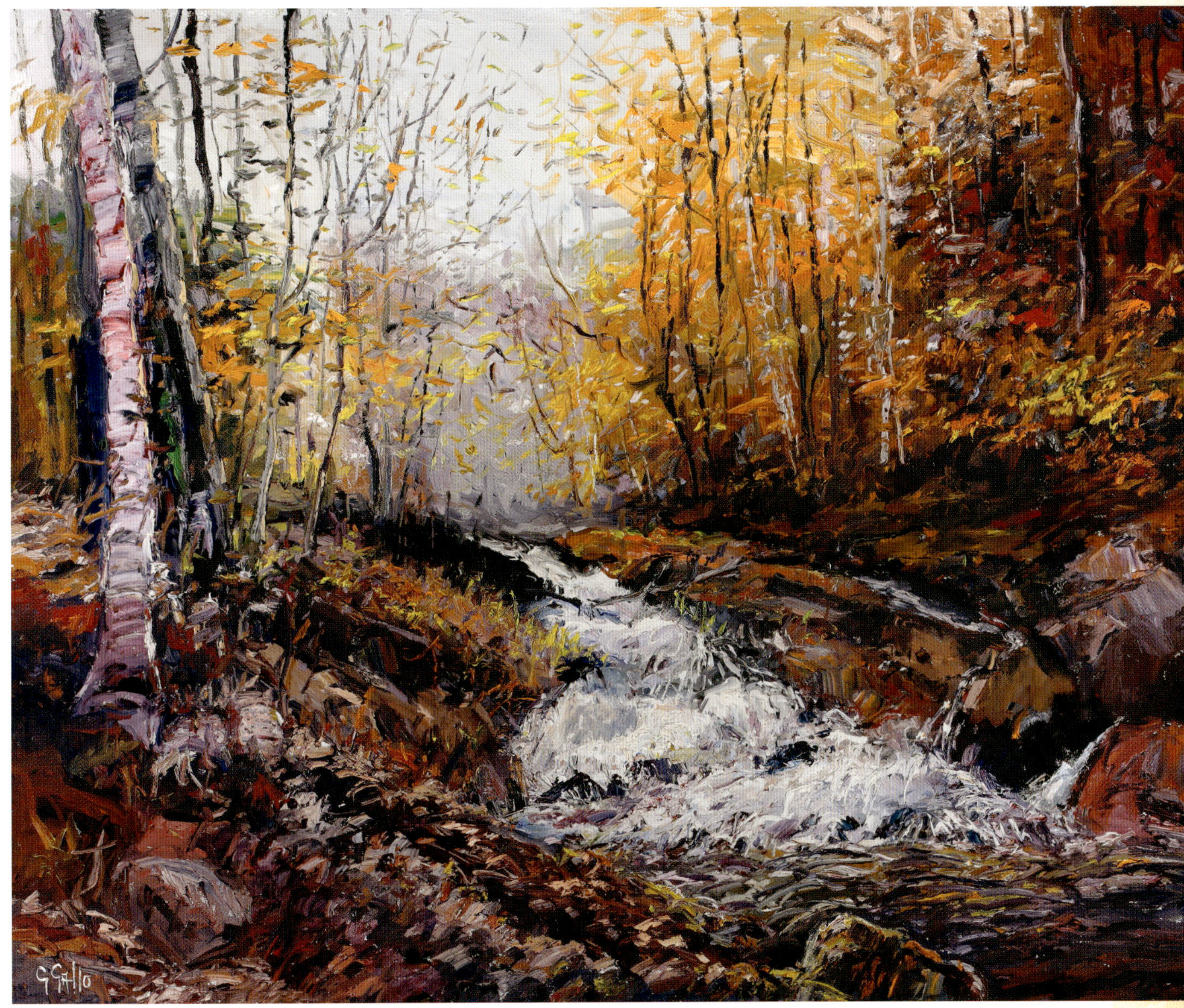

AUTUMN CASCADE
Oil on Canvas · 48" × 60" (122cm × 152cm)

Painting large will force you to create your own language with brushstrokes. Don't be timid. Enjoy using all the paint your brush can hold. As I'm sure you've realized, I'm an advocate for taking chances. It's the only way to grow as an artist and find your own voice. The Old Masters took their large canvases outside. I advise you to do the same. They were concerned with finding new ways to see and expressing in paint the beauty around them. You'll never achieve greatness if you keep doing 4" × 6" (10cm × 15cm) paintings the rest of your life. Edward Redfield would paint outdoors in subzero weather on canvases as large as 50" × 56" (127cm × 142cm) and complete the painting in one session! I'm not saying that you should take a canvas the size of a garage door outside at first, but I'm convinced working large outdoors will free you. Working large forces you to get the composition right, find new and inventive ways to express yourself, and if you do it well, it will bring you incredible joy as an outdoor painter.

Free Yourself

If you attack your work with gusto, the viewer will feel your excitement. The brushstrokes you choose are among the best tools you have to express yourself loud and clear. Don't be timid. Just let go. I find painting to be a joyful experience. In fact, I feel it is as close to God as I can get. When I am out in a field working with a light breeze blowing and the sunlight warming the land, I find myself in a wonderful state. Some of what I feel is the privilege of being alive. I also feel a great deal of accomplishment when I work with abandon because I imagine all of the years it took me to get to the place I am now.

Painting is in many ways not so much about the work but more about living with a certain kind of optimism.

Many of the Impressionists, both European and American, lived long and happy lives. I think the joy of pursuing something beautiful somehow keeps the body and mind going.

I implore you to keep the child within you very much alive as you work. That is where all of the curiosity of the human heart dwells. Keep that inquisitive voice active, and you will never tire of your work. It will always be fresh and new, a well that will never run dry. If you fall into formulas, live by rigid do's and don'ts, or never get past just copying what you see in front of you, you will eventually tire of painting. It will become boring because of the limits you've put upon yourself. There will be no way to grow, and frankly, little point in continuing.

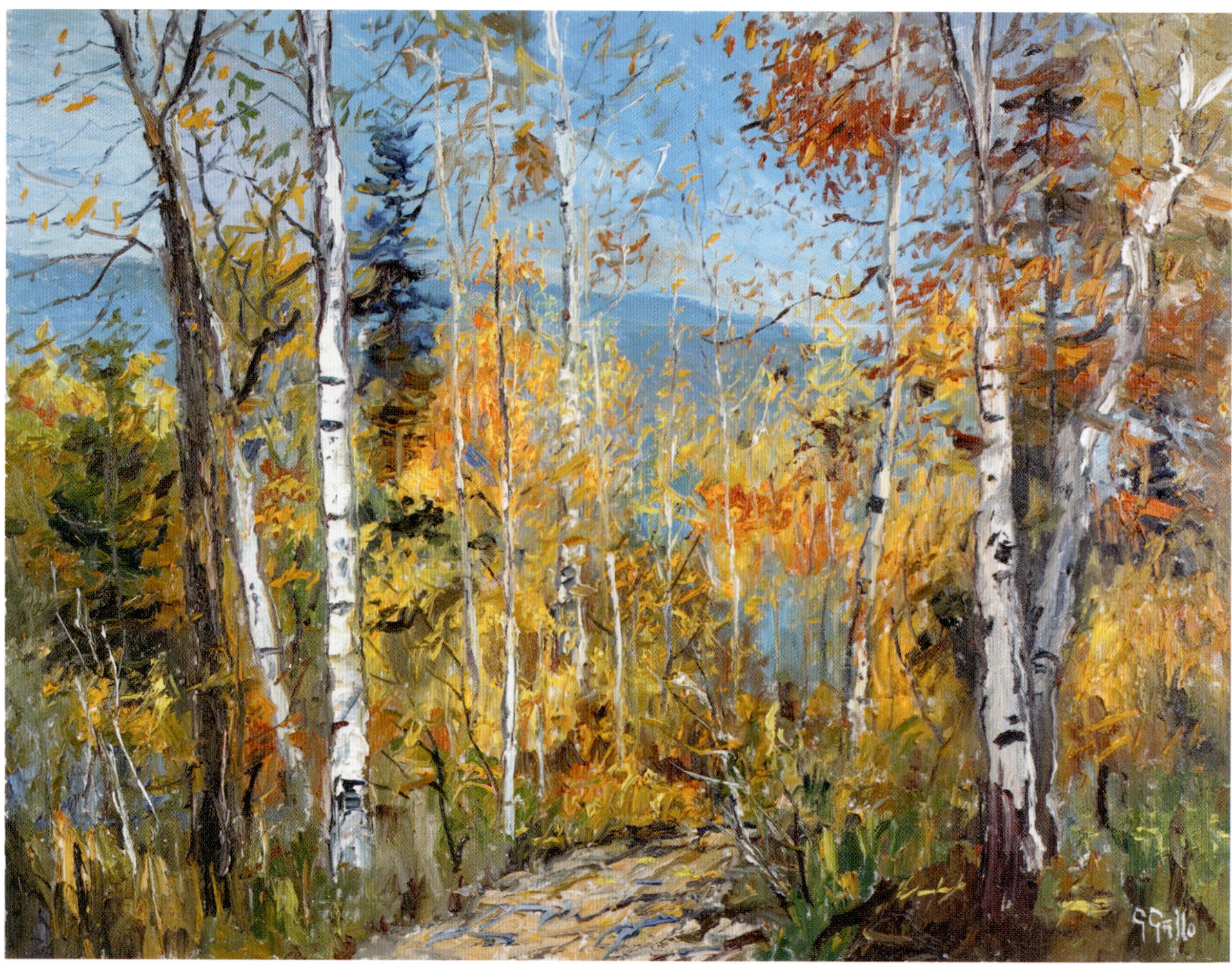

VIEW FROM BELLYACHE RIDGE
Oil on Canvas · 36" × 48" (91cm × 122cm)

This painting was done outdoors at 10,000 feet (3,048m). The light was incredibly clear and created a mosaic of color. I decided to communicate this using hundreds of little dabs of pure color.

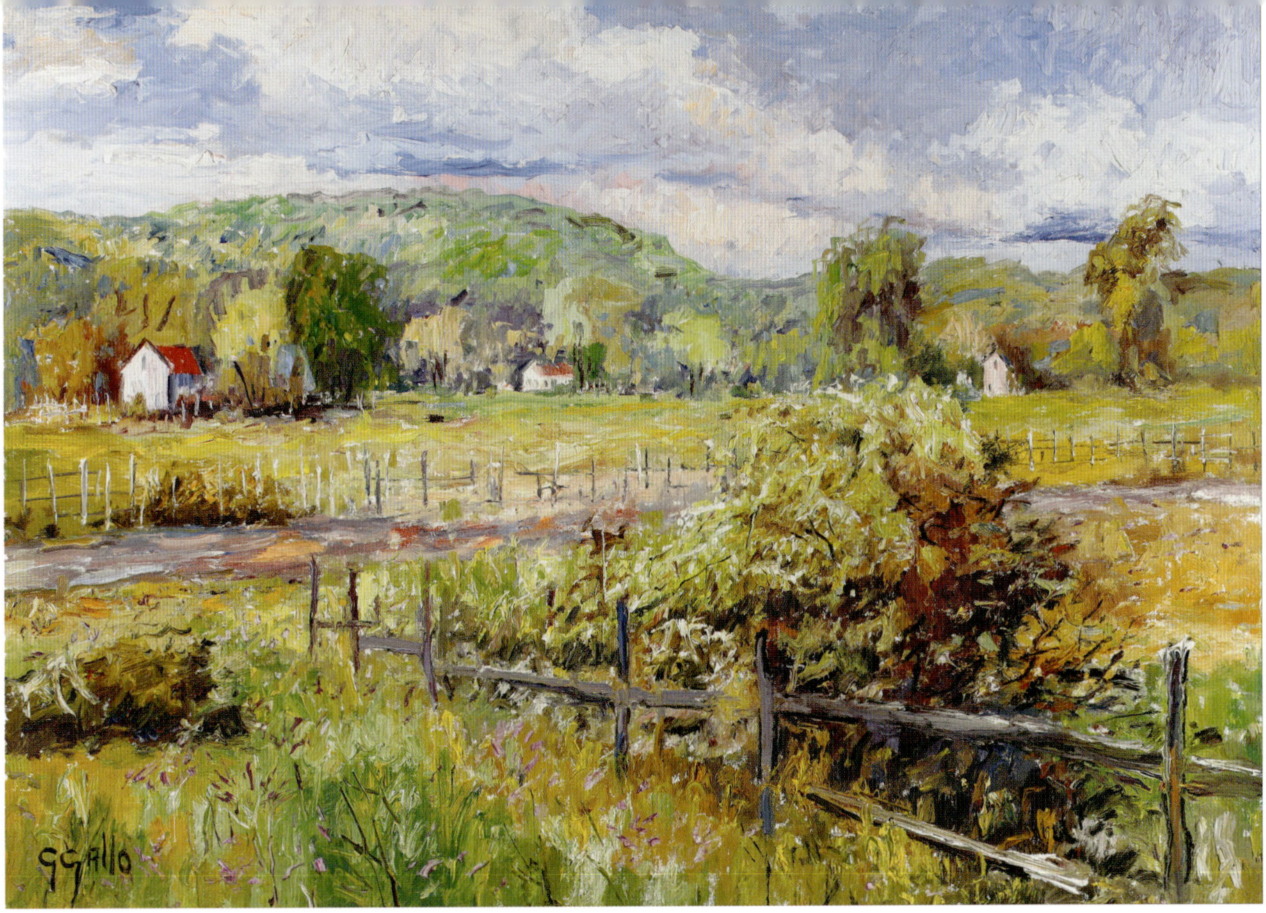

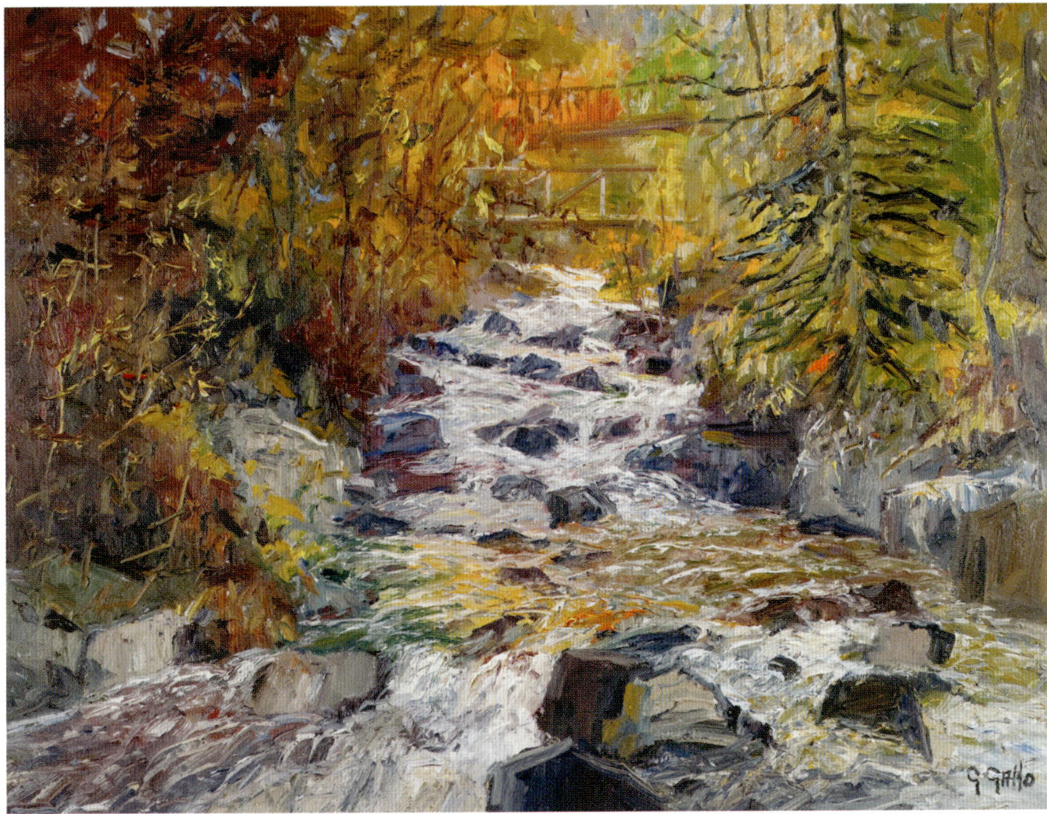

SOUTHERN JERSEY IN SPRING
Oil on Canvas · 30" × 40" (76cm × 102cm)

I used a similar treatment to *View from Bellyache Ridge*. The place appeared to have so much going on in terms of color that I put it all down using staccato-like strokes to communicate what I was feeling.

FROM THE COVERED BRIDGE
Oil on Canvas · 36" × 48" (91cm × 122cm)

The water was so lively and full of color that I loaded my brush and re-created its movements with slashes of paint.

Create Expressive Brushstrokes

So if the brushstrokes are the words of the painting, then they are also the punctuation—periods, commas and exclamation points. It is far more exciting to see how an artist feels about a place rather than just look at what he sees. See brushstrokes as something joyful and expressive unto themselves. Always imagine the different ways to put them down. There is terrific excitement in the juxtaposition of vertical strokes alongside horizontal strokes combined with choppy strokes and smooth strokes, all deliciously expressing your excitement about everything around you. This, to me, is where the greater art lies because it is produced by the fire of the heart as opposed to the cold and removed intellect of the mind. Of course painting can't be all heart; knowledge must be acquired to let the heart roam free. But as you gather more and more knowledge, imagine the freedom you will feel as you cut loose and create without judgment. You'll be able to just react and work joyfully faster than the speed of thought. This should be your goal. Your life and your paintings will be much better as a result.

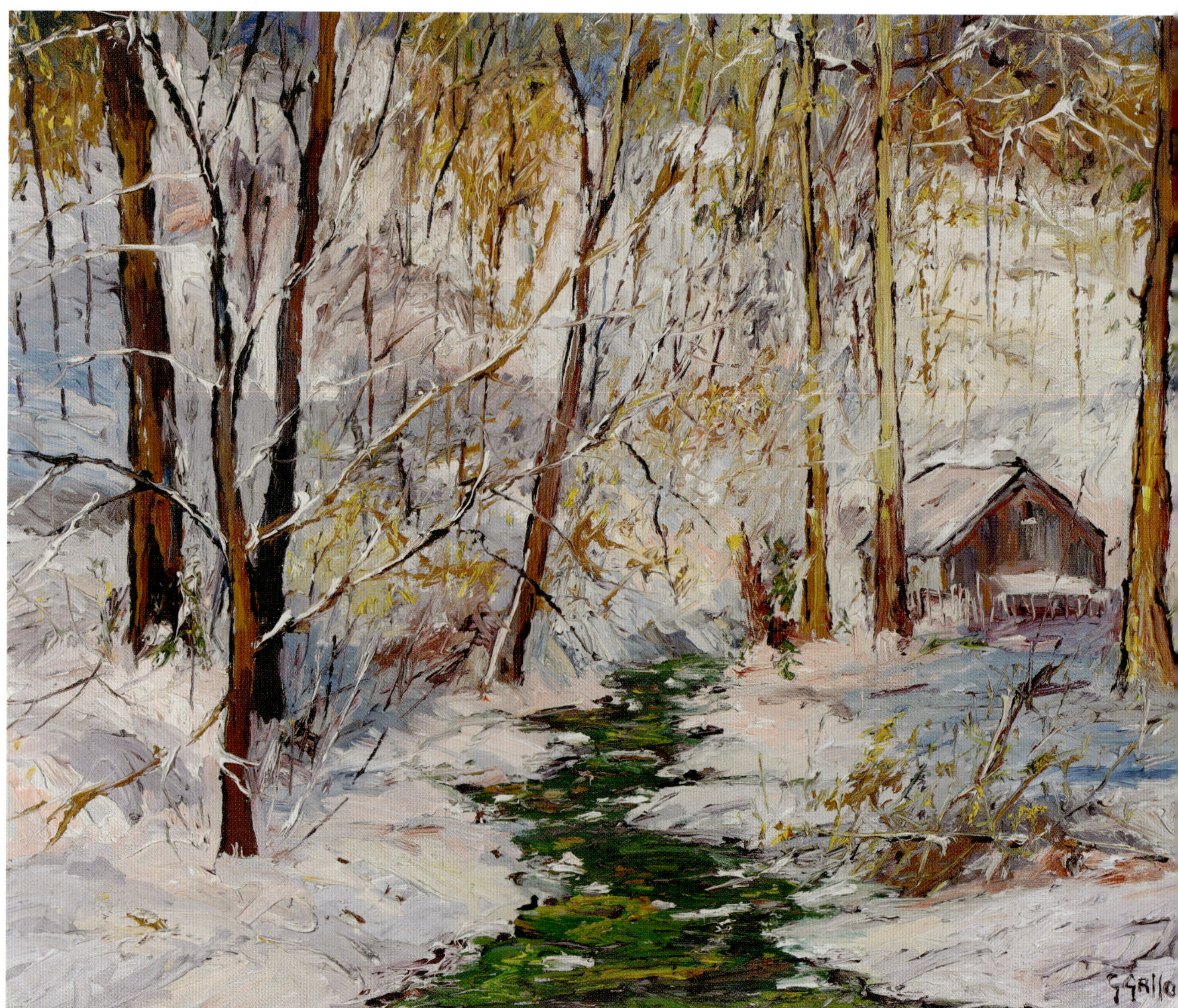

EMERALD STREAM, NEW HOPE · Oil on Canvas · 30" × 36" (76cm × 91cm)

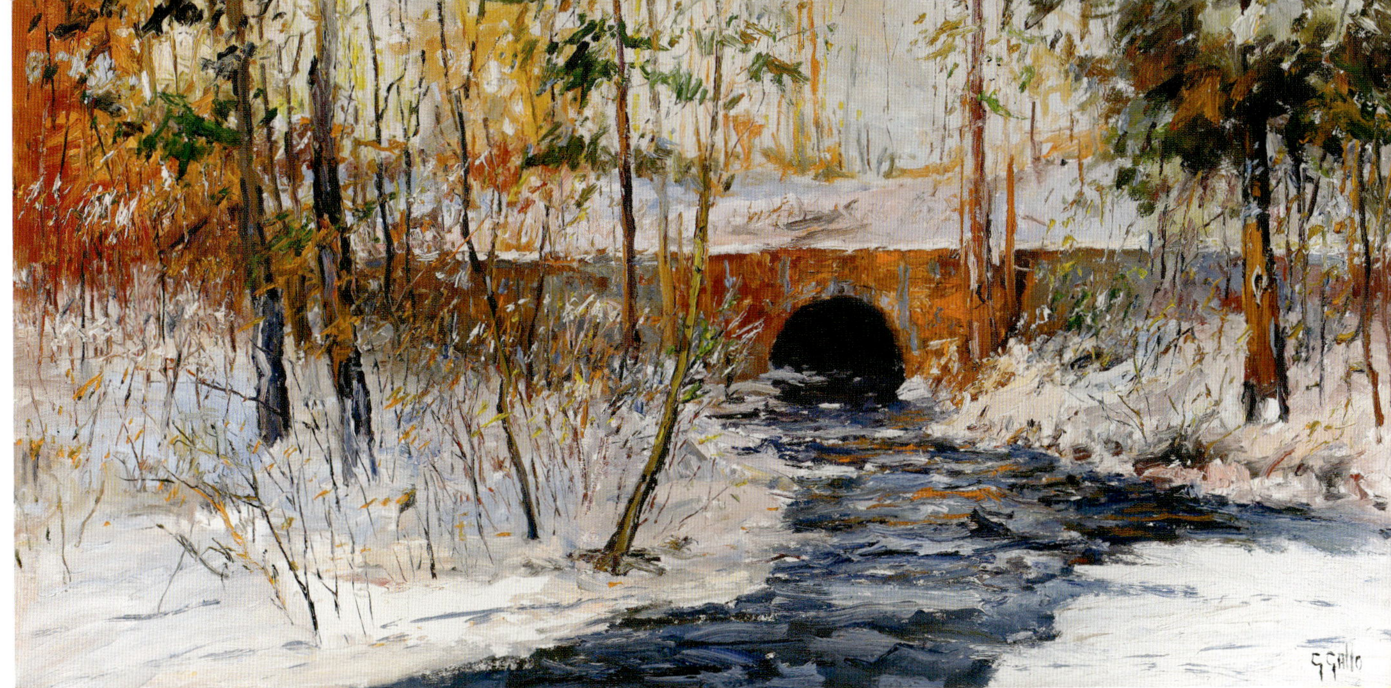

PHILLIPS MILL BRIDGE, WINTER
Oil on Canvas · 24" × 48" (61cm × 122cm)

The foliage here is painted using small energetic strokes versus the more broadly painted areas, the stream and the snow. These choices create contrasts.

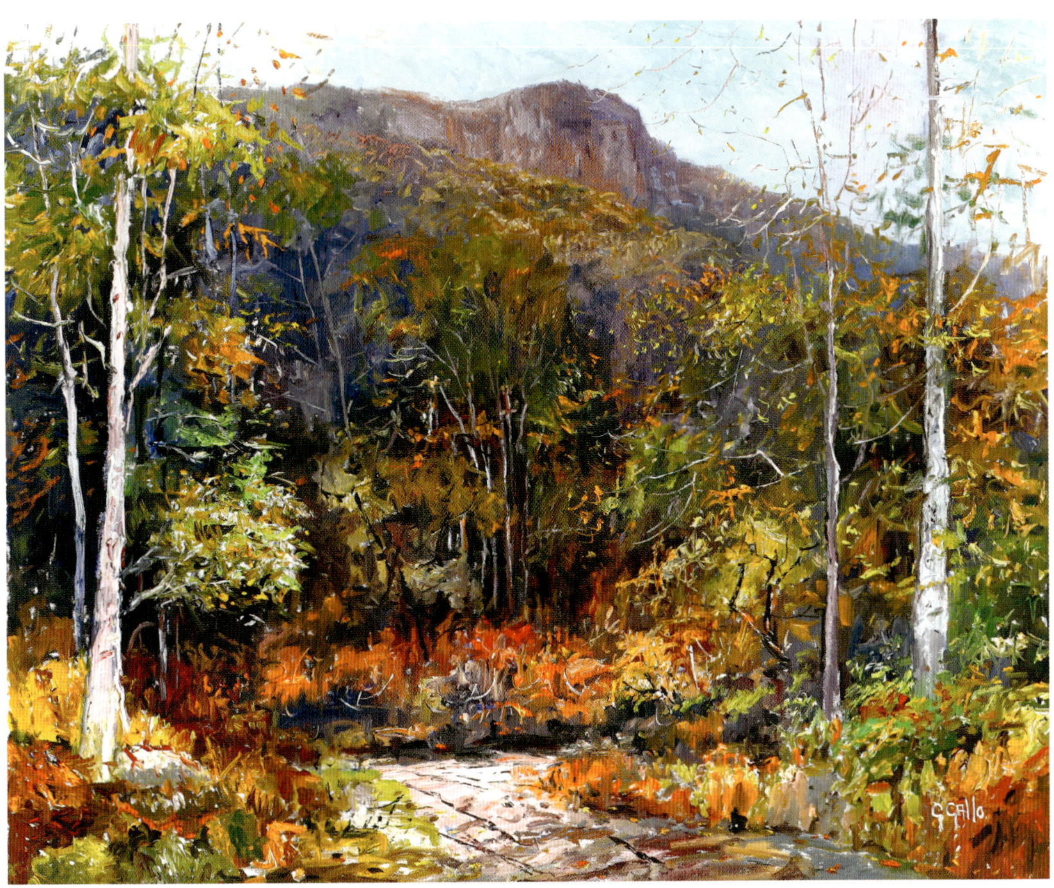

I was practically looking into the sun while I painted this scene. The light created a flat sky and mountain. The foliage caught the light from more of an angle, creating a wonderful, scintillating effect. I used what I saw to my advantage, painting the sky and mountain with flat strokes and the foliage with hundreds of thick dabs.

PETER STRAUSS RANCH IN AUTUMN
Oil on Canvas · 48" × 60" (122cm × 152cm)

Smaller Brushes and Dynamic Shifts

Many of the Impressionists used smaller brushes even on larger paintings because of the wonderful color shifts they could accomplish in doing so. Don't just accept a tree trunk as a certain brown or gray. Inside of that mass there can be many color shifts of similar values. A tree trunk can have warm spots, cool spots and bits of reflected light, all interacting with the local color of the tree. If the day is breezy and things are moving, there can be a dance of colors occurring, colors that are always changing and moving. Instead of mindlessly blocking out those areas with a big brush, it's fun to use smaller bristle brushes such as filberts, flats and daggers to express all of that wonderful movement. This is precisely what the Impressionists did. Look at the work of Monet, for example. He achieved a sense of lively movement in his work by way of the rhythms of his brushstrokes. The same is true of Redfield or Garber. Garber's 50" × 60" (127cm × 152cm) paintings are stitched together with little dabs of color. This is how he achieved a great feeling of sunlight in his work, by laying warm and cool notes side by side. He also saw the same dynamic color shifts in the sky. You, too, can see these colors and nuances if you look. I am always amazed at all the different specks of color I see in what we call a blue sky. Smaller brushes can help you achieve all of these wonderful Impressionistic dabs.

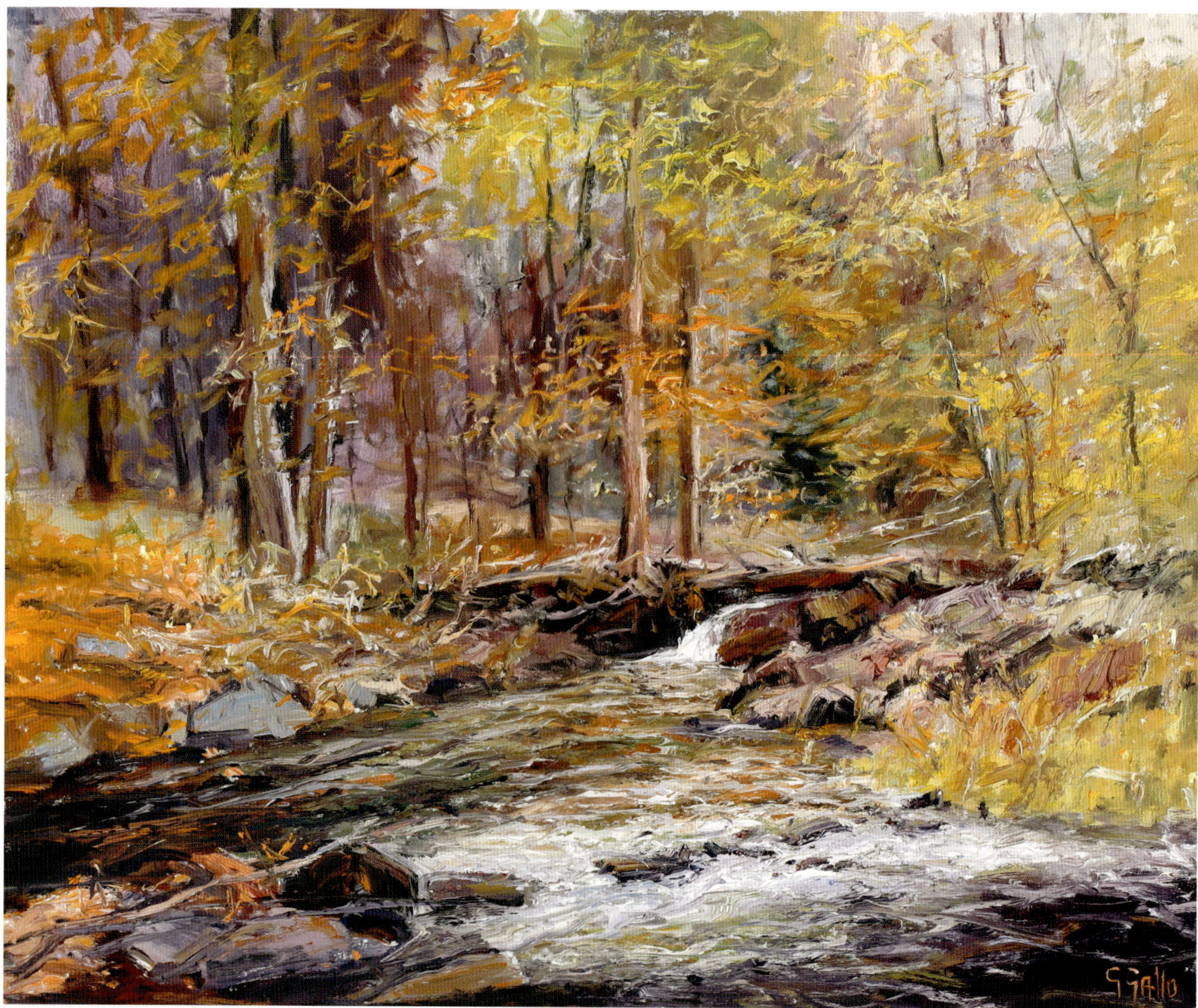

STREAM, EARLY SUMMER
Oil on Canvas · 24" × 30" (61cm × 76cm)

The day was high overcast, creating a quiet, silvery light. I kept my heavy paint application down to a minimum to create something more moody.

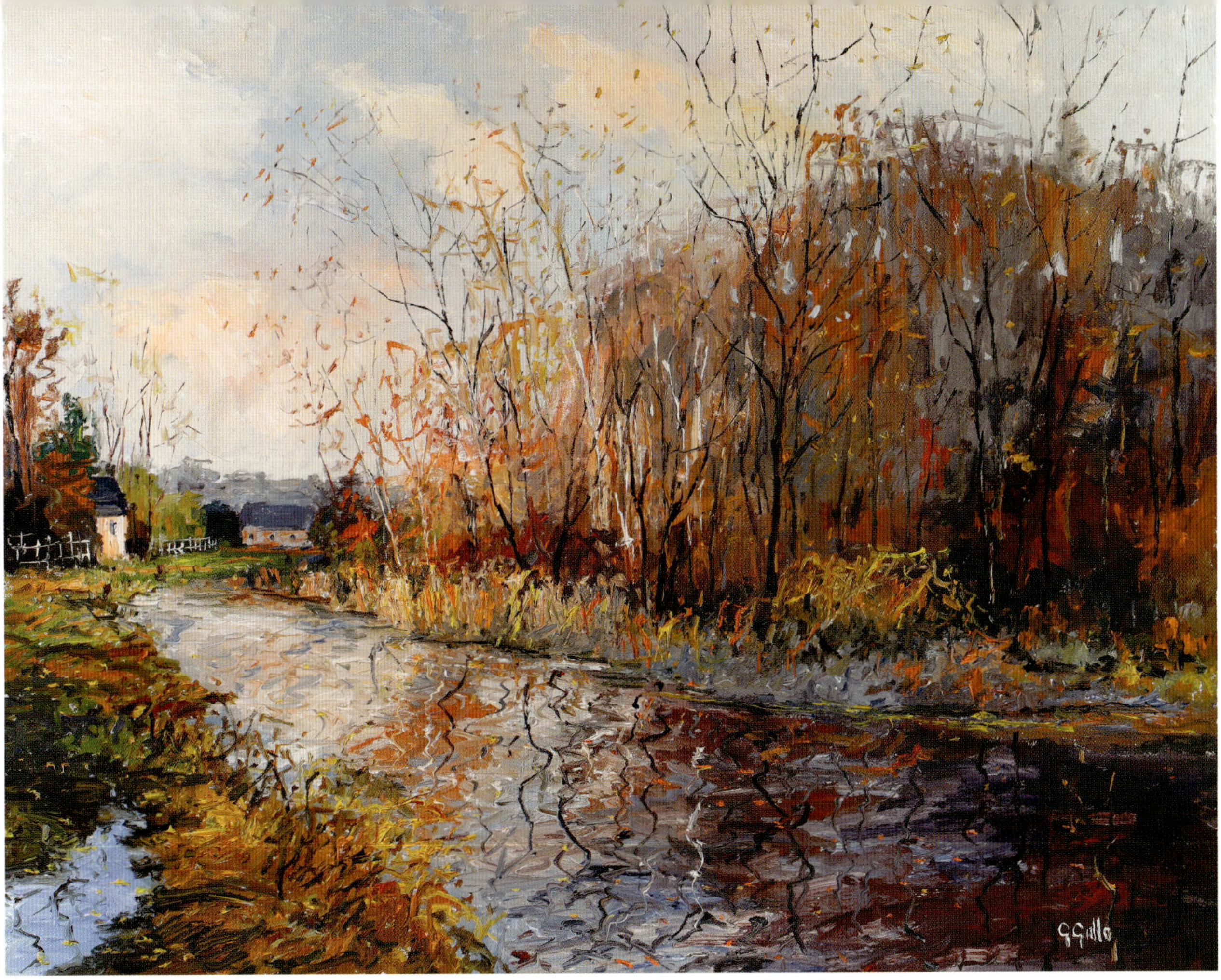

The bare trees and their reflections created a wonderful dance of lines. I used lots of heavy paint and swirling strokes to define what I saw.

TOW PATH IN AUTUMN
Oil on Canvas · 40" × 50" (102cm × 127cm)

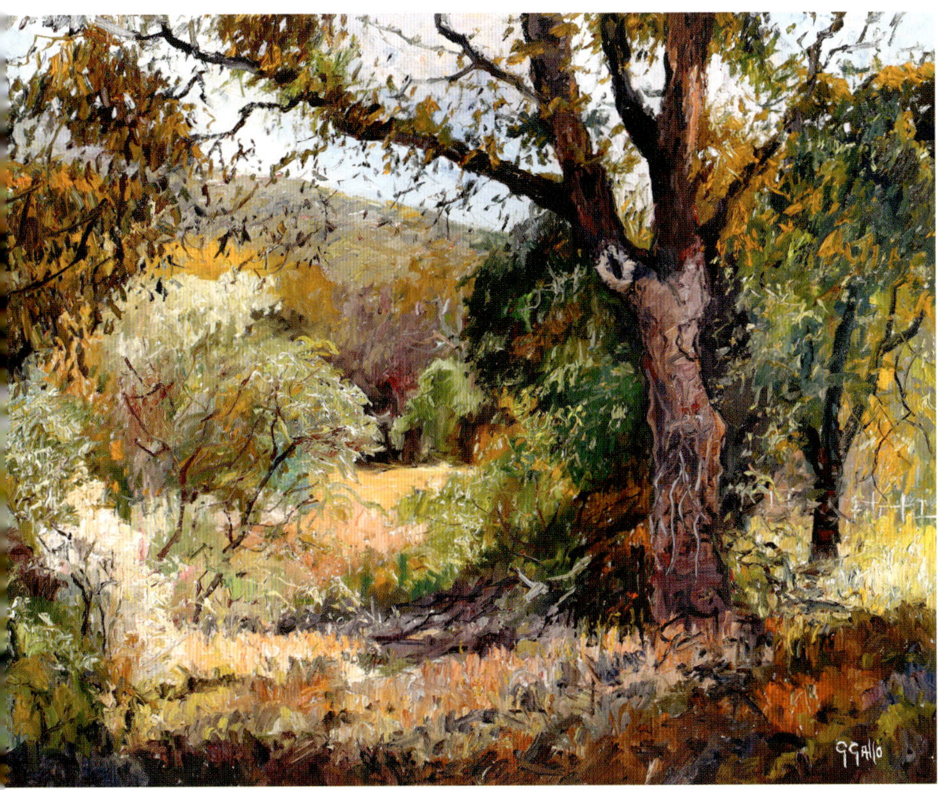

Nearly all of this painting is done with classic staccato-like Impressionistic brush strokes. The exception is the large tree, which is painted more broadly. It acts as an anchor holding the painting together.

**SUMMER AFTERNOON,
PETER STRAUSS RANCH**
Oil on Canvas · 38" × 50" (97cm × 127cm)

Lost and Found Edges

Being aware of edges is a great tool for adding a sense of romance and mood to your work. Most edges will occur naturally in your painting if your values are correct. And sometimes you can blend one edge into another to make it "lost." Lost and found edges are a great way to achieve movement in your work. For instance, an ocean wave will have many hard and soft edges, and defining their character will give your work a sense of both movement and reality. However, you should also be cautious about edges. The interplay of edges has become very much *en vogue* in recent years. Some painters have created works that are largely about edges. If you're not careful, you can get carried away with them, and your work may look like you have cataracts.

The American Impressionists used edges sparingly. In fact, John F. Carlson believed that all edges should be hit hard. I believe this is because he and many other artists at that time were producing very large paintings, and therefore their work had to hold together from a distance. Soft edge work, although compelling, is akin to whispering. If you're too far away, you simply won't hear it.

But make no mistake, observing edges in nature is a key to producing powerful work. Edges are a close cousin to values. To judge the hardness or softness of an edge, merely squint. As you close your eyes, the last thing you see will not only be your brightest value but also your hardest edge.

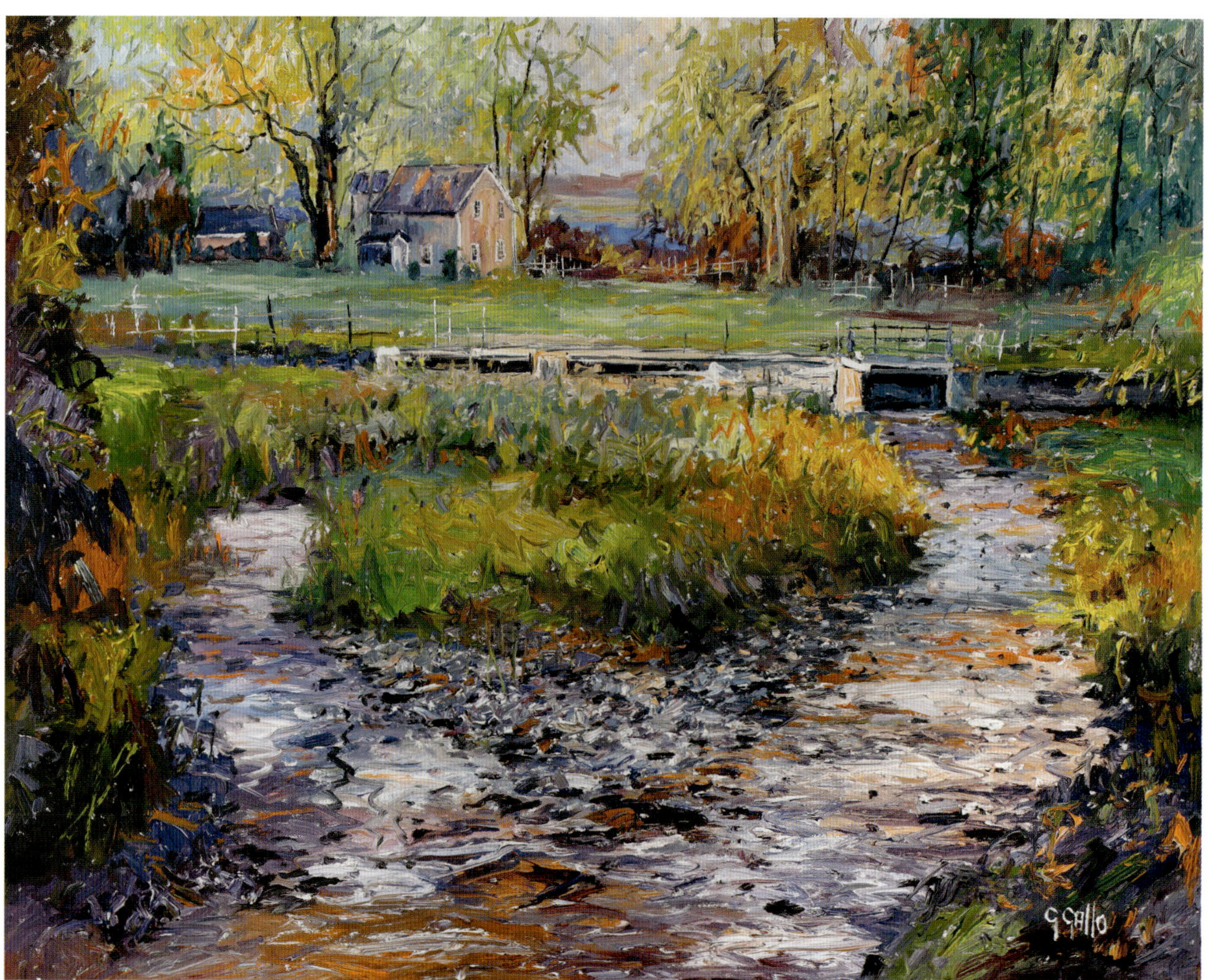

Much of this painting is about vertical strokes juxtaposed with horizontal strokes. The building and the trunks of trees in the distance are painted more flatly so they don't compete with the energetic handling of paint in the foreground.

OLD MILL STREAM
Oil on Canvas · 40" × 50" (102cm × 127cm)

A Last Thought on Color

Some painters might tell you that cutting complementary colors into one another will not produce a neutral color. This type of thinking has little to do with the reality of painting. This is the equivalent of saying there is no such thing as a true warm red. Color is relative. A warm red in one painting could be a cool red in another. We perceive colors and color temperatures based on what is next to them. The same is true for mixing neutrals or grays for your paintings. Your neutral might appear green in one color universe and brown in another. It is color relationships that you should be shooting for not only in landscape painting but in all painting. Your neutral colors, born on the palette of the day's work, are fun to mix. When you mix complement into complement, you are really painting and can come up with unique and honest color combinations, especially in terms of neutrals. Understanding this will be one of the major keys to your success.

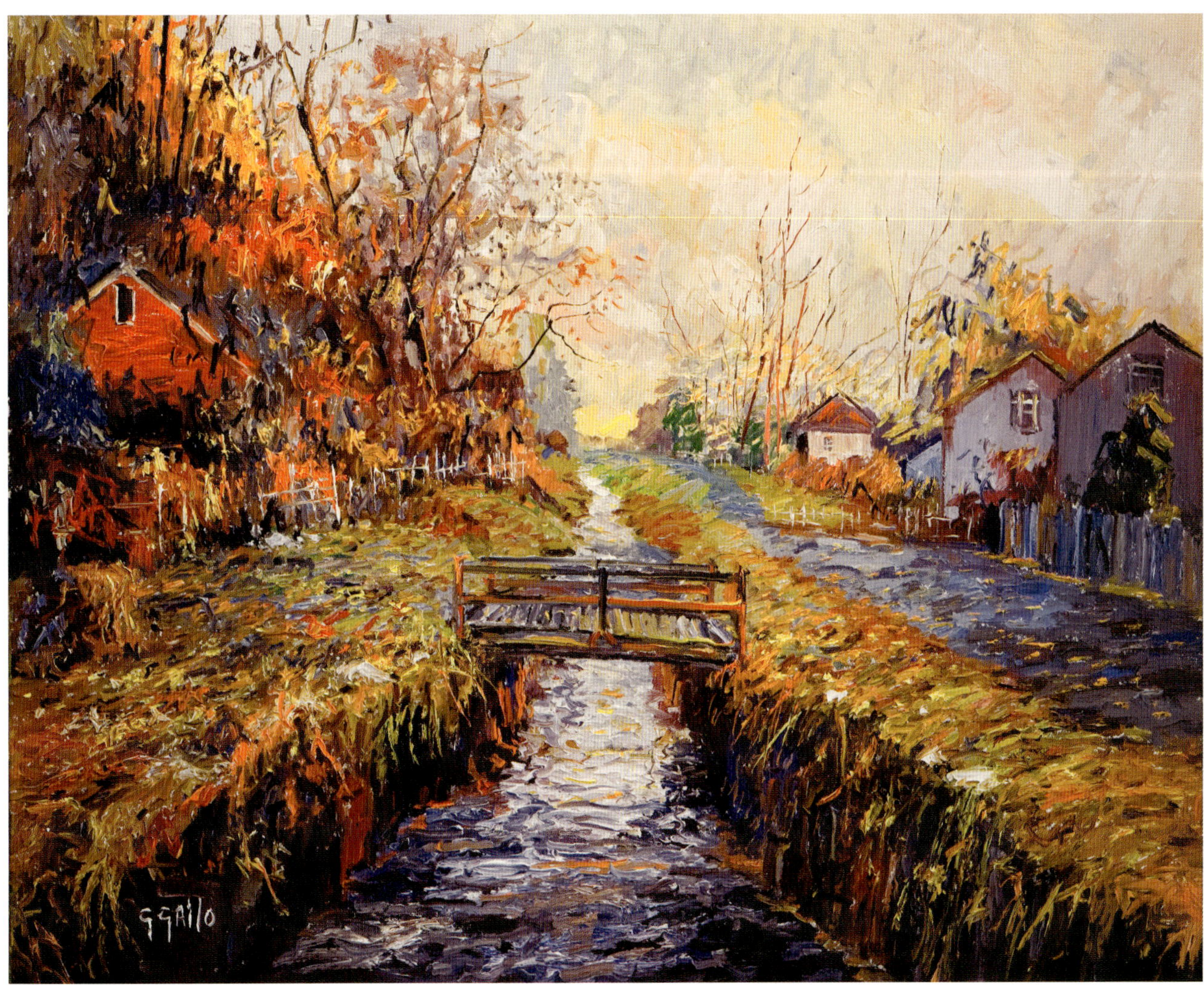

BUCKS COUNTY FOOTBRIDGE
Oil on Canvas · 40" × 50" (102cm × 127cm)

The foliage looked like hundreds of little dabs. The grass looked like longer, more graceful strokes. The water simply swirled toward me. So I merely put down what I saw and felt.

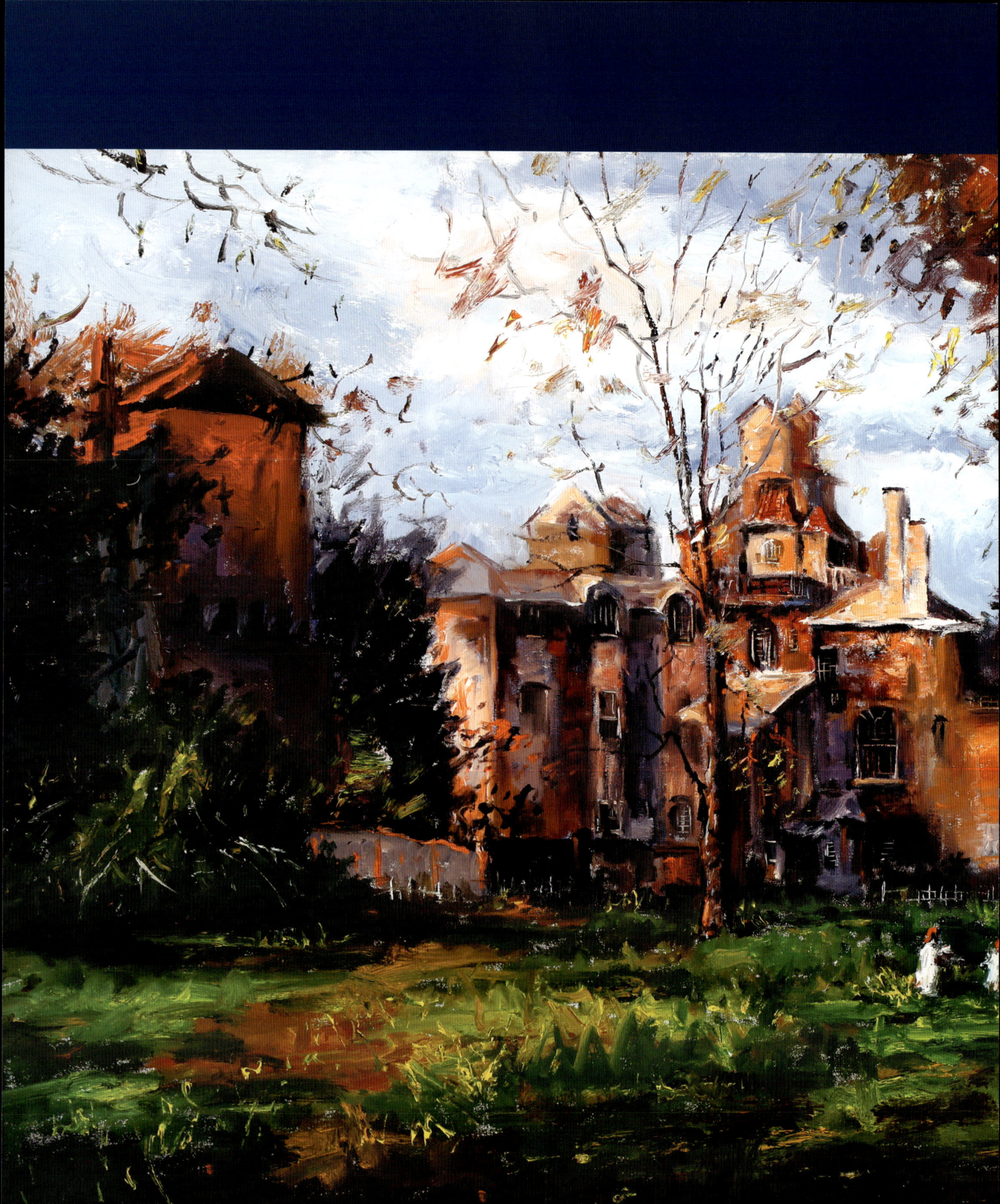

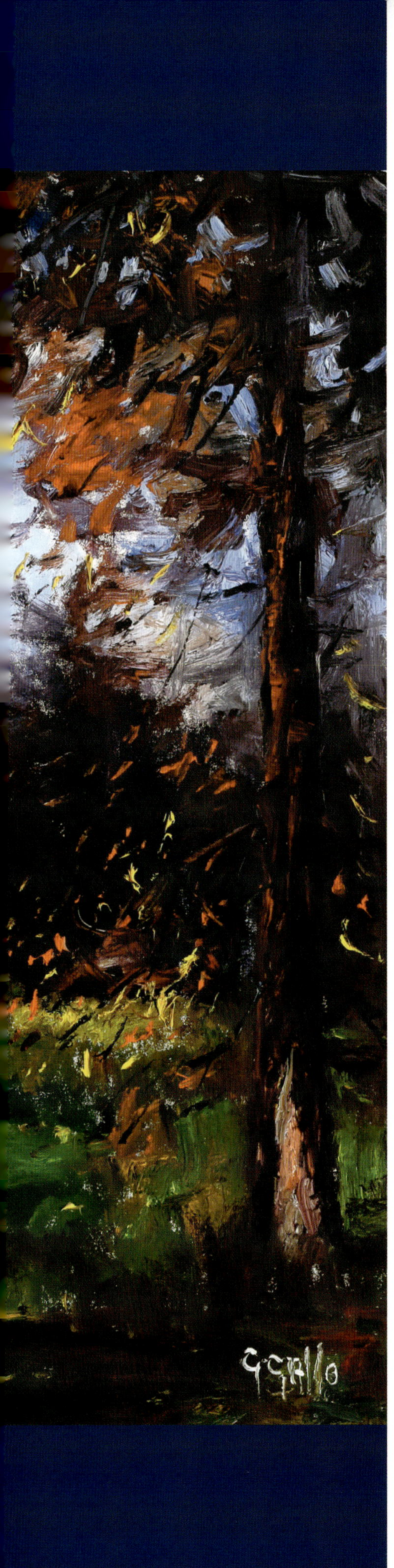

CHAPTER 6

THE PROCESS OF PAINTING

Do your best to have the finished picture in your mind before you start, and you'll have a much clearer path to the finish. You wouldn't get into your car and drive aimlessly around hoping you'll somehow arrive where you want to go. Painting is no different. I work in a true *alla prima* style: I finish as I go. I do this for one simple reason: The idea is to get one thing finished and right and completed as soon as possible because then finishing the rest of the piece becomes easier. If you paint something inaccurate next to something that's accurate in terms of drawing, value or color, the thing that is wrong will jump out at you. I've never understood painters who had things that were half right all over their canvas. How will they ever know that something is correct?

The quickest and clearest way to the painting process is to compare one set of brushstrokes to another set side by side. I was told as a student by many well-intentioned instructors that this approach was wrong. At one point, I almost gave up painting because I adopted their methods and it got me so confused I could never bring any painting to a fruitful conclusion. Then luckily I saw a few half-finished paintings by two of my favorite artists, Claude Monet and Edward Redfield. There were passages in their works that were totally complete while other sections of their canvases were still white. As soon as I began painting in this manner, I began to do better work. Now I'm not telling you to paint like me. You should approach a painting in a way that makes sense to you and not adopt any idea that goes against your nature. But for my way of thinking, finishing as you go, comparing one passage to another, simply makes more sense.

HAUNTED · Oil on Canvas · 36" × 48" (91cm × 122cm)

Country Road at Evening: A Lesson in Design

MATERIALS

SURFACE
stretched oil-primed linen

BRUSHES
no. 4 filbert

no. 2 rigger

¼", ½" daggers

PIGMENTS
Ivory Black, Ultramarine Blue, Alizarin Crimson, Cadmium Red Deep, Cadmium Orange, Cadmium Yellow Deep, Cadmium Yellow Lemon, Phthalo Blue, Titanium White

OTHER
medium cup

odorless mineral spirits

paper towels

wooden or paper palette

The inspiration for this painting demonstration comes from a photo of a peaceful place during the last moments of daylight. An image like this can be very powerful not only because of the mood it sets, but because of the emotions it elicits. I am frequently drawn to subject matter like this. Farmland and country roads bring up notions of simplicity and as a result, the painting should be executed accordingly.

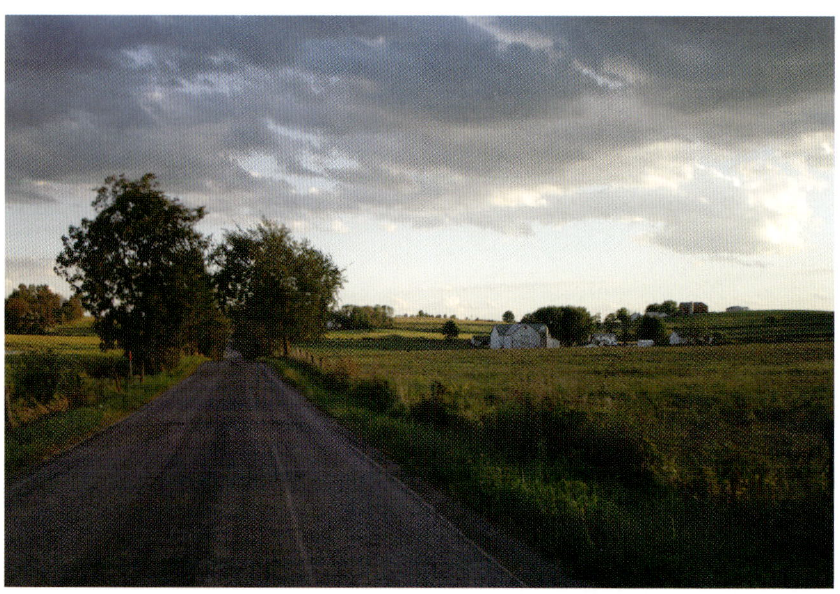

A road leading the viewer's eye into a painting is a classic compositional device and helps create a strong design.

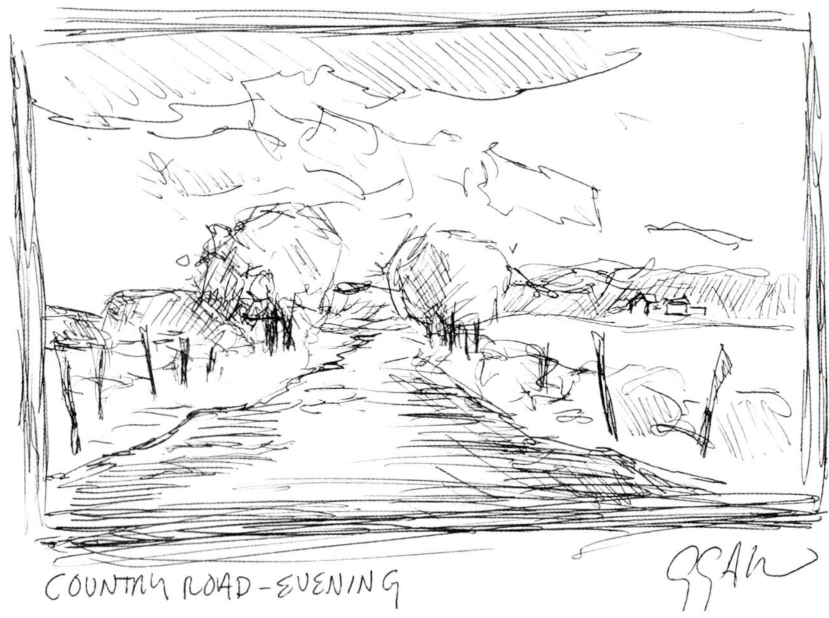

In the sketch I widen the road at the bottom of the composition to pull the viewer's eye in even more. This creates a more dramatic design.

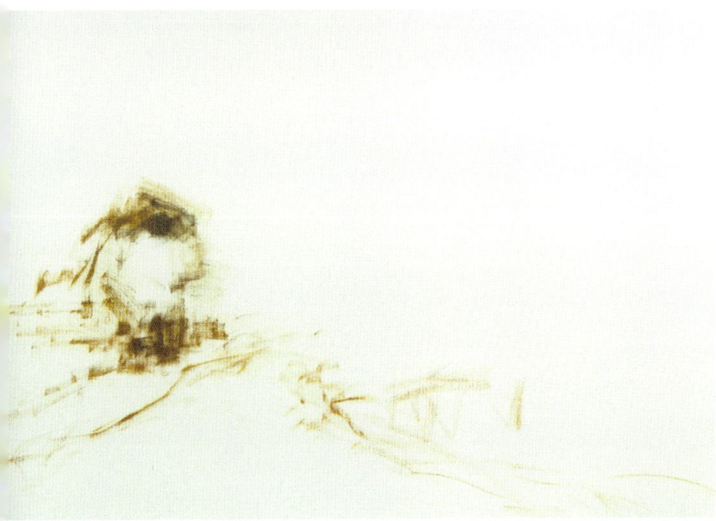

1 BEGIN SKETCHING ON YOUR CANVAS

When putting together a good design, exaggeration is certainly one of the best tools you have. Start by making the road much wider at the bottom than it actually is in the photo. Use a ¼" dagger brush with a thin wash of mineral spirits, Ultramarine Blue, and Alizarin Crimson. Step back and you'll see that by widening the road, the vanishing point becomes more dynamic and draws your eye into the piece. Establish the basic shape of the tree on the left.

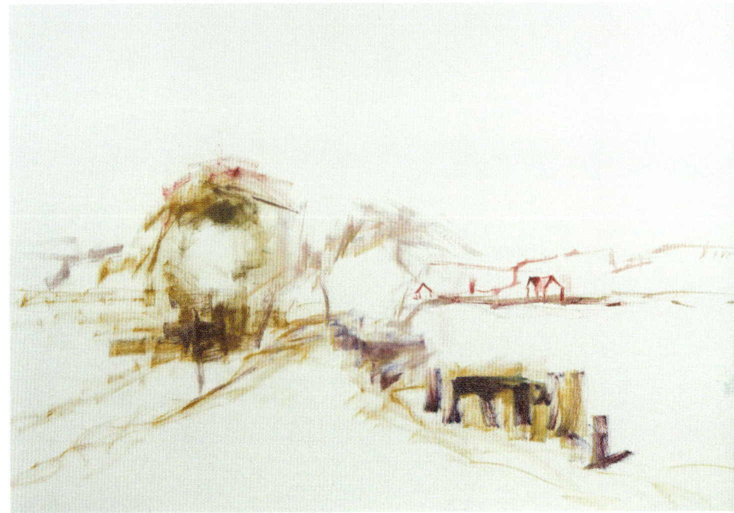

2 ESTABLISH THE COMPOSITION

Since design is the most important thing in painting, it's essential to start by putting everything in the right place. This keeps repainting at a minimum. It also keeps everything looking fresh and spontaneous because you don't have to go back and move things around. Establish the horizon line, the distant tree line and the location of the main farmhouse in the background. Continue establishing the composition and once you are satisfied, you are ready to move to the next step.

3 ESTABLISH WARMS AND COOLS

Still keeping the colors to washes and not adding heavy paint yet, establish some of the warms and cools with a ½" dagger or no. 4 filbert. You want to see as quickly as possible whether the color harmonies are going to work. The deep purples and warm orange-greens are a beautiful contrast. Keep your cooler colors in the distance (purples, blues and cool greens) and warmer colors up front (orange-greens). The more you work out now, the less you have to work out later. Once you know this is working, you can move to the next step, which is to add heavier paint. The important thing is that you need to know what the finished painting is going to look like based on this strong beginning.

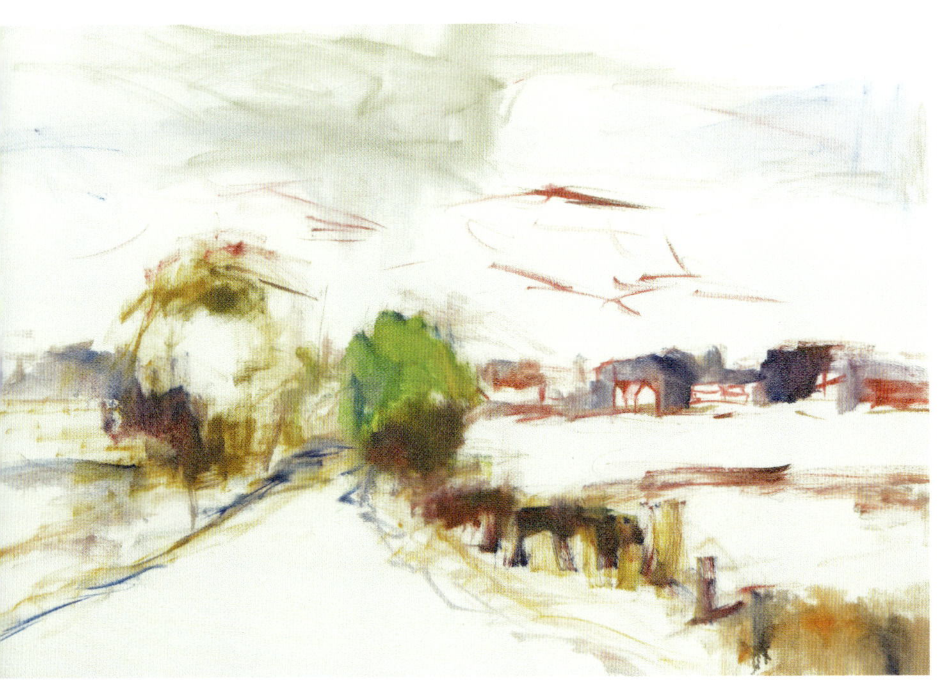

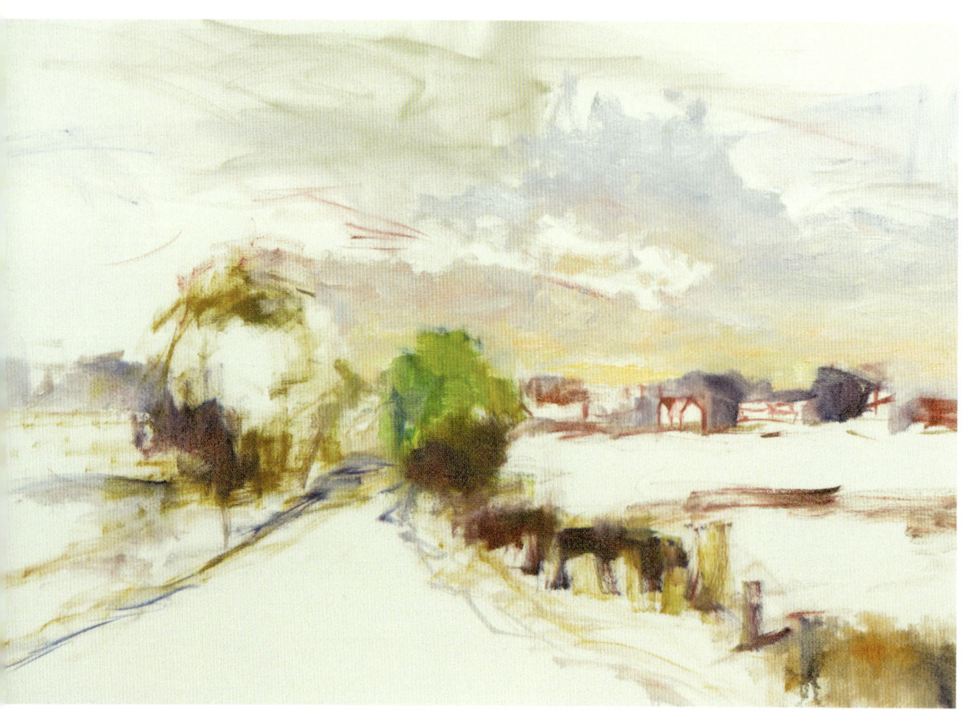

4 TIE THE SKY AND LAND TOGETHER

Now use heavier paint in the sky, a combination of Titanium White, Ultramarine Blue, Alizarin Crimson, Cadmium Orange and just a hint of Cadmium Yellow Lemon. The harmonies are working well for two reasons. One is that much of what is going on in the sky is also going on in the land below. Work using many of the same color combinations, adding only white as needed. Too many students dissect areas when they paint and don't think of them as one completed thought. See everything as a unit. The other reason is that all the colors on the palette harmonize naturally (see Chapter 3 for a refresher on color).

5 COLOR PATTERNS

Alternate between your ¼" and ½" daggers to create color and value variation as well as different textures. Complete the cloud using the same color combinations but add more white and Cadmium Yellow Deep. Make sure to keep the edges of the clouds soft. You don't want them to compete with the trees that are closer to us. Keep all of this in mind as you work. Move on to the other parts of the sky using Ultramarine Blue and Alizarin, leaning towards blue. Everything is harmonizing because you're keeping it simple and making sure that you're putting down the same color patterns that you established earlier. Add a touch of Ivory Black to your purple mixture, graying it out near the top of the canvas. Begin to establish the distant tree masses using combinations of purple and green.

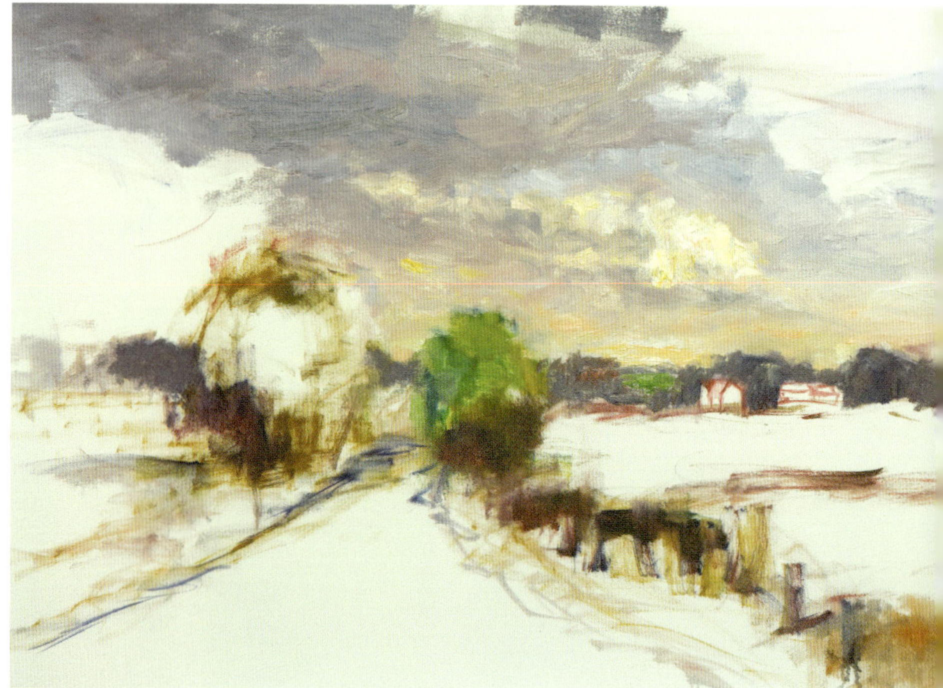

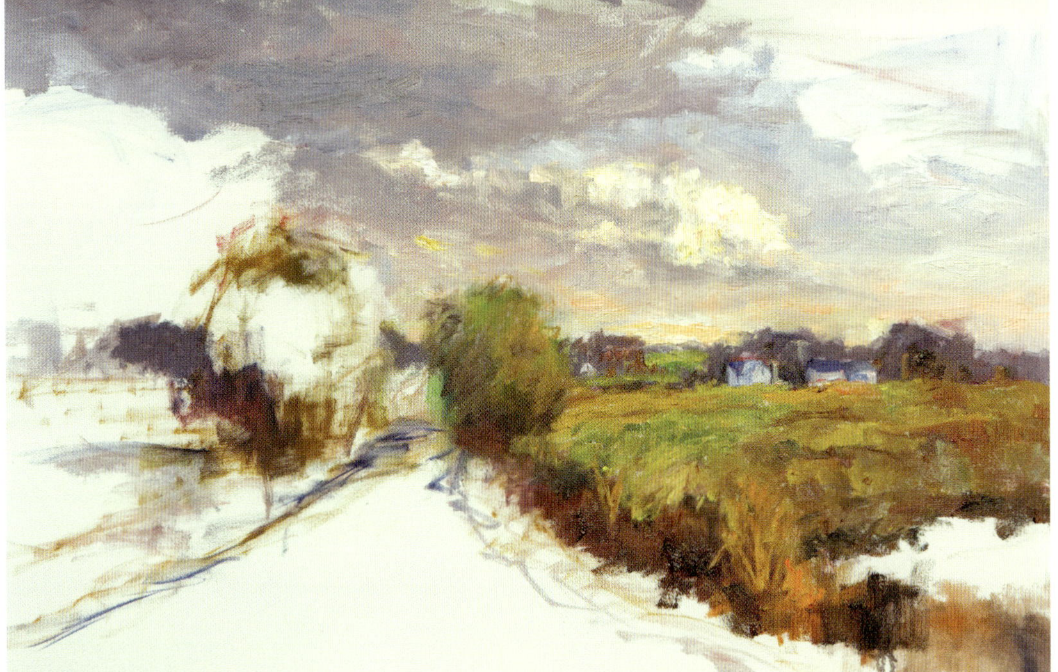

6 ADDING LOCAL COLOR

Continue working on the distant tree mass. The reason there's harmony is that you're re-creating the same basic color patterns of the sky, only adding more local color to the mixtures (the local color here being the real green of the trees). This isn't a trick; this is how nature behaves. The air between where you are standing and the distant trees has moisture. The moisture picks up color. The color it picks up is the color of the sky. Imagine a series of veiled curtains hanging between you and various objects.

Continue with the field on the right using Phthalo Blue, Cadmium Yellow, Lemon Cadmium Yellow Deep and Cadmium Orange with a touch of white. The Cadmium Yellow Lemon has a touch of blue in it and reflects what's going on in the blue parts of the sky. The Cadmium Yellow Deep reflects the warmer or more orange parts of the sky.

The darks in the field are merely the purples or cool sections of the sky that are reflected below, again achieving harmony. Use the ¼" dagger to create the detail in the bushes. It's a very versatile brush with sharp edges. Paint the distant farmhouses, being very cognizant of how far away they are from you. Keep them cool and grayed out using various shades of white, purple and blue. Don't make them all the same exact value; you want there to be variety between them.

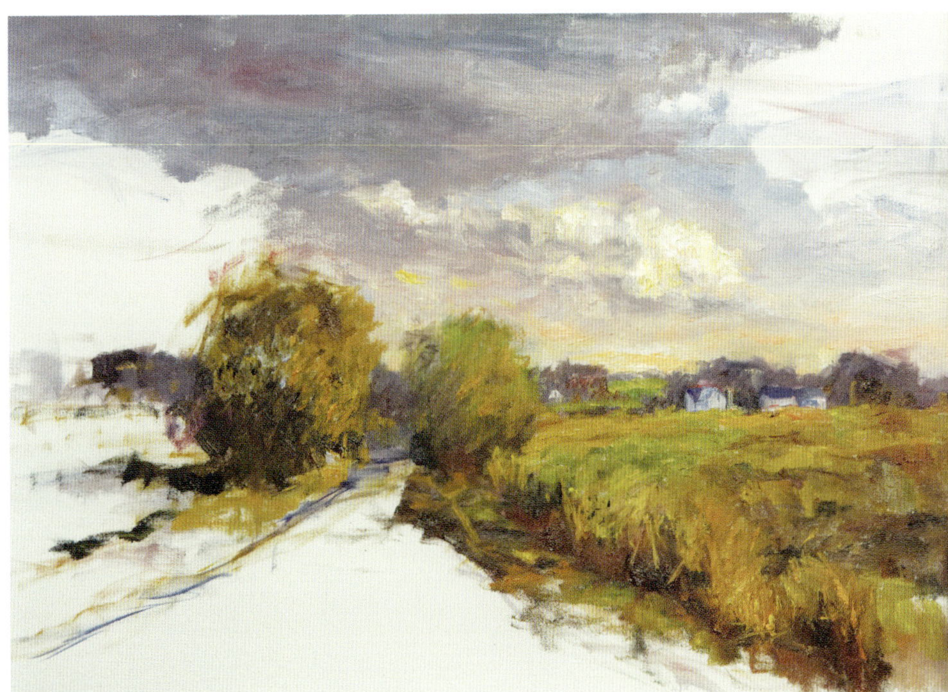

7 PAINT THE TREES

Go to work on the main trees. Remember, they are simply color masses with soft edges. Use purple in the shadowed areas to be consistent with everything else you're doing. Put the tree on the right more in shadow than the one on the left so they don't look exactly the same, adding variation to the painting.

Continue working on the distant treeline on the left. Make it even cooler and more in the Ultramarine Blue family since it is farther away from the sun than the tree mass on the right. It's always a good idea to cool objects in your painting that are farther away from the sun since that's what happens in nature.

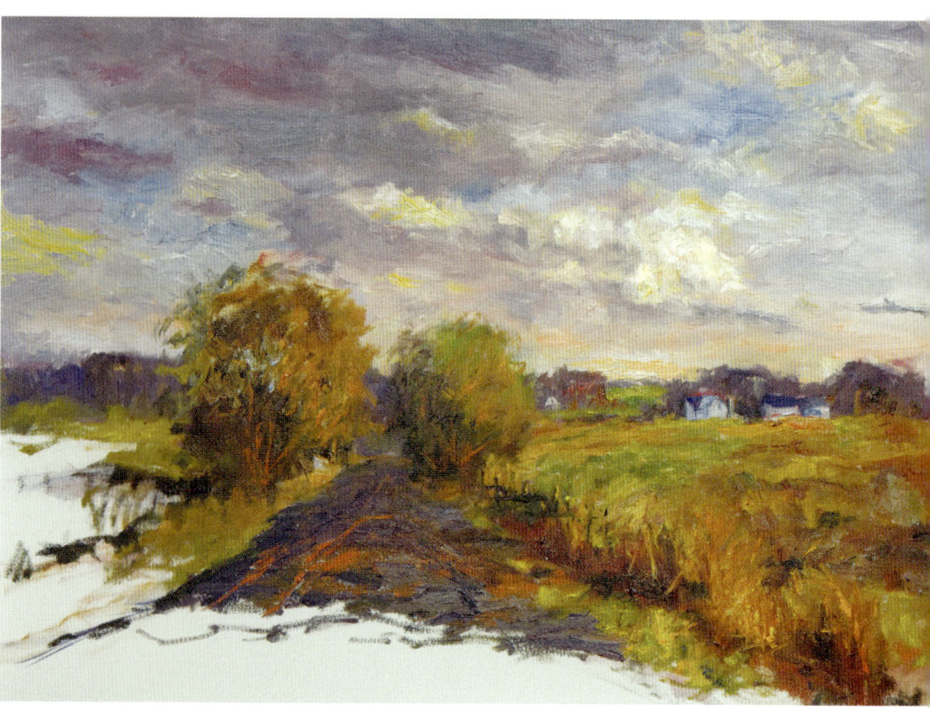

8 PAINT THE ROAD

Finish the sky and go to work on the road. The road simply consists of the same color patterns that you've already established. The road, much of it being in darkness, takes on the colors of the coolest parts of the sky, the purples. Use variations on this, either warming it or cooling it, with subtle additions of Cadmium Orange or Cadmium Red Deep.

Blend a few spots of green to suggest the road picking up some of the color from the trees and grass around it. Suggest a few fence posts, keeping the values dark.

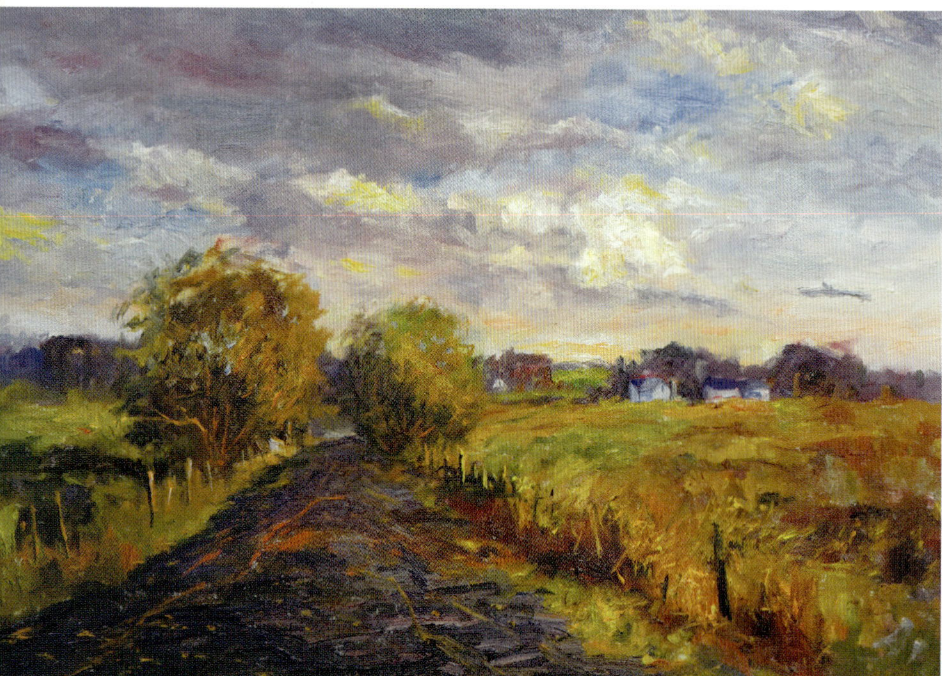

9 FOCUS ON THE EDGES

Complete the road and add a few hot spots of Cadmium Orange to suggest reflections and direct sunlight. Keep your edges mostly soft because you don't want to draw too much attention from what's going on in the foreground. If you make things too sharp in the foreground, your eye will go toward it and keep it from focusing more in the middle distance, which is the focal point of the piece.

Add a few flecks of Cadmium Yellow Lemon and Cadmium Orange mixed with a touch of Titanium White to suggest leaves in the grass that are catching sunlight. Continue working on the fence posts using Ultramarine Blue, Alizarin Crimson, Cadmium Orange and white, the same color patterns that were established at the very beginning of the painting process.

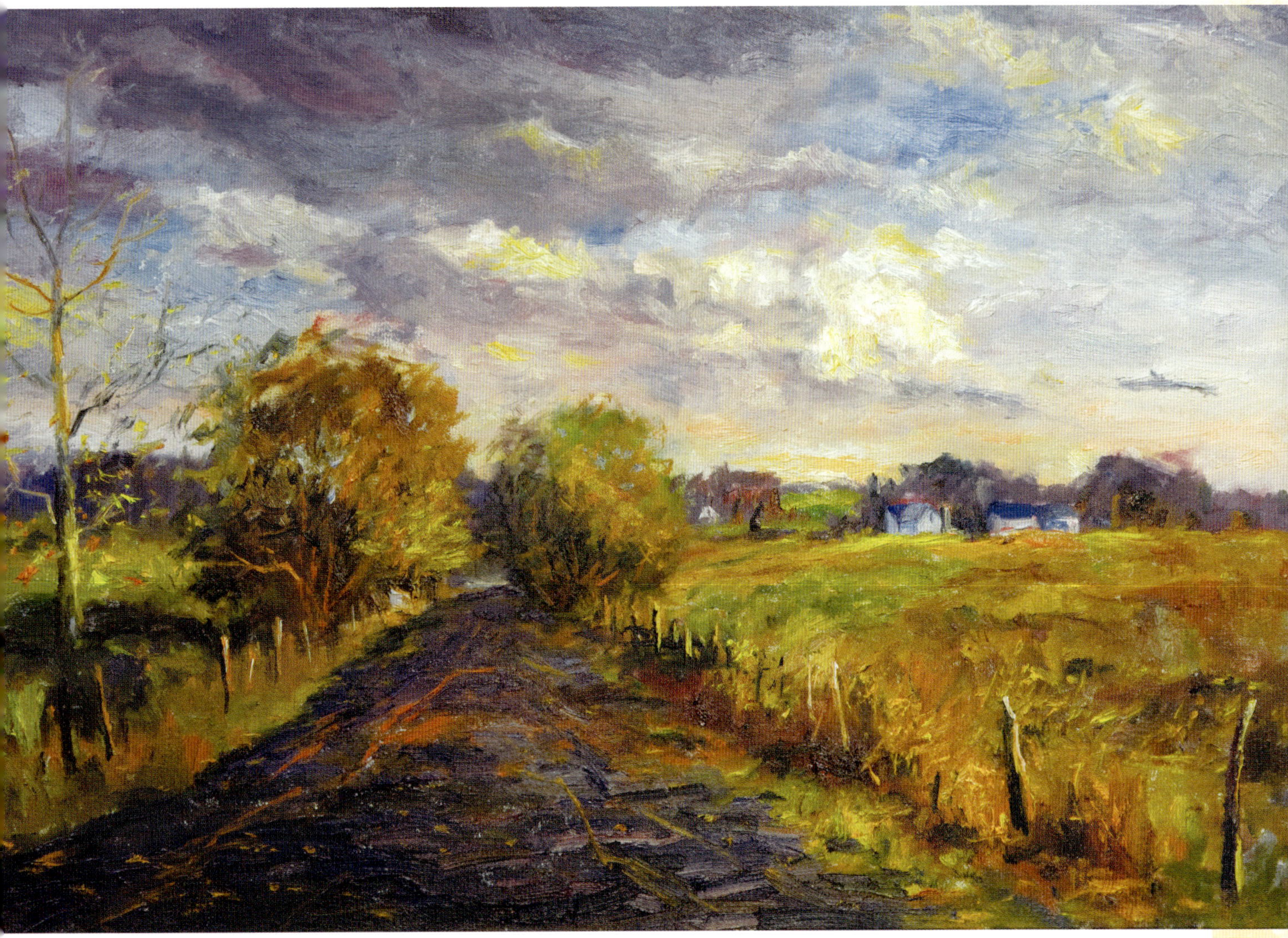

COUNTRY ROAD AT EVENING
Oil on Canvas · 24" × 36" (61cm × 91cm)

10 FINISH THE PAINTING

This is always a dangerous part of the painting process. It's very easy to ruin something by adding too much stuff. Part of what happens is that we just get bored looking at something we've been looking at for hours. You have to really ascertain whether you're adding something to make it better or just adding something. Add a tree to the left side of the canvas to keep the viewer's eye from going too far into the background. Use a ¼" dagger to paint the tree and a no. 2 rigger to suggest individual leaves and branches. Paint a few highlights showing leaves catching sunlight. Add a strong highlight on the trunk, a couple of dabs here and there, finish up the fence posts and *stop*. This painting has a strong sense of mood because the values are close and lots of attention was paid to edge work. Also, the design choice to widen the road at the bottom of the frame is a wonderful way to invite the viewer into the painting.

Chagrin Falls: A Lesson in Movement

I've always enjoyed waterfalls. They are full of life and energy. They are also both fun and challenging to paint, as they are filled with visual contradictions. They move with tremendous power but at the same time have a tendency to have soft edges. Lots of great painters have used them as subject matter. Here's my version of a waterfall.

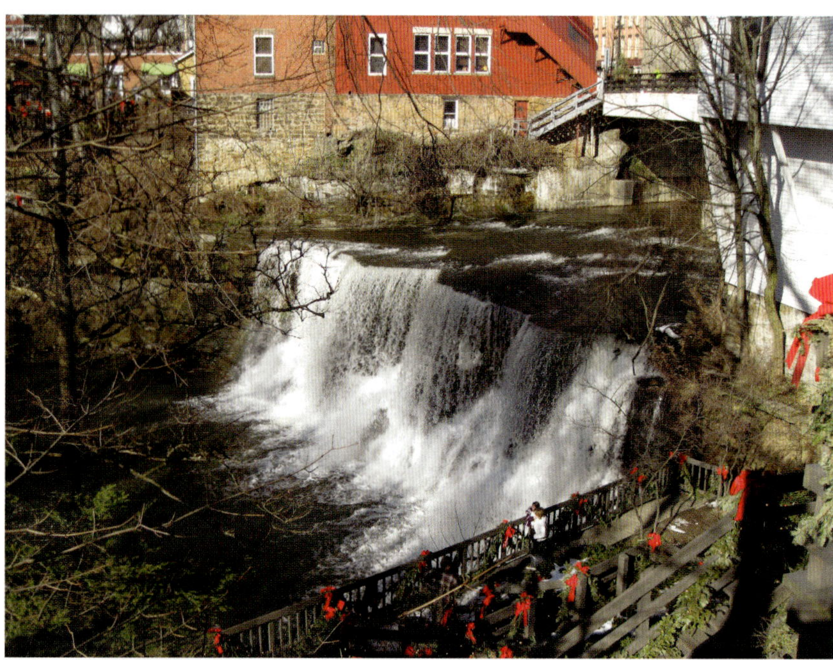

This is a classic circle pattern. The viewer's eye follows the direction of the falls. The large tree on the left keeps your eye from leaving the composition. The branches lead your eye back into the painting and to the red structure. You'll notice the staircase on the right leads your eye back toward the falls, thus closing the circle.

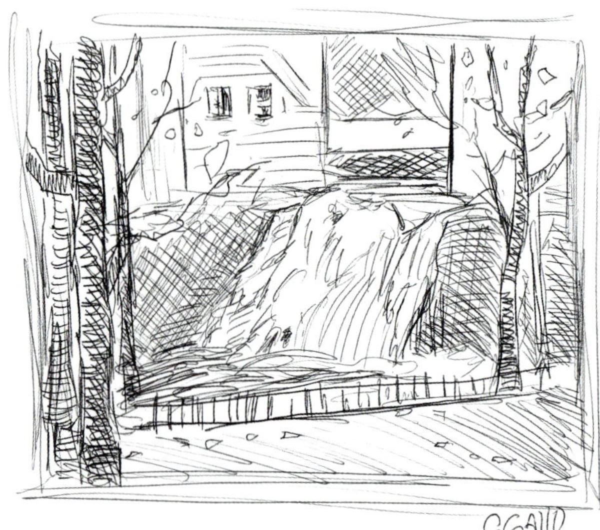

This is a lively subject. Therefore, I use lively, playful lines to create movement.

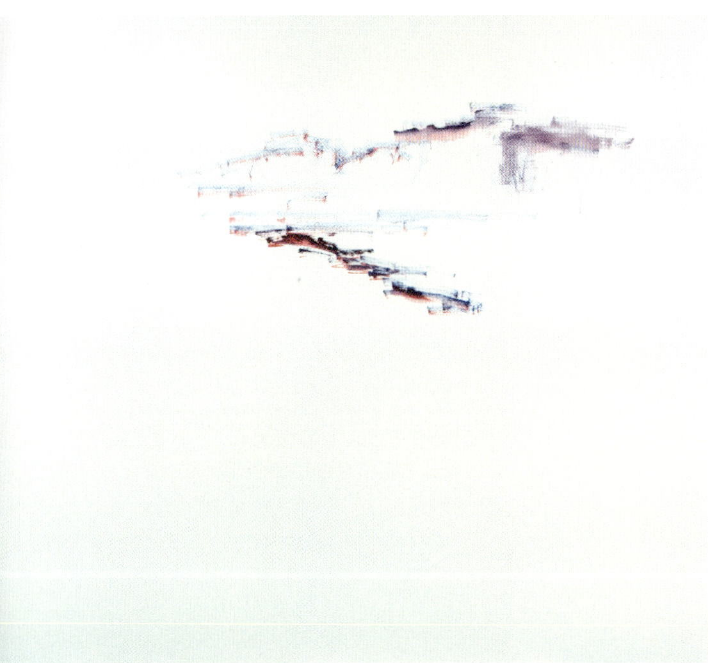

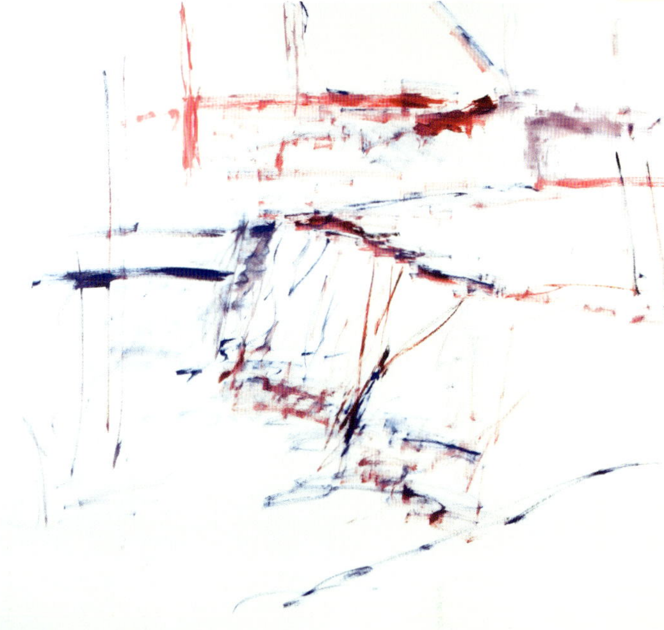

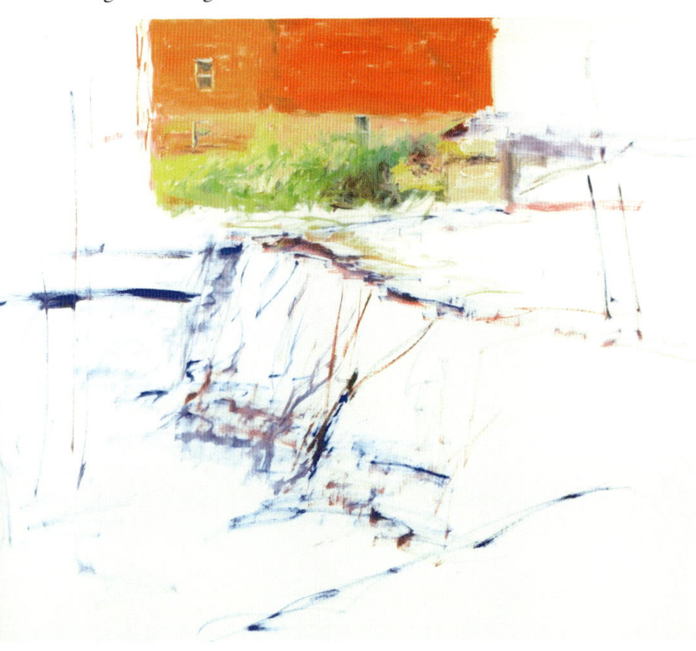

1 BEGIN SKETCHING

Start sketching with a ¼" dagger bristle brush. Use Ultramarine Blue and Alizarin Crimson. The placement of shapes is of utmost importance. You'll notice some lines are hard and others are soft. This is very important because you want to try to get the feel of the painting as soon as possible. To achieve the hard lines, push down on the canvas with more pressure. For the softer lines, use less paint and drag the brush against the grain of the canvas.

2 FINISH ROUGHING OUT THE DESIGN

Continue working out the design. The most important thing now is the focal point, which is the waterfall. It will end up being your lightest light and your warmest light as well. Work out the placement of your biggest shapes. Be very aware of the rhythmic nature of the lines that will lead the viewer's eye through the painting.

3 LAY IN THE FIRST SHAPES

Use a ½" dagger and a small triangular painting knife for this step. Use the knife not only to lay down paint, but to scrape paint away, creating a combination of sharp and soft edges. This is useful because there is a lot of mist in the air. If the background edges are too sharp, you won't get the feeling of the water misting up from the falls.

Lay in the background buildings using Cadmium Red Deep and Cadmium Yellow Deep with a touch of white. Make the shrubs greener than they really are. Since green is the complement of red, this will make both colors pop.

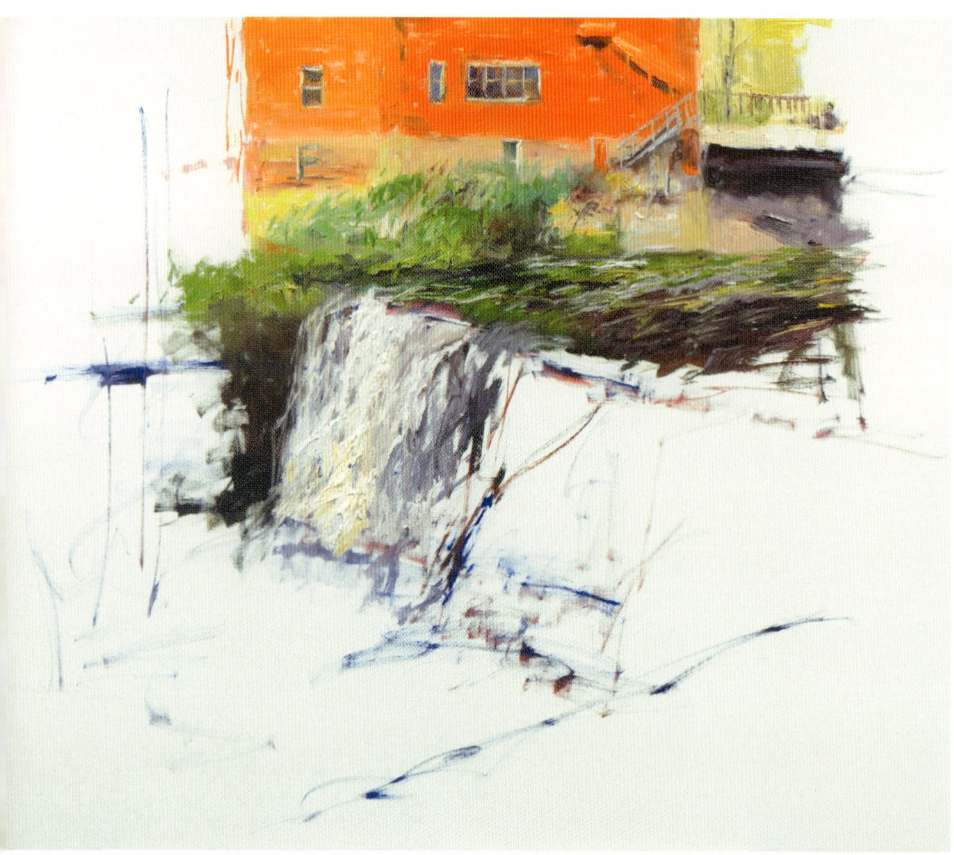

4 PAINT THE WATERFALL
Now work on the water with purple using a ¼" dagger brush. Use a mixture of Ultramarine Blue and Alizarin Crimson. By using big strokes you'll get the feel of the water. Take a bit of the red and green mixtures from the shrubs and the building and work it on top of your purple mixture. Add a few touches of white to get the feeling of the whitecaps. Then go to work on the falls. Use vigorous brushstrokes to get the feeling of water. To simulate the sunlit parts of the falls, use Titanium White, a touch of Cadmium Yellow Lemon and a touch of Cadmium Orange. Use a lightened mixture of purple to build the shadowed areas. Now you have all of your complements working together, ensuring harmony in the piece.

5 CONTINUE WORK ON THE FALLS
As you continue to work on the waterfall, make sure no area is brighter and warmer than the one just left of center. Nothing should compete with this brightest of values from here on out. This will ensure interest in the main subject, which is the light hitting the water.

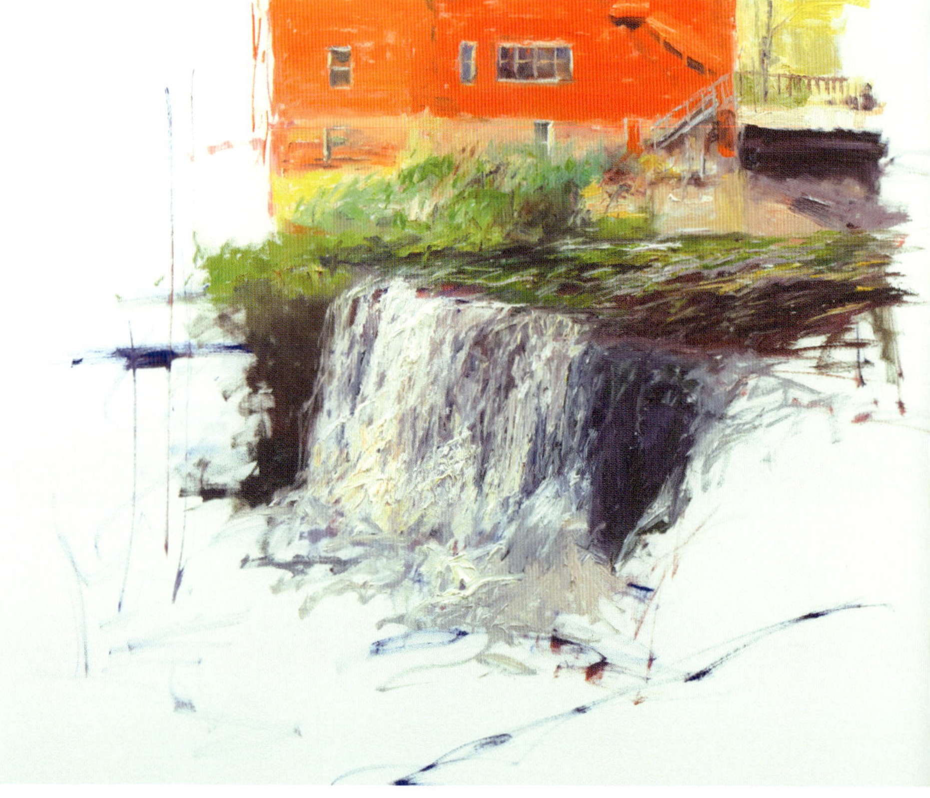

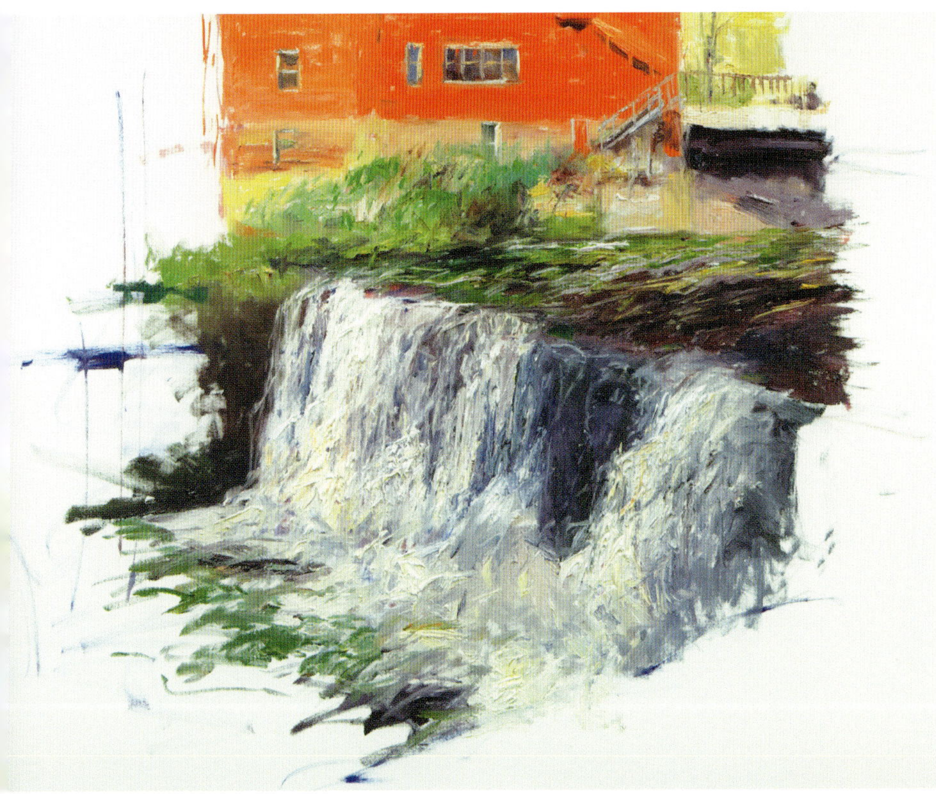

6 KEEP THE FOCUS ON THE MAIN SUBJECT

Continue working on the falls using the same color combinations, always remembering to keep them darker in value and cooler in color temperature so your eye stays on the main subject. (Always use at least two brushes when painting greens and purples, keeping the same brush for each color so they don't intermix and turn to gray.)

7 PAINT THE BACKGROUND

Set up the background area where you are going to overlay the large tree. Render the background in an abstract manner because of the strong foreground elements. Use a combination of a ½" dagger and a larger trowel-shaped painting knife. Paint in the background building with greater detail. Its value should be darker than that of the falls. Add hits of green mixed with Phthalo Blue, Cadmium Yellow Lemon, and Cadmium Yellow Deep to the water below the falls. All complements will work beautifully together.

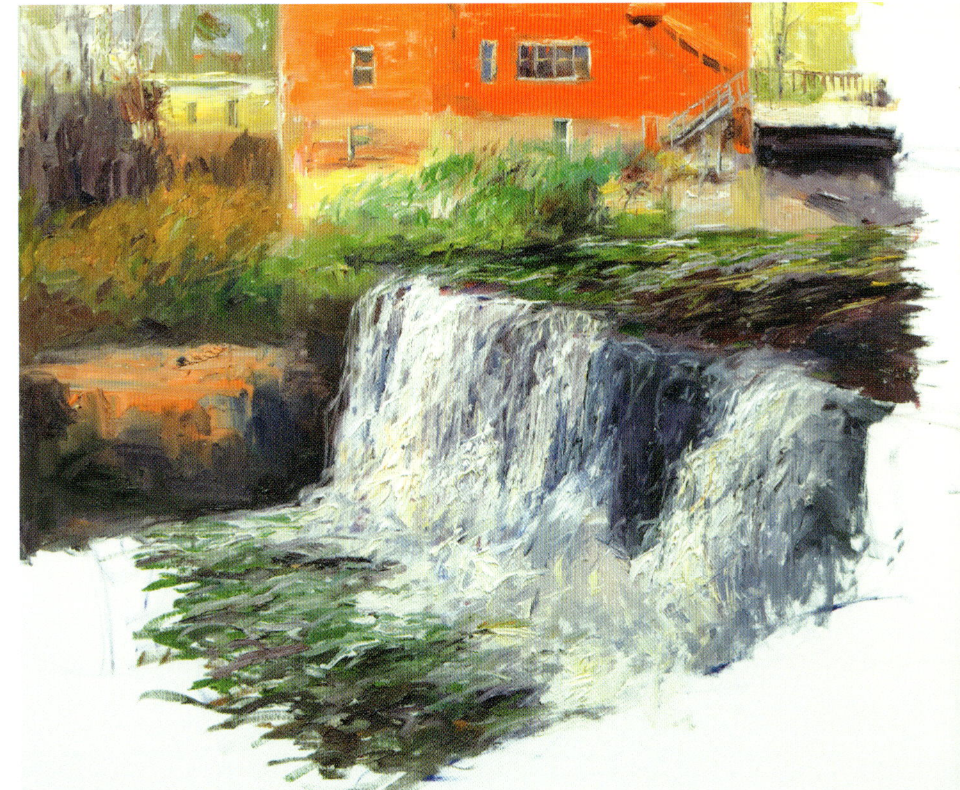

8 ADD THE TREE

Now add the foreground tree with a medium filbert brush. Your focus at this point should be on values, keeping them all close. Use a small dagger and a rigger to paint the branches, some darker and cooler (the ones in shadow) and others warmer (the ones in sunlight). Use purple for the dark branches and orange with a touch of purple for the lighter branches. Using these complements assures harmony. Using a small dagger, put down a few flecks of Cadmium Yellow Lemon and Cadmium Yellow Deep to simulate leaves.

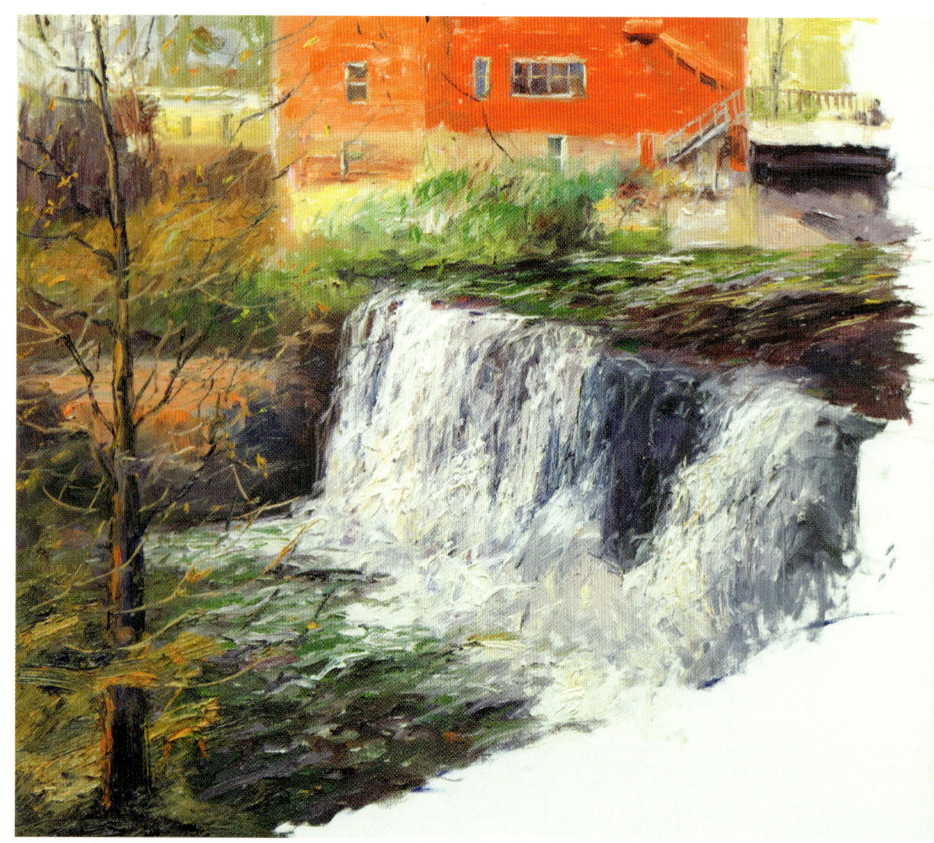

9 PAINT THE WHITE BUILDING

Establish the building on the far right using Titanium White, Ultramarine Blue, Alizarin Crimson and a hint of orange to neutralize it. Over that, with a small dagger lay in the trunks of the trees. Use the side of the dagger for the smaller branches. The idea is to make sure the value of this building does not compete with the value of the waterfall. Now lay in the foreground deck. Since many of the edges in this painting are soft, a hard object in the foreground should set everything off beautifully and ensure a strong atmospheric perspective.

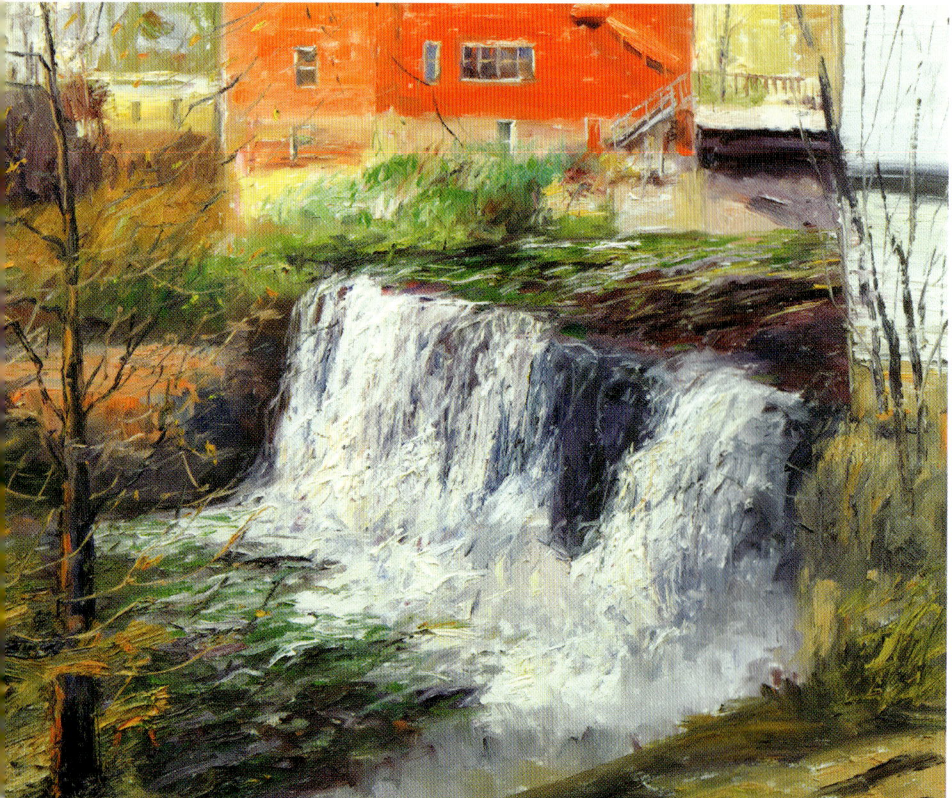

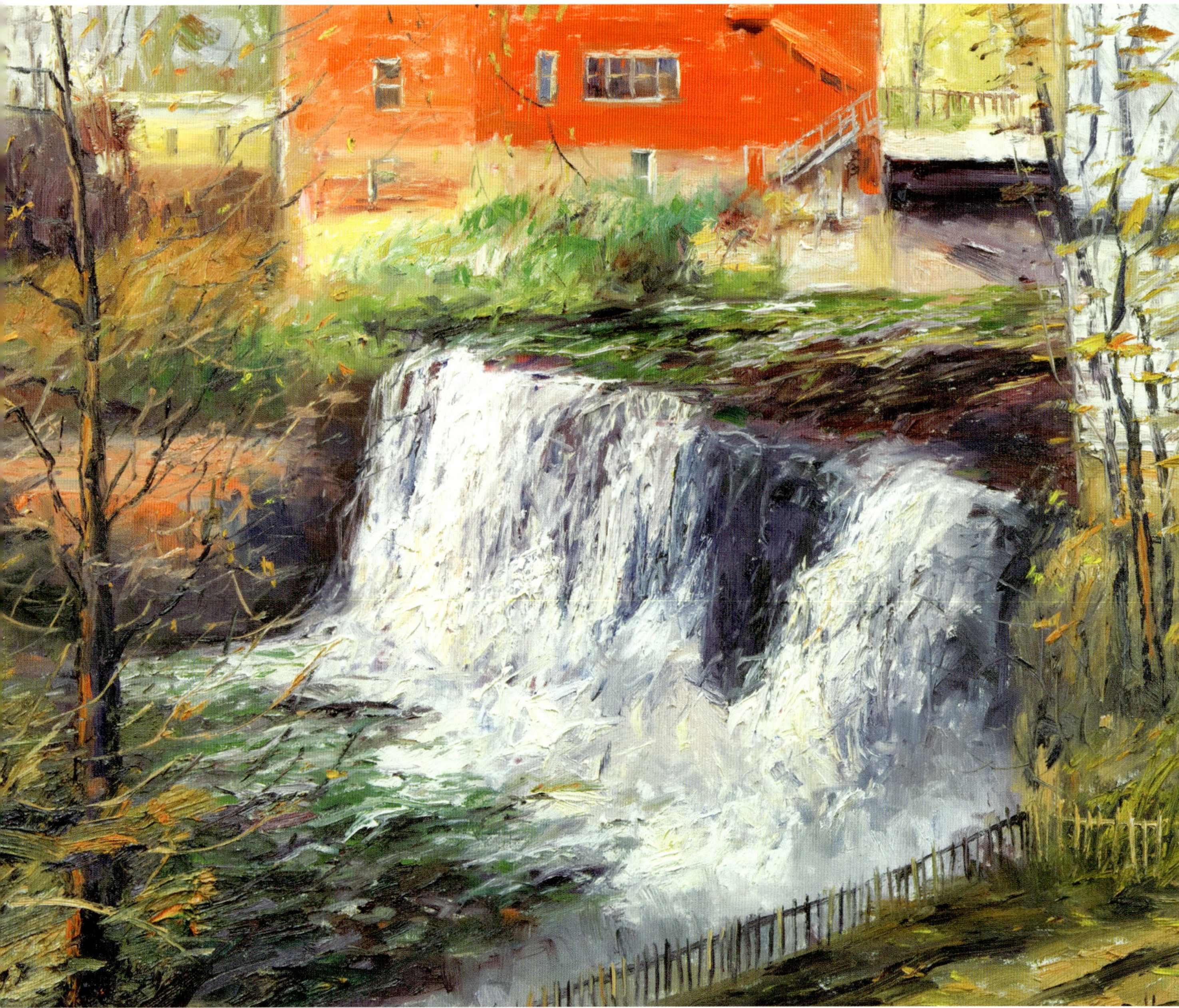

10 FINISH THE PAINTING

Finish the foreground by adding the fence with a ¼" dagger brush. Using this brush should help you get the fence right the first time, and believe me, you don't want to overpaint it. Add a few highlights here and there because the fence is in intermittent light and shadow. Use your neutral mixtures of purple and orange for the midtones and purple for the darks. Add a few more leaves to the tree on the right, keeping them in the mid-value range so they don't become too interesting. Now sign it and put your brushes away.

CHAGRIN FALLS · Oil on Canvas · 30" × 36" (76cm × 91cm)

Eagle, Colorado, in Winter: Snow Is Anything but White

MATERIALS

SURFACE
stretched oil-primed linen

BRUSHES
no. 4 filbert

nos. 2, 4 riggers

¼" dagger

PIGMENTS
Ultramarine Blue, Alizarin Crimson, Cadmium Red Deep, Cadmium Orange, Cadmium Yellow Deep, Cadmium Yellow Lemon, Phthalo Blue, Titanium White

OTHER
medium cup

odorless mineral spirits

paper towels

wooden or paper palette

While hiking with my artist friend James Van Fossan we came across this wonderful, quiet scene. Although I would have preferred to paint this from life, I couldn't because time was limited and it was also 7°F (-14°C). The moment I saw this scene I knew it had to be painted. The combination of the cool gray sky against purple mountains along with the yellow structure being hit by sunlight was just sublime.

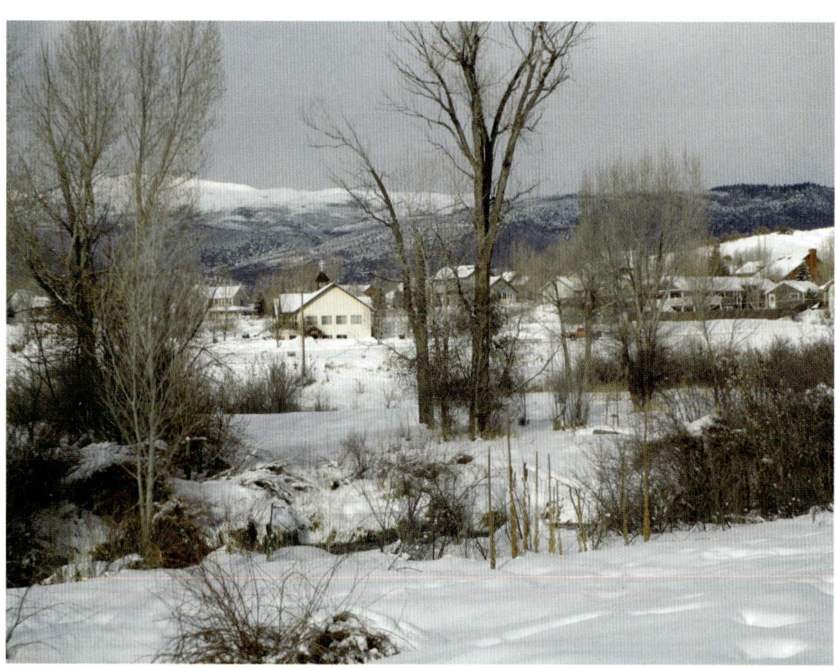

When painting snow you must reserve your color notes of pure white. Otherwise you'll end up with something very harsh and unrealistic. Snow always reflects the sky and everything else around it.

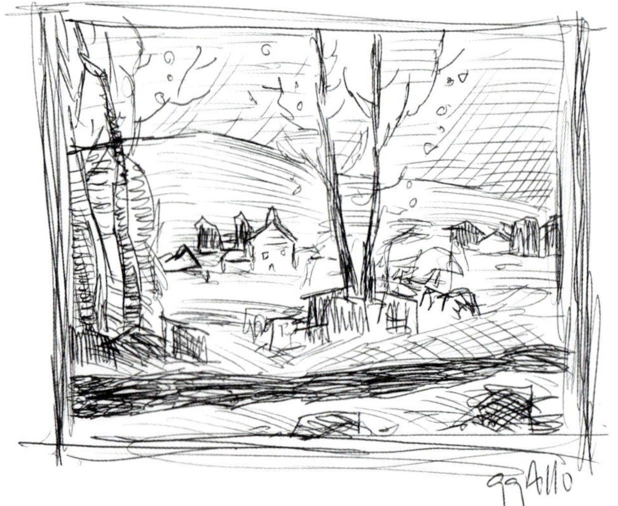

In this sketch I widened the stream at the bottom of the composition to help create something that would tie the entire design together. A painting with so many elements can easily become spotty if there isn't one unifying element.

1 SEPARATE SKY AND GROUND PLANES

Establish the composition by figuring out where the mountain meets the sky. Use Alizarin Crimson with mineral spirits and a ¼" dagger brush to sketch in your horizon.

2 SKETCH IN THE FOCAL POINT

With Ultramarine Blue and Alizarin Crimson on your brush, dip the brush into your mineral spirits. Sketch out the proportion of the house and the main group of trees. The correct placement of these shapes is essential to the success of the painting.

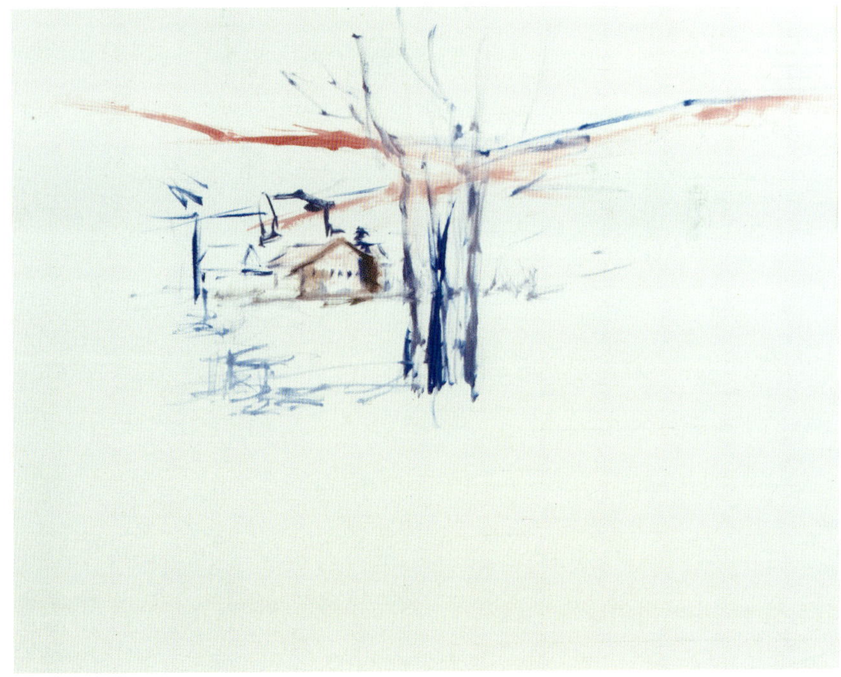

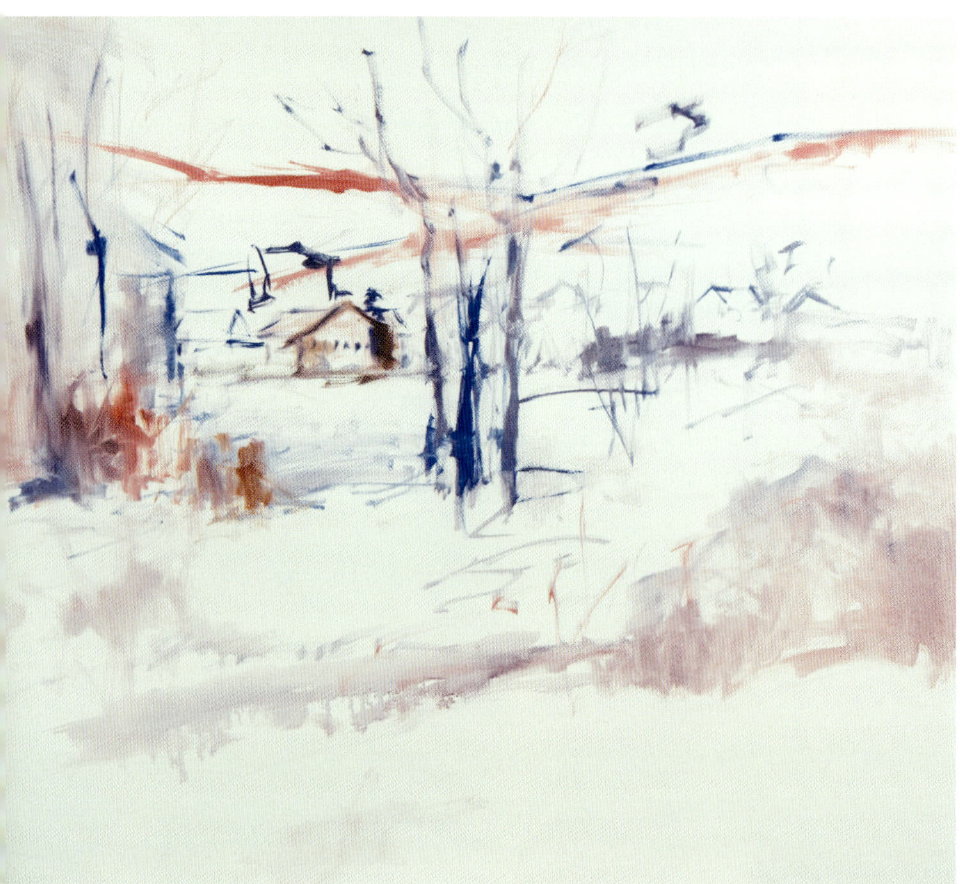

3 CREATE MORE SHAPES
Continue sketching in the shapes using Ultramarine Blue and Alizarin Crimson. The key is to see the painting as close to complete as possible from the very beginning. If the design is working, the only other things you need to get right to create a successful painting are values and color.

4 PAINT THE SKY
Lay in the gray sky by mixing Ultramarine Blue, Alizarin Crimson and white with a touch of orange to make it go neutral. Use both your ¼" and ½" daggers to create texture. Where the sky is cool, lean your mix towards purple. Where the sky is warm, lean towards orange.

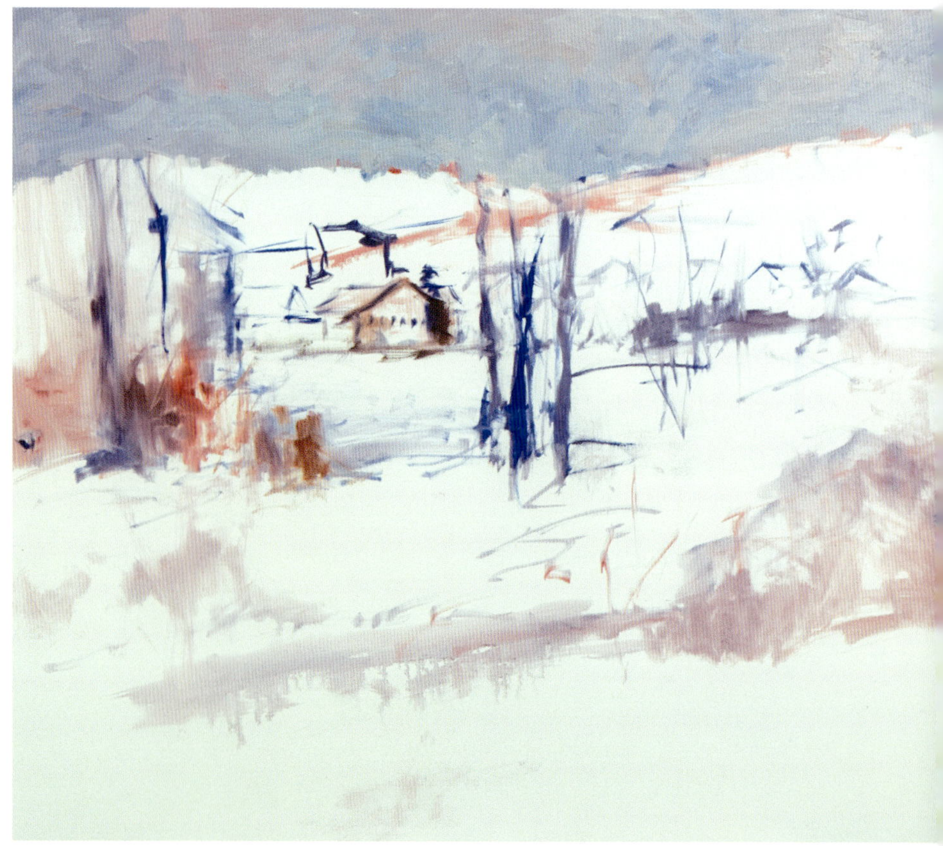

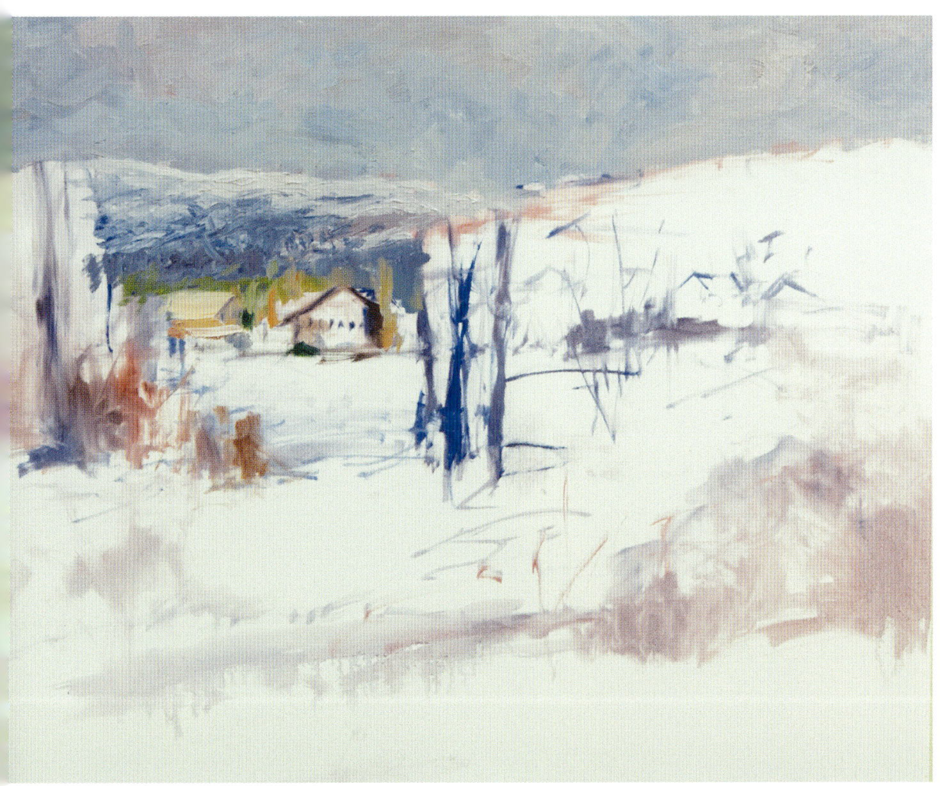

5 PAINT THE MOUNTAINS
Using the same brushes and the same colors, lay in the background mountains, leaning more towards purple. Add white to suggest the snow, but keep the value down to create a feeling of atmospheric perspective. Don't make it too warm or it'll jump forward. Add a few warm notes to suggest the evergreen trees using Phthalo Blue and Cadmium Yellow Deep. Notice how the warm colors come forward and the cool ones lay back. At this point you should already see that your three secondary colors are working.

6 PAINT THE MAIN SUBJECT
Paint the house with Titanium White, Cadmium Yellow Lemon and Cadmium Yellow Deep. Neutralize it with your purple mixture where you need to. Underneath the house, paint the snow in the distance, keeping the value higher. Then paint the snow in the middle ground with cooler tones, making sure to keep the values in the medium range so they will not compete with the main subject—the house—and the snow just beneath it. Paint the trees on the right using Ultramarine Blue, Alizarin Crimson and Cadmium Orange. These neutral tones will remain harmonious with your other colors. Paint the trees paying close attention to edges.

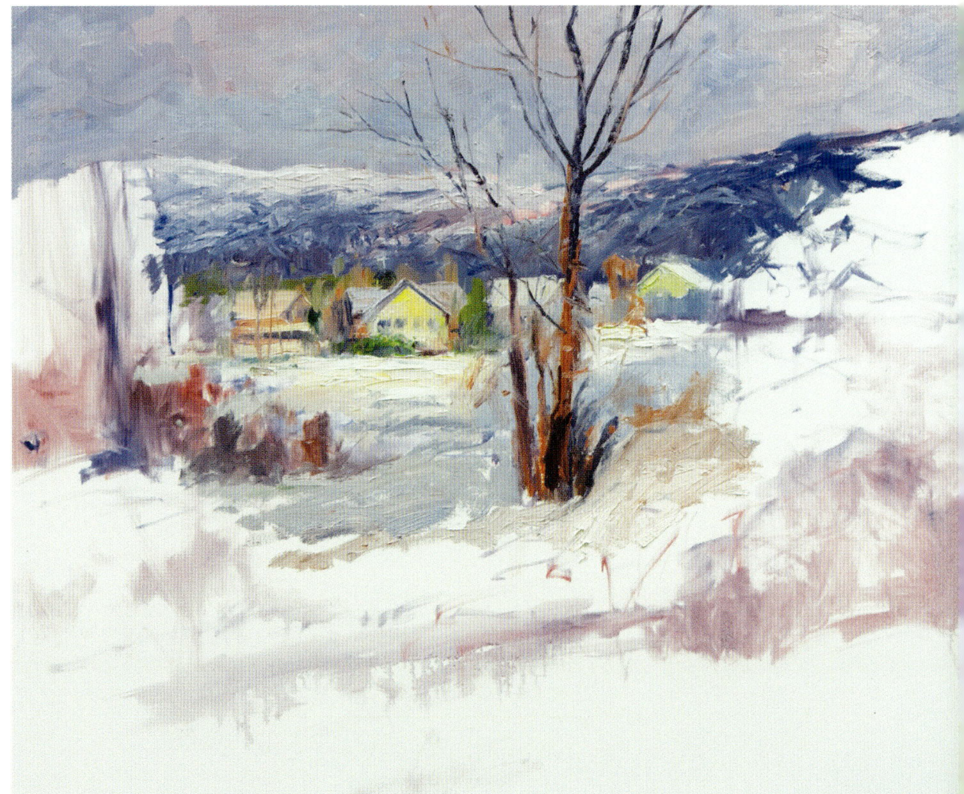

7 REFINE THE PAINTING

Continue working on the snow, alternating between warms and cools. Work on the shrubs, paying close attention to the edges and to their color temperatures. Are they warm or cool? Continue working on the background mountain using the same colors as before but leaning more towards Ultramarine Blue. Use your nos. 2 and 4 riggers to create the thinner branches and occasional leaves.

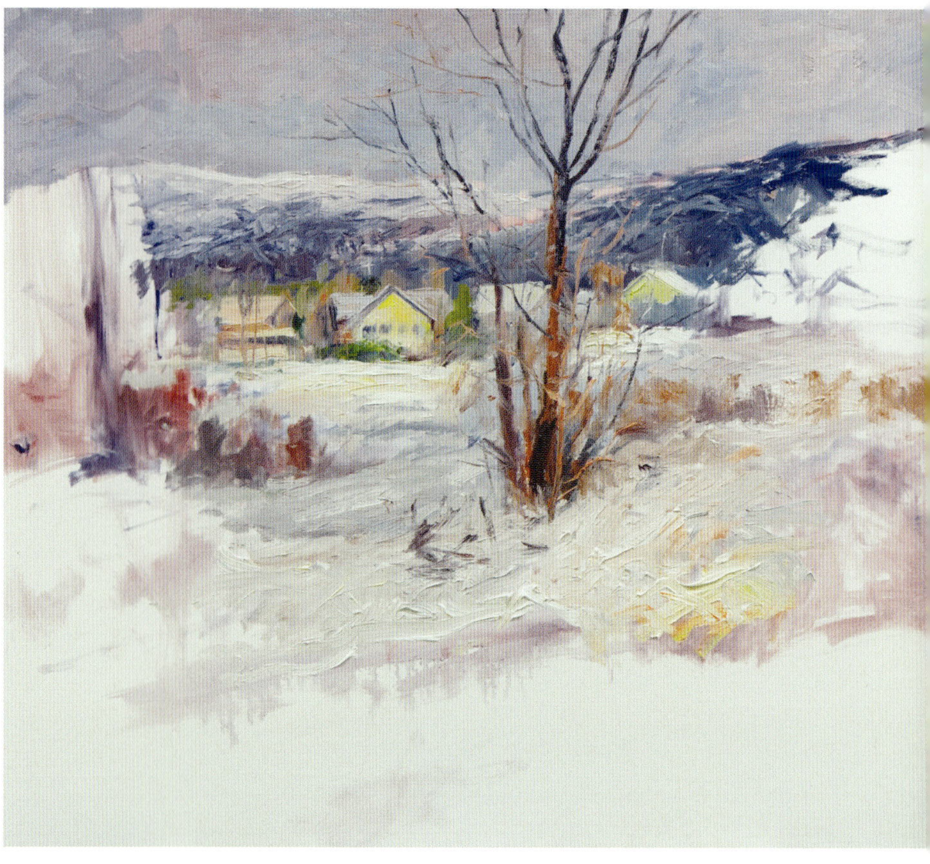

8 FOCUS ON THE FOREGROUND

Now work on the foreground using your ¼" dagger. Include more of the stream that cuts across the bottom than is in the photo to create a unifying element that holds the picture together. Lay in the rest of the trees and a few nice hot spots in the foreground using Cadmium Yellow Lemon mixed with Cadmium Red Deep and bits of your purple mixture to unify this section with the rest of the painting.

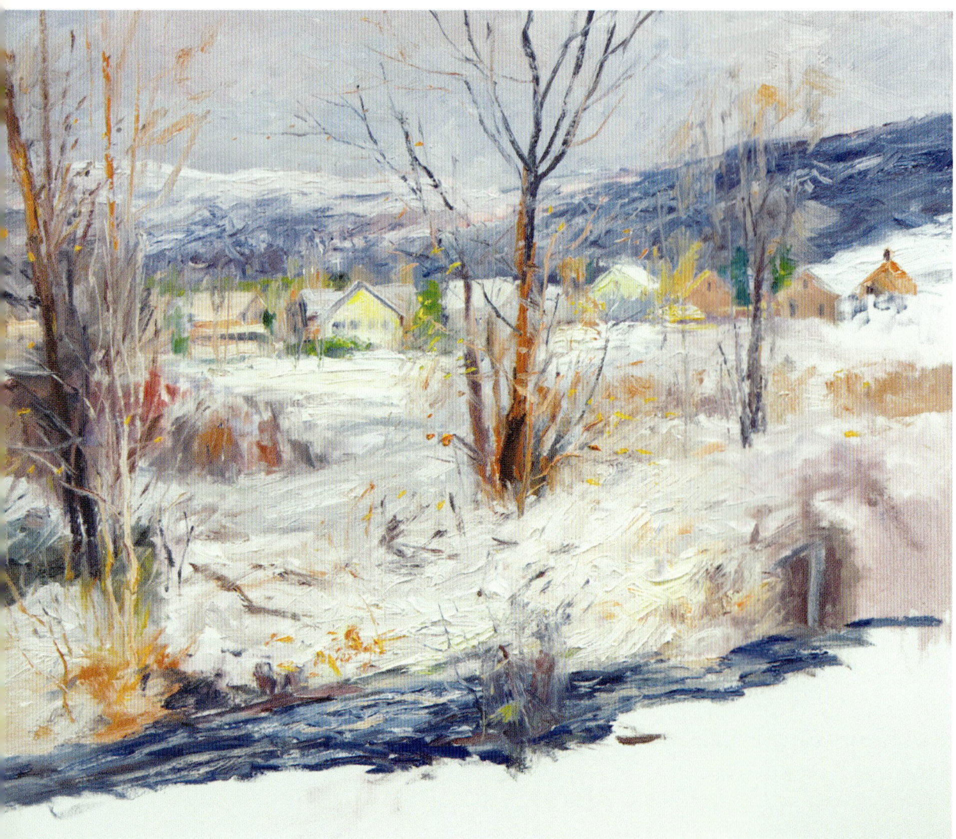

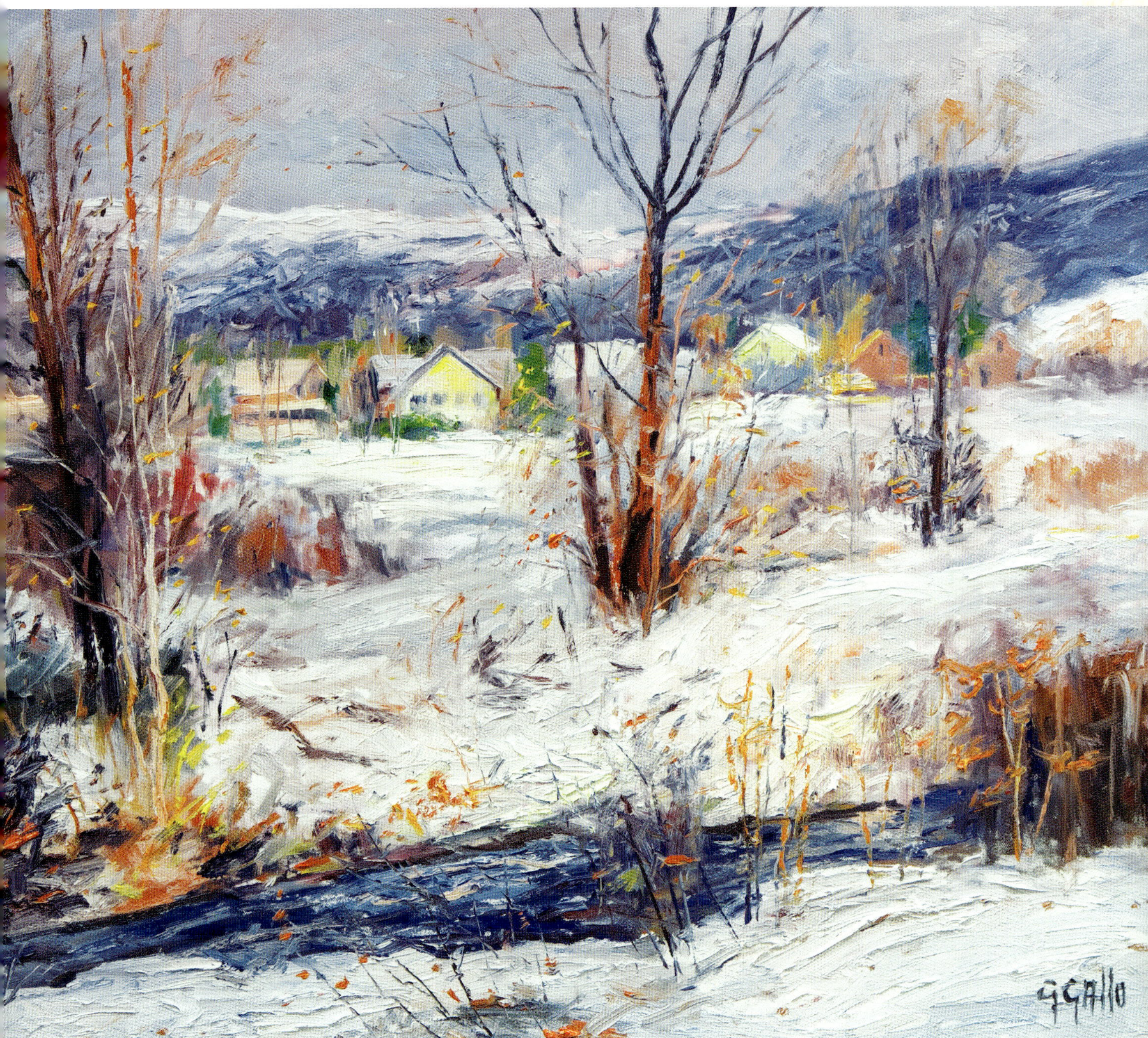

9 FINISH THE PAINTING

Now pull it all together. Smudge the background house on the right and turn it into a distant group of trees because the edge is too hard and you don't want the viewer's eye focusing on the right side of the painting. Continue adding highlights and cool notes throughout the piece, pulling it all together. A small dagger, a medium filbert and small rigger for details are the only brushes required to finish this painting.

With a painting as complicated as this, there's always some correcting to do. A lot of this painting is about making sure soft edges remain soft and hard edges remain hard. You don't want the viewer's eye to become confused and not know what the main focal point is, which is the yellow house in the distance and the snow just beneath it.

EAGLE, COLORADO, IN WINTER
Oil on Canvas · 24" × 30" (61cm × 76cm)

Savannah Park: Painting a High Overcast Day

Savannah Park is a painting of a spring subject in which there is not only a high overcast sky but the air is thick with moisture. This creates wonderful color combinations and rich atmospheric perspective.

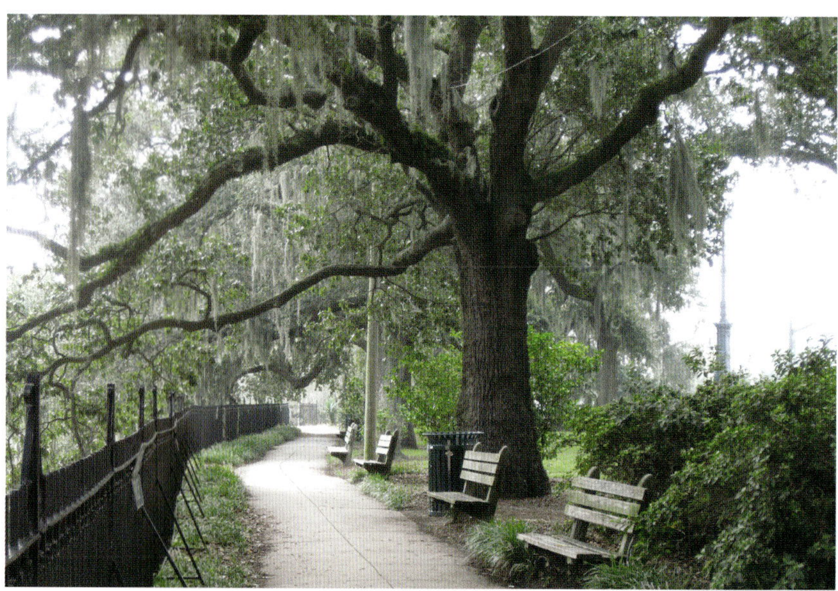

This place seems both cozy and contemplative. The high overcast light makes everything a touch more gray, bringing the values closer and therefore helping illustrate these emotions.

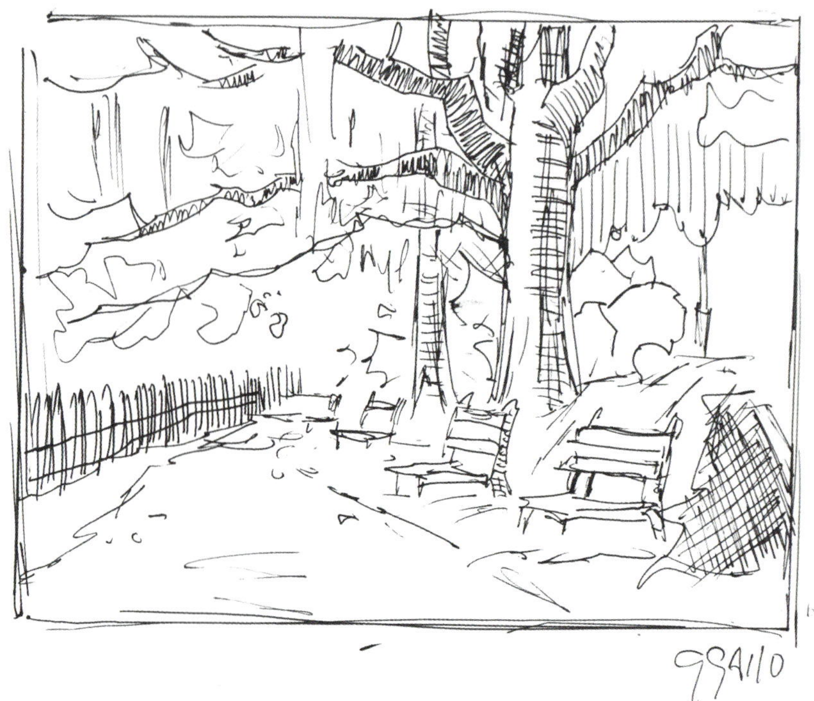

In the sketch I played up the size of the tree, widened the road at the bottom and made the first bench a bit lighter to help atmospheric perspective.

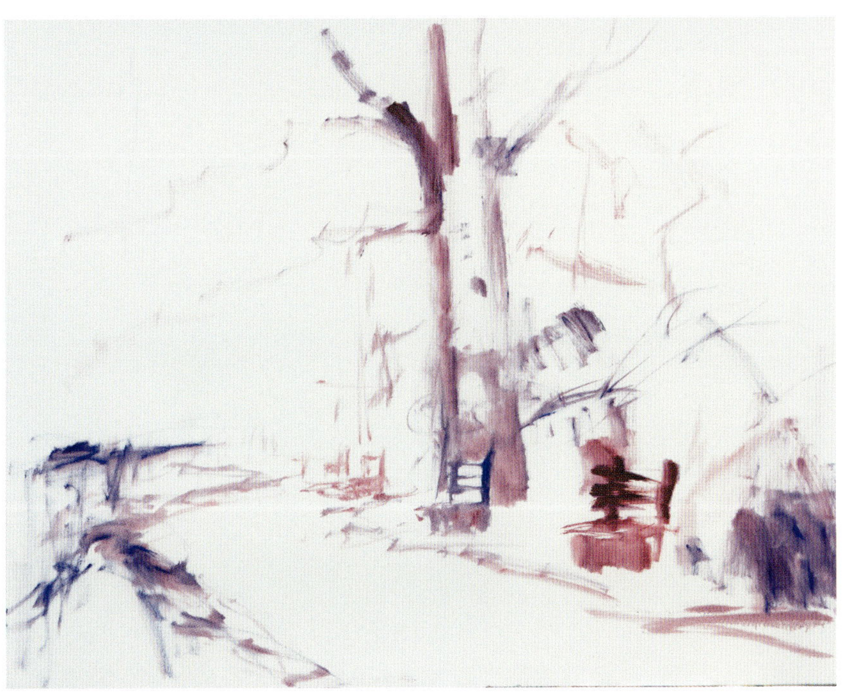

1 CREATE YOUR COMPOSITION

Start out by placing your shapes using Ultramarine Blue, Alizarin Crimson and lots of mineral spirits. Use a ¼" dagger brush. Since much of this painting is about the large tree, it is essential to position it properly. Make sure it is slightly off center and doesn't cut the canvas in half. In placing a solid mass such as this, it is also important to recognize the negative space on either side of the tree. You don't want two halves of equal proportions.

2 SCRUB IN THE DARK MASSES

Scrub in the dark masses using the same colors with a ½" dagger. Much of the tree is in darkness and in cooler tones. The shadowed areas under the bush are all rendered in the same value as the tree. Lay in a few of the mid-values such as the sky to get a good idea how they will interplay. Place the benches, making certain that their scale works as they recede.

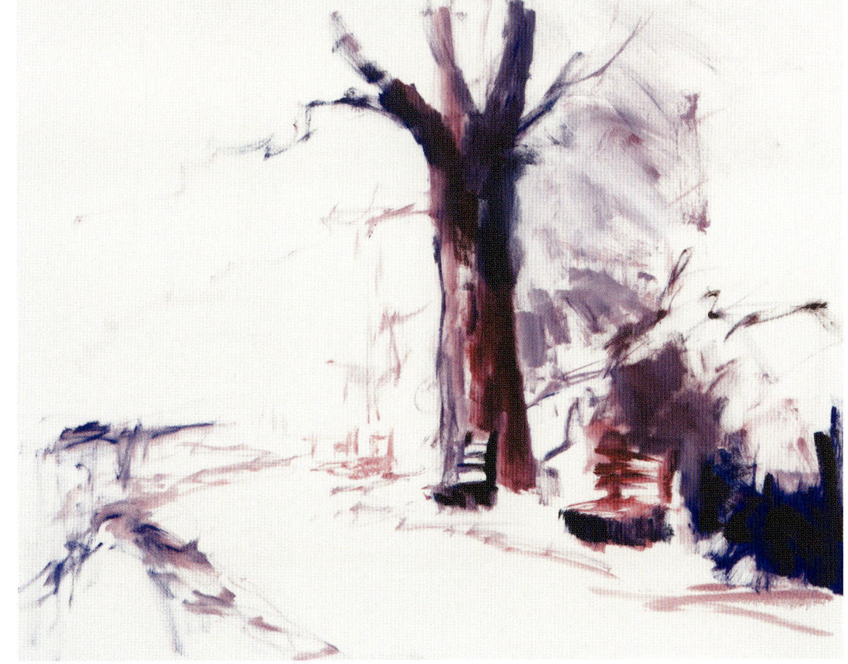

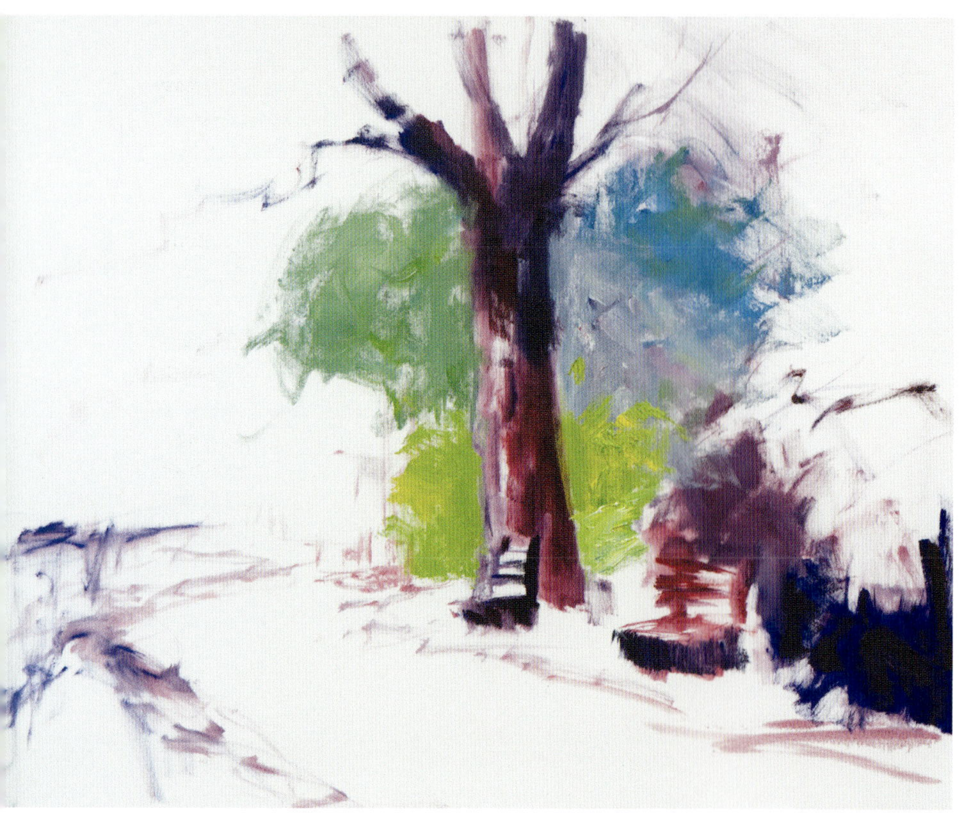

3 CREATE MORE SHAPES

Now go with more opaque paint. Using Cadmium Yellow Deep and Phthalo Blue, lay in the warmer areas of the leaves with your ¼" dagger. The darker areas are Phthalo Blue, a touch of Alizarin Crimson and a hint of Cadmium Yellow Deep. The warms and cools of the painting should already be working beautifully.

4 PAINT THE TREE

Continue working on the tree. Add some warm notes with Cadmium Yellow Deep, Phthalo Blue and a touch of Cadmium Yellow Lemon. The distant area is nothing more than a haze. Render it with Titanium White, Ultramarine Blue and Alizarin Crimson. The cool purple color forces the distant area to lay back. Add a few hits of Cadmium Orange to neutralize the color. Then work on what is one of the most important parts of the painting, the light landing to the left of the base of the tree. It's essential to get the colors and values right in this section. Work carefully on the edges where the tree meets the ground.

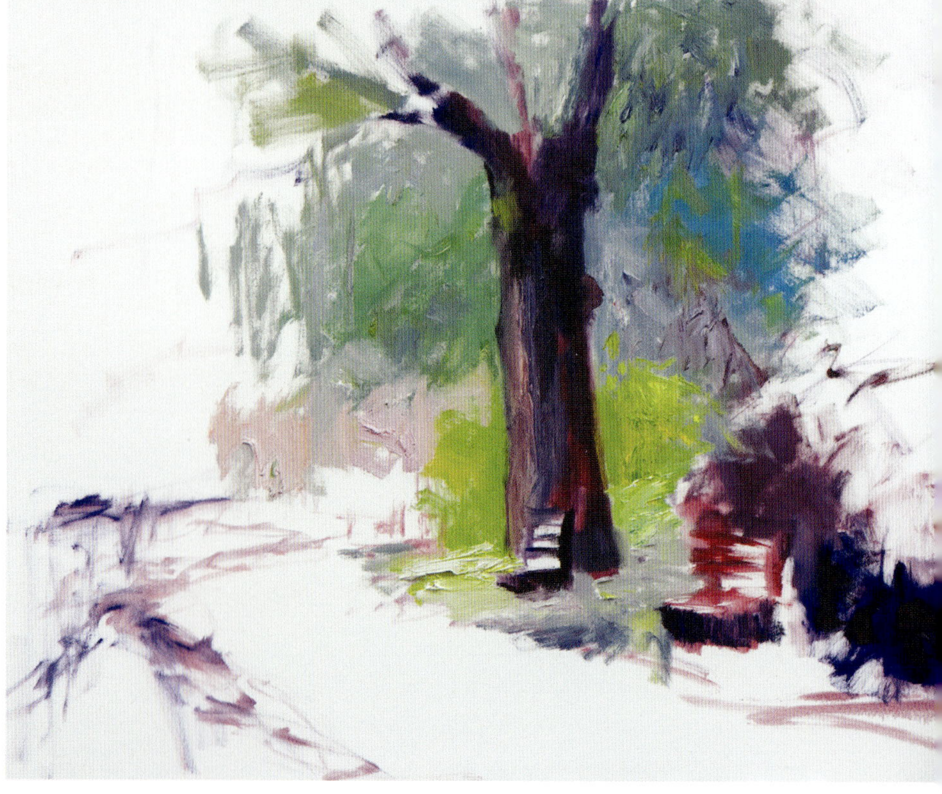

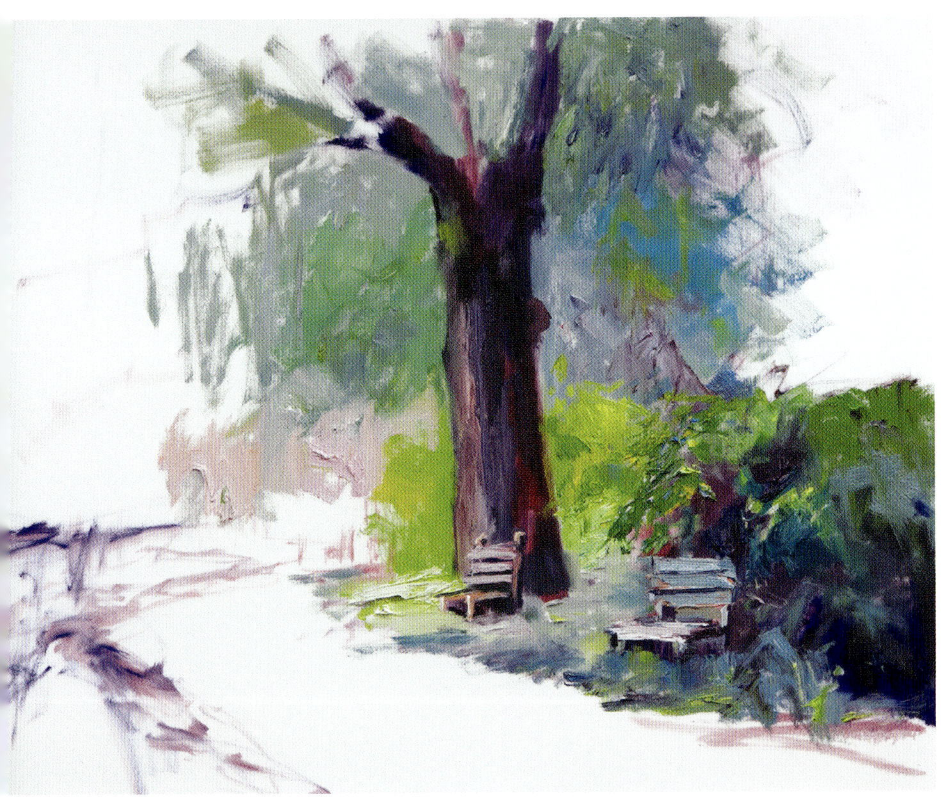

5 CREATE NEUTRAL TONES

Now that the basic colors of the painting have been established, it's easy to mix more neutral tones. Dip bits of sky color into your neutrals. Paint the benches using white, a touch of Ultramarine Blue, a touch of Alizarin Crimson and Cadmium Orange. Shift from warm to cool where needed. Then start to render the bush on the right. It's important that you get the color and value of the leaves against the background grass correct. If you can get this right, it will be easier to get other values and colors correct. All you have to do is compare them.

6 PAINT THE SKY

Now work on the sky. Since there is so much green in the painting, the gray sky will automatically lean to the red family. Since you need to keep it cool, use your cool red, Alizarin Crimson, which has a touch of blue in it. At this point, your color harmonies should be working well together. Continue sketching in the leaves of the trees and some of the wisteria. The idea is to keep the edges soft to give the foliage a lacy quality. Continue using the warm and cool mixtures you've laid down already.

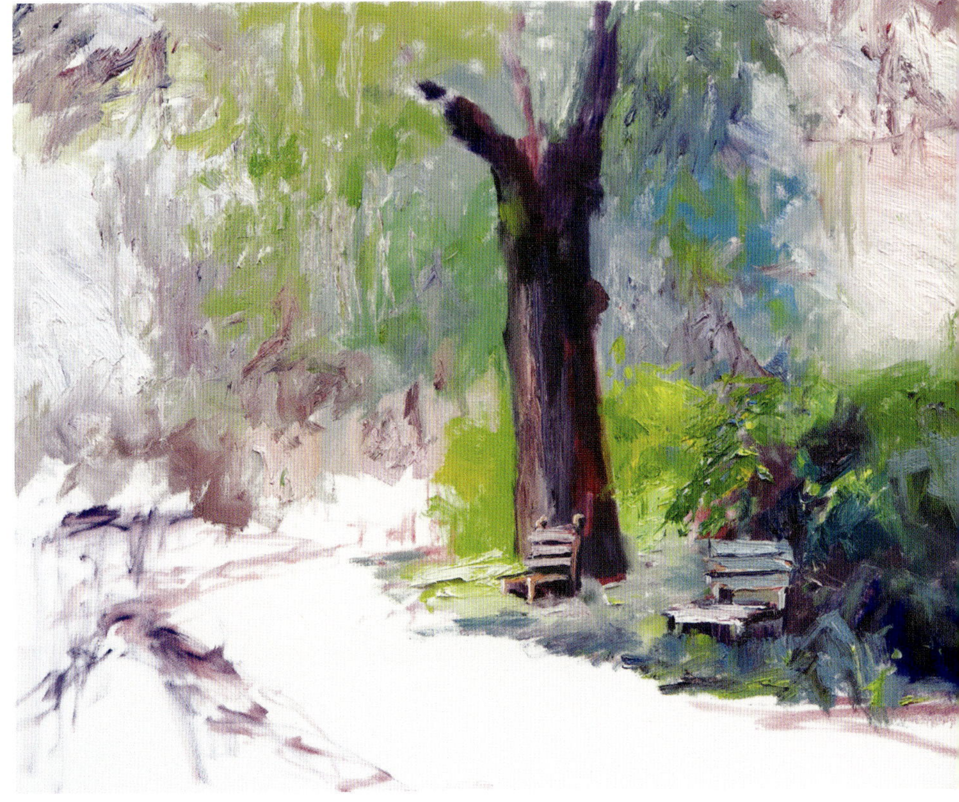

7 CREATE THE TREE BRANCHES

Now work on the design of the tree. The branches reach out in all directions. Their movement is key to determining the personality of the tree. Use your dagger brush and twist it around to get the different variations of thickness in the branches. Change some of the branch movements and simplify others in order to make a better design. Use your dark purple mixture of Ultramarine Blue and Alizarin Crimson. Keep the paint thinner in these areas to avoid glare; you don't want anything in the dark passages to catch unnecessary light. Continue working on the wisteria, dipping into your greens with the addition of white, and just drag the brush down. Use your rigger brush to get the smaller strokes of the branches.

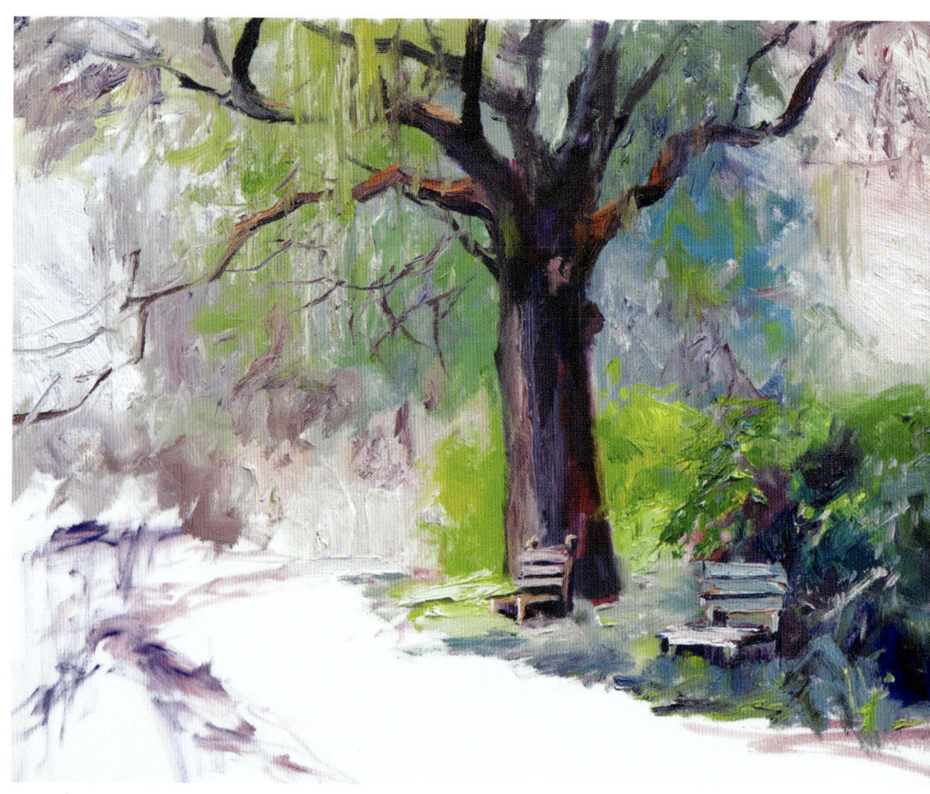

8 GUIDE THE VIEWER'S EYE TOWARD THE FOCAL POINT

Lay in the grass on the left side using Cadmium Yellow Lemon, Cadmium Yellow Deep and Phthalo Blue. Use a touch of Titanium White here and there to get the feeling of the white, cold sky overhead. Then work on the road using a mixture of Ultramarine Blue, Alizarin Crimson, white and a touch of Cadmium Orange to neutralize it in places. Use a ½" dagger for the broad areas of the road. Make sure to change the feeling of your brushstrokes between the grass and the road so you feel the difference in texture. Using a painting knife, add a few strokes of white in the road to create more interest near the tree, which is the focal point.

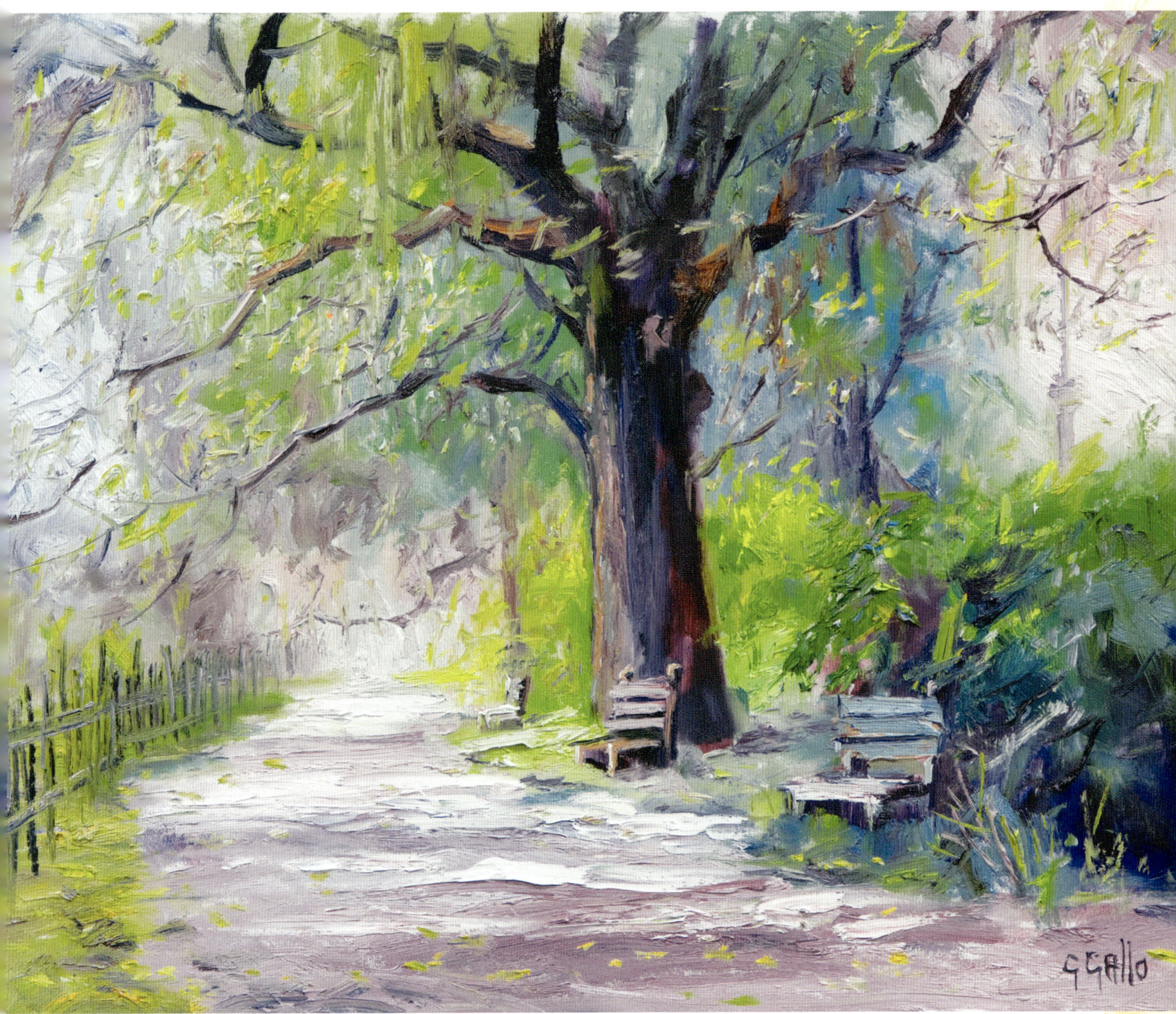

9 ADD FINISHING TOUCHES
Add the fence on the left using a no. 2 rigger and a ¼" dagger. The mixture is Ultramarine Blue, Alizarin Crimson and a touch of Ivory Black. Make sure to keep it sketchy because you don't want the viewer's eye to focus on it. The fence should be nothing more than a suggestion and not painted with the same kind of detail as the tree and the benches, which are the subjects. Add a few dabs here and there to suggest leaves on the road. If you don't do this, the roads in your paintings will look too clean and antiseptic.

SAVANNAH PARK
Oil on Canvas · 22" × 28" (56cm × 71cm)

Bachelor Gulch, Autumn:
A Lesson in Secondary Colors

MATERIALS

SURFACE
stretched oil-primed linen

BRUSHES
no. 2 rigger

¼", ½" daggers

PIGMENTS
Ultramarine Blue, Alizarin Crimson, Cadmium Red Deep, Cadmium Orange, Cadmium Yellow Deep, Cadmium Yellow Lemon, Phthalo Blue, Titanium White

OTHER
medium cup

odorless mineral spirits

wooden or paper palette

I came across this scene in Colorado. It was the perfect time of the year to paint. It snowed in the mountains overnight, and all the aspens in the valley below were afire with reds, yellows and oranges. In other words: a landscape painter's dream.

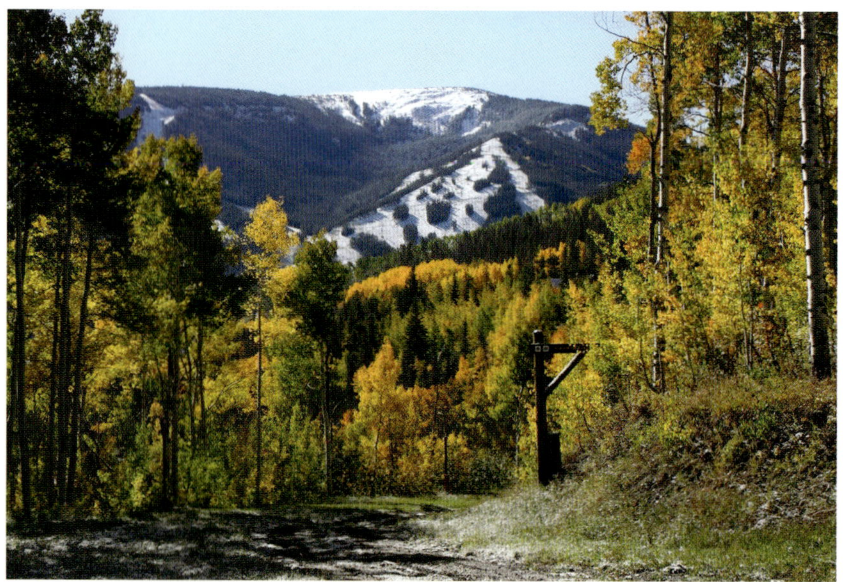

This scene is magical and a great way to play with the interaction of your secondary colors: green, purple and orange. The trick is to not make it look too garish.

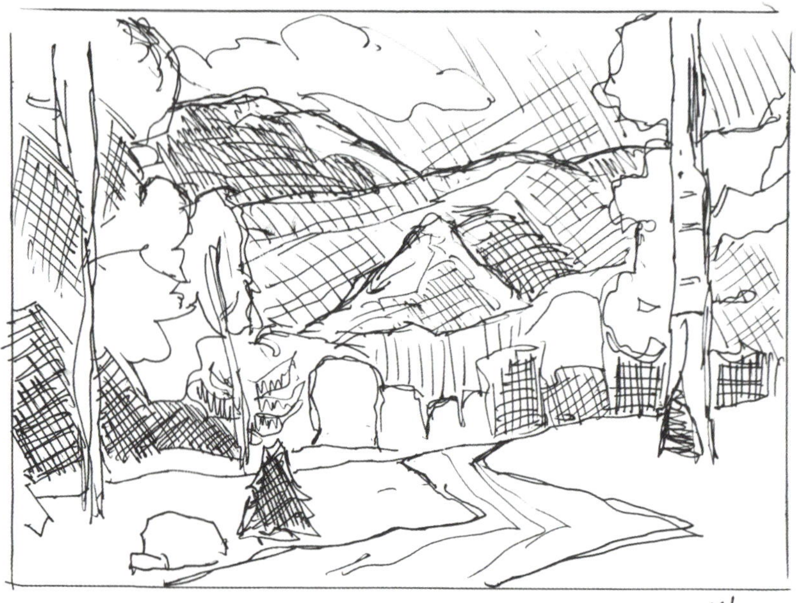

I gave the road an S curve to play up a sense of mystery.

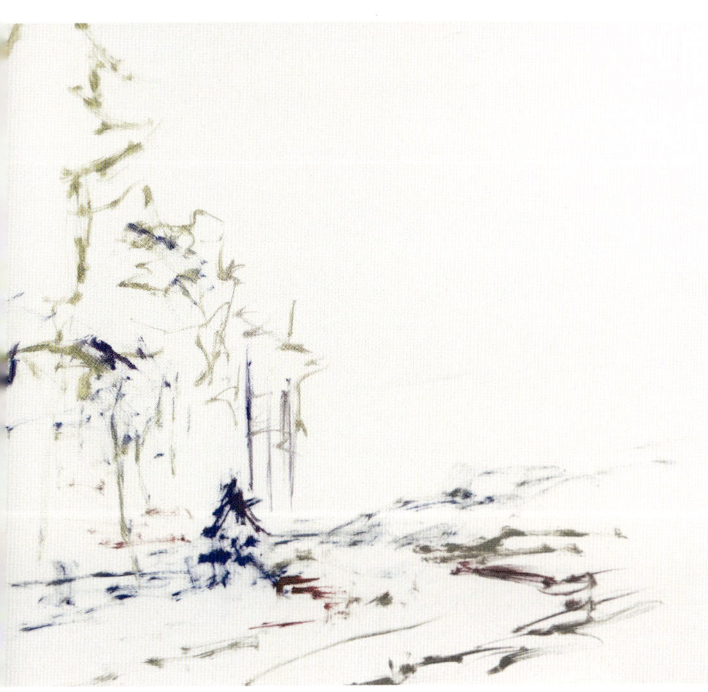

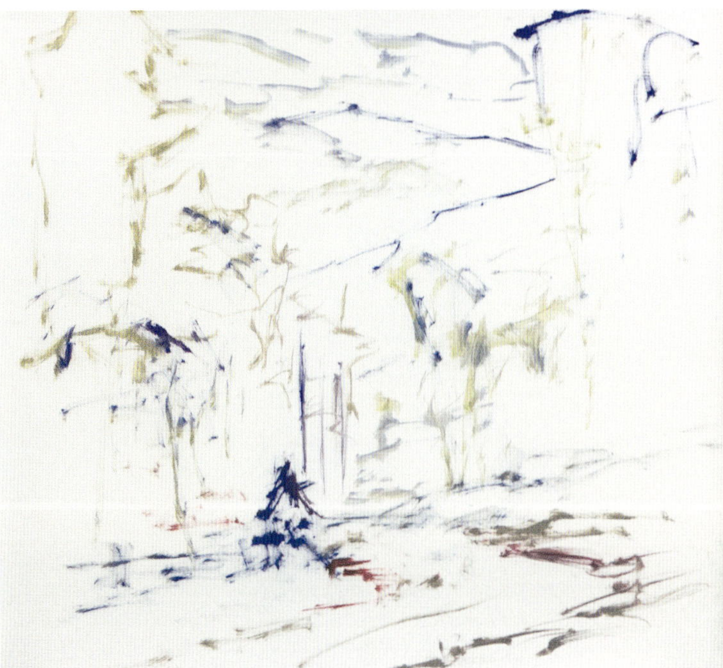

1 CREATE THE BIG MASSES

In terms of design, this is a complicated piece with a lot of components. The key is to see everything in masses, not separate units. Tone down all the yellows so you don't make it too overwhelming. Your intention should be to add a bit of mystery to the painting. Mystery will keep viewers looking at a piece. Too much yellow would be like too loud music. Use a ¼" dagger for this step. Make the path not only narrower, but give it an S curve, which also adds a sense of mystery. Then sketch in the shape of a small evergreen tree in the foreground so there is a strong element up front to help push everything else into the background. The forethought on design helps ensure a successful outcome. Do this block-in using Ultramarine Blue, Alizarin Crimson and mineral spirits.

2 SKETCH IN THE MOUNTAINS AND CLOUDS

Sketch in the mountains making sure to keep the lines strong to counterpoint the softness of the tree lines. Add a few clouds to give the sky a bit more interest.

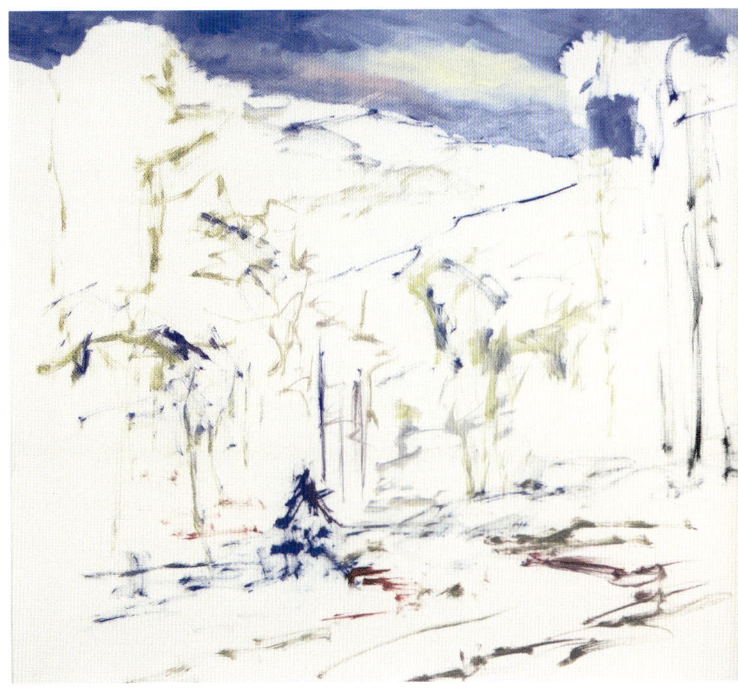

3 PAINT THE SKY

Lay in the sky using Ultramarine Blue, Alizarin Crimson and Titanium White with your ¼" and ½" daggers. Add a touch of orange to make the sky more neutral. The clouds are painted with the same mixture, leaning heavily towards white. Make sure the value and color temperature of the sky do not fight with the snow, which is much brighter and warmer and will be added next.

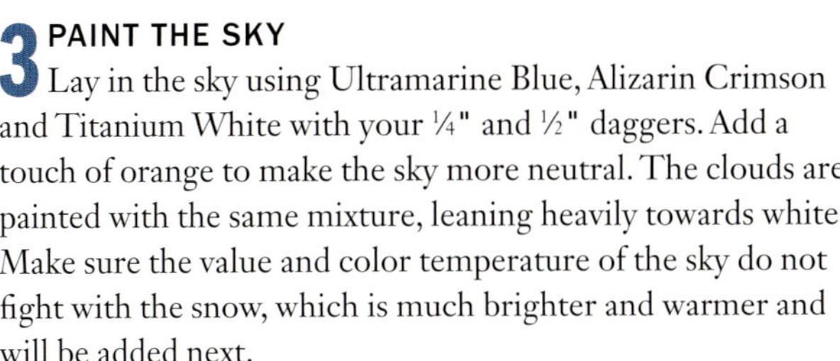

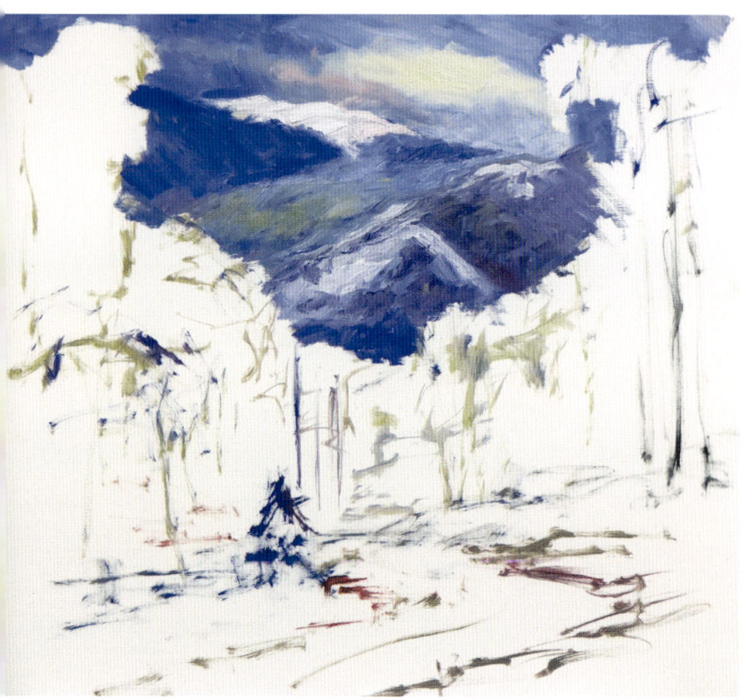

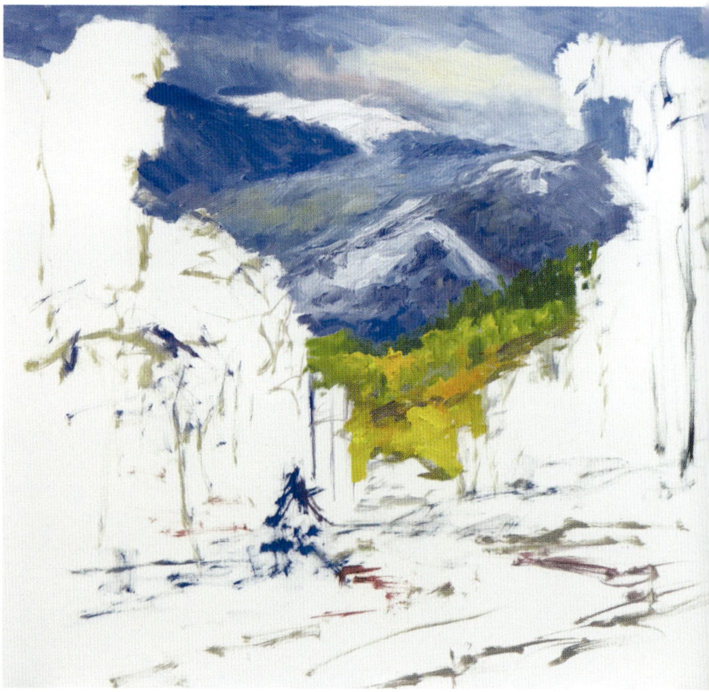

4 PAINT THE MOUNTAINS

Paint the mountains with a ¼" dagger using much of the same mixture of Ultramarine Blue, Alizarin Crimson, Titanium White and a touch of orange. Use one of the daggers for your purple mixtures and the other for your green mixtures. (This keeps the painting from getting muddy.) The snow is painted with Titanium White, a touch of your purple mixture and the slightest hint of Cadmium Yellow Lemon. The distant evergreens are painted with Phthalo Blue and Cadmium Yellow Deep with a touch of Titanium White to keep them cool and distant. Continue painting the mountains in shadow using variations of the same mixtures as before, Ultramarine Blue and Alizarin Crimson with a lot less white. You'll notice the difference between the snow in the middle distance as opposed to the snow at the top of the mountain. They don't fight for interest because the snow at the top of the mountain is brighter in value and also warmer.

5 FOCUS ON THE MIDDLE GROUND TREES

Paint the evergreens and aspens in the middle ground using Phthalo Blue, Cadmium Yellow Deep and a few touches of your purple mixtures. This ensures harmony since you are using the same basic mixtures, making changes only for local color. For the brighter areas use Cadmium Yellow Lemon.

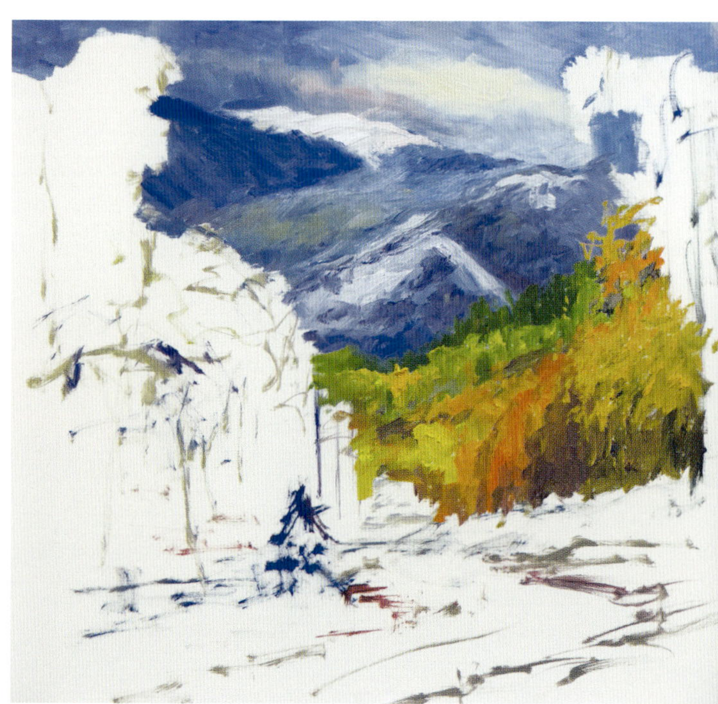

6 CREATE SHADOWS WITH NEUTRAL COLORS

Add Cadmium Orange along with your other mixtures. Where the trees fall into shadow use purple mixtures, keeping them more neutral by mixing in Cadmium Orange.

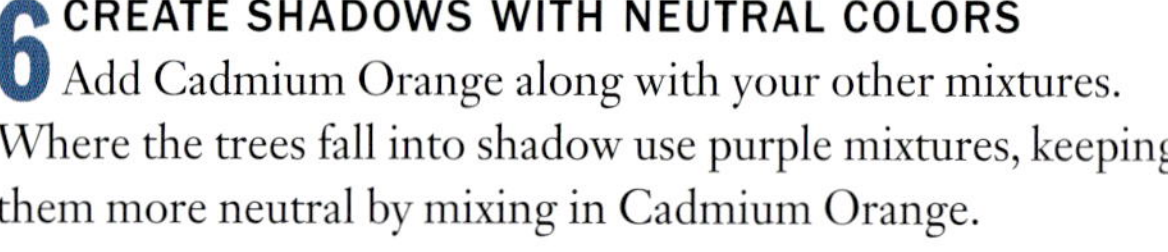

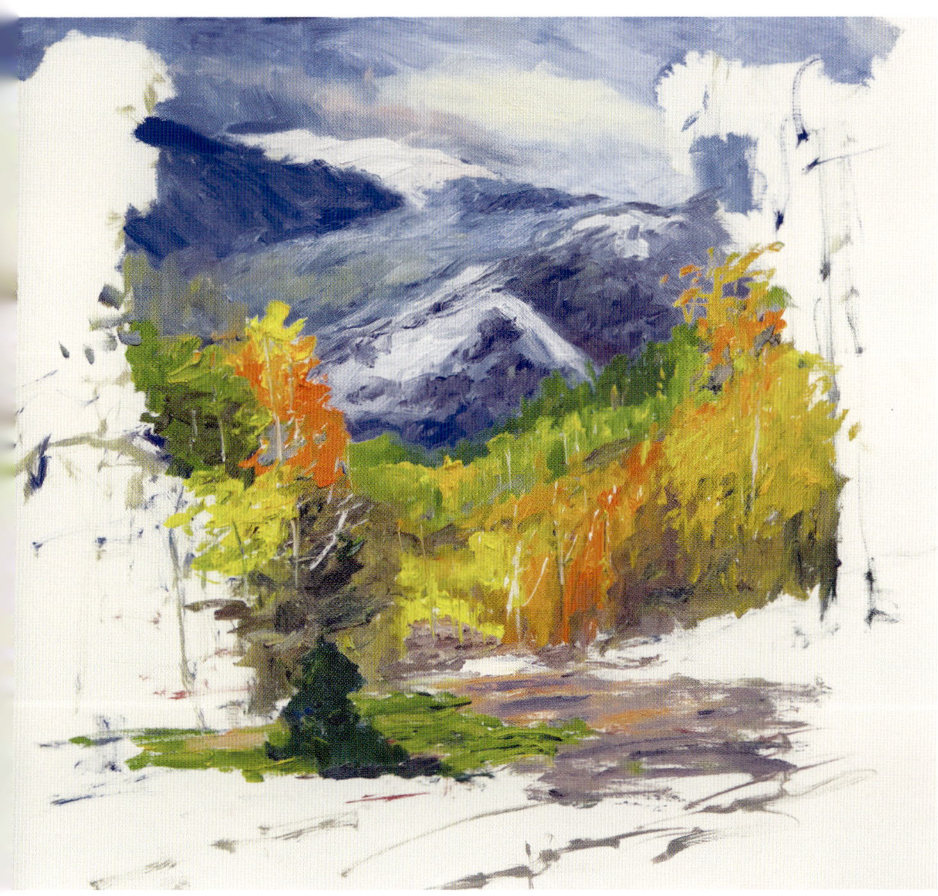

7 CREATE THE FOCAL POINT
Add a focal point using Cadmium Yellow Lemon. This gives the feeling of light slamming into the middle distance. Add some white to the curve in the road to help the focal point. The road, which is all cool, is a mixture of purple and orange alternating back and forth. Begin working on the trees on the left and the grass behind the evergreen. Use a ¼" dagger and no. 2 rigger to suggest tree trunks and branches. Alternate with Phthalo Blue, Cadmium Yellow Deep and Cadmium Yellow Lemon. Add Cadmium Red Deep to neutralize the greens. This creates lovely color harmony and gives the feeling of deep rich shadows.

8 PAINT THE TOPS OF THE TREES
Paint the tops of the trees on the left using Cadmium Yellow Lemon, Cadmium Yellow Deep and a touch of Cadmium Orange. Mix in a few dabs of purple to cool it in areas. Keep in mind that the yellow will be too strong if you carry it throughout the whole painting.

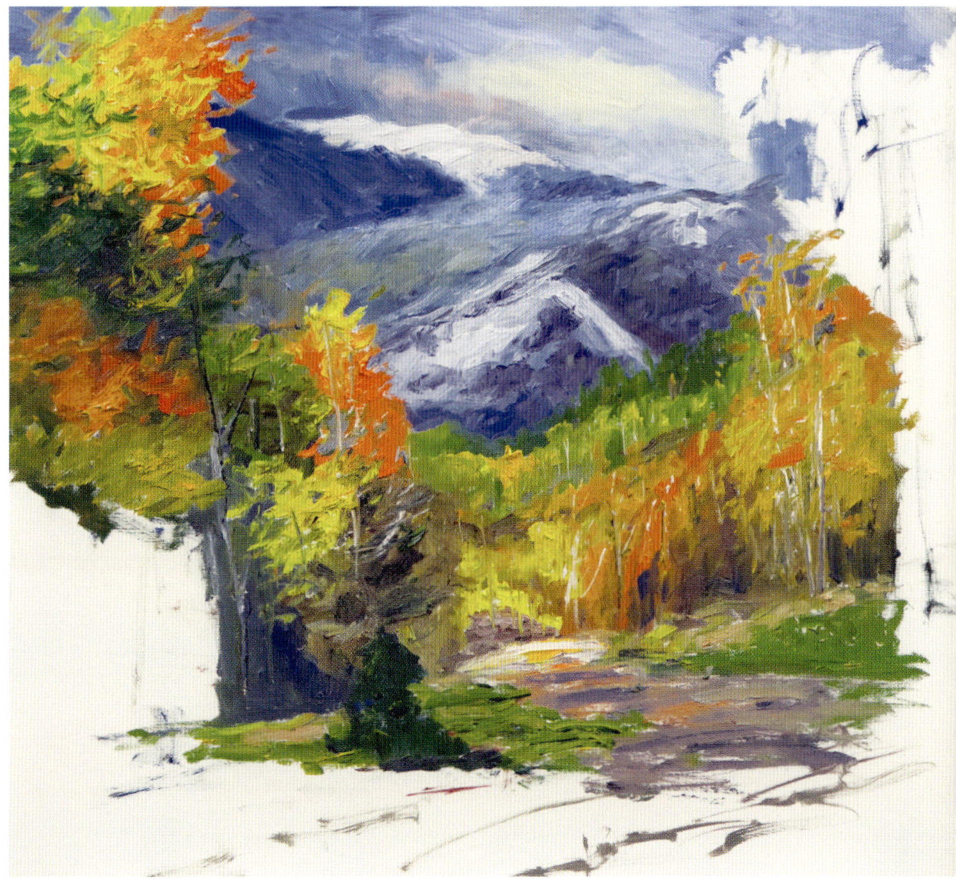

9 CREATE TREE TRUNKS AND BRANCHES

Using your dagger and rigger, suggest tree trunks and branches, tying in all the masses, adding a feeling that the trees are in rows. Suggest a few leaves here and there using a rigger. Masses are always defined by their edges. If the edges are correct in terms of sharpness and value, they will properly describe what you're looking at. Continue working on the grass on both the left and right. Use Titanium White in the cooler sections. Don't forget: White doesn't warm things up; it cools things down.

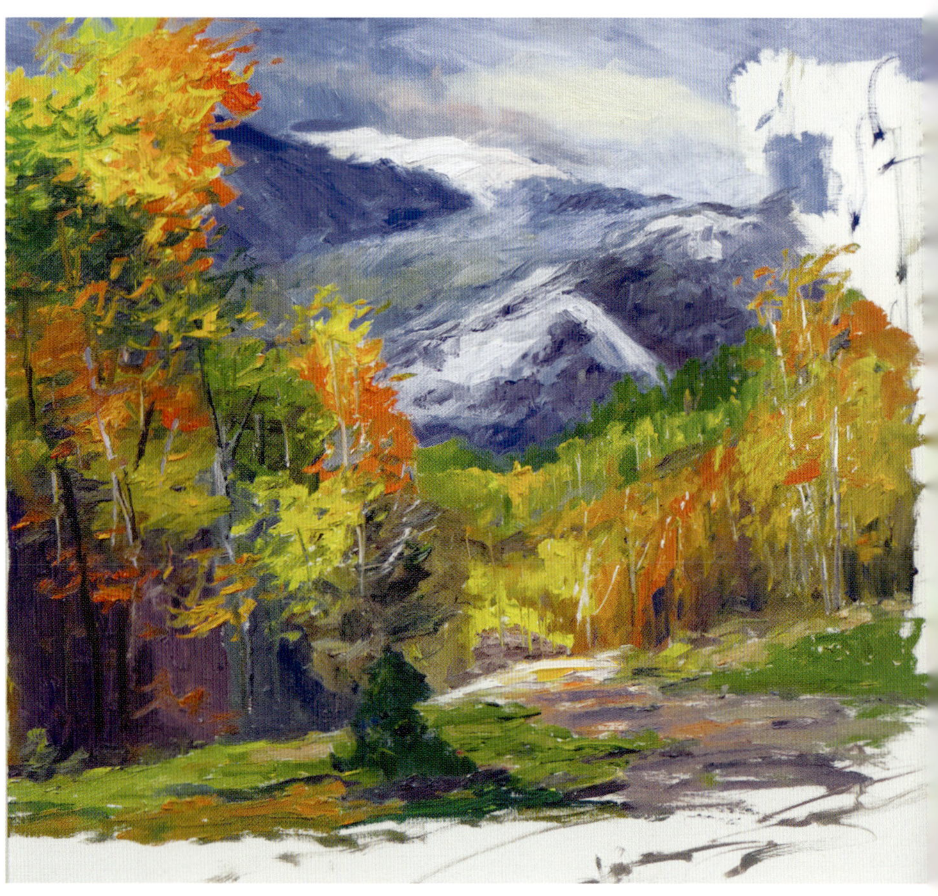

10 UNIFY THE COMPOSITION

Paint the large aspen tree on the right. This tree acts as a unifying element for the entire composition. Use many of the same colors you've used throughout the piece. Titanium White, purple and a bit of orange will neutralize the colors. Keep it simple to ensure harmony. Everything in nature is always harmonious because it is all bathed in the same light. As a painter you can get this effect by keeping all of your colors in the same harmonious family.

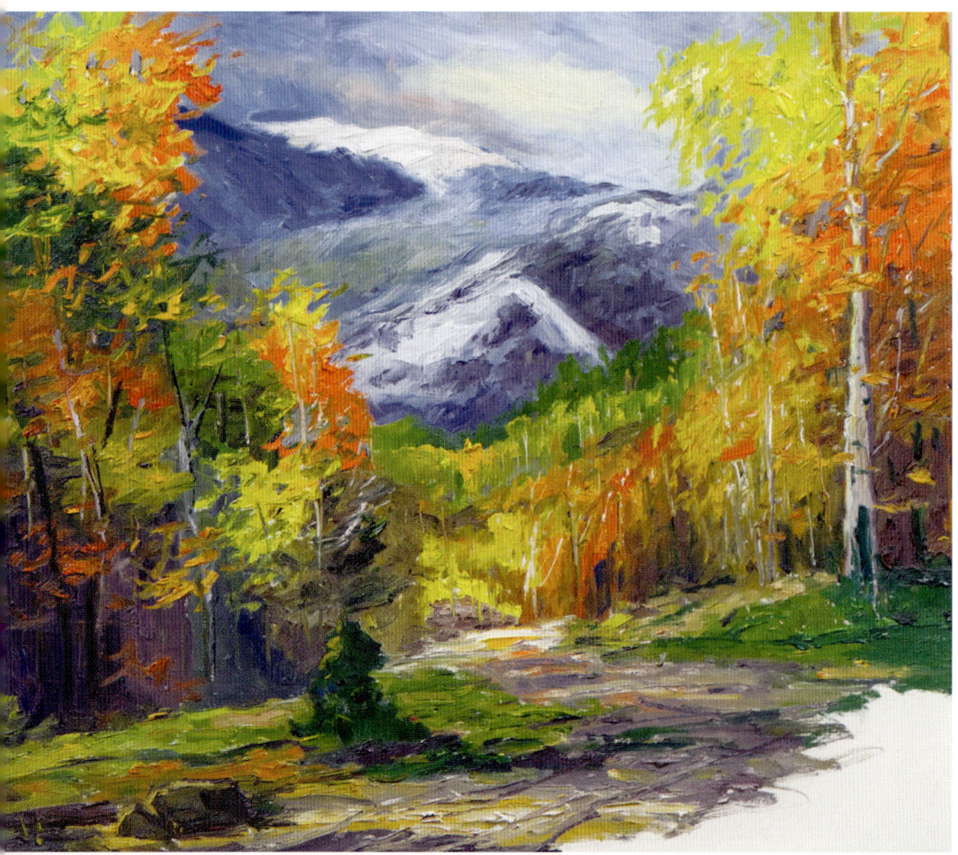

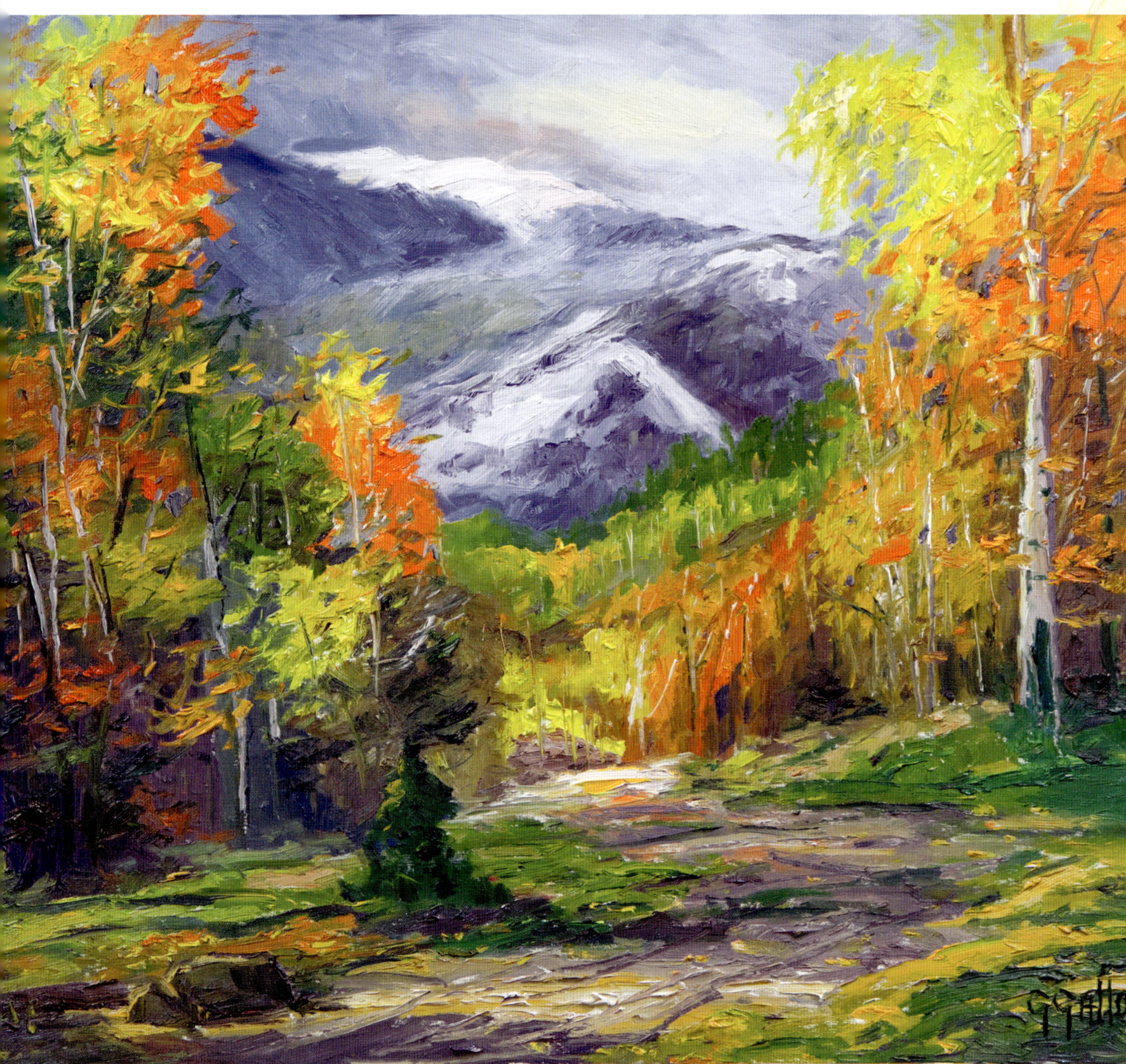

11 FINISH THE PAINTING

Finish the road, the rocks on the left and the foreground on the right. Keep the values down so they will not compete with the other areas of the painting. Remember, to create successful paintings you need to plan ahead. You can paint with freedom and abandon only if you have a clear idea of what you want to say before you begin to paint.

BACHELOR GULCH, AUTUMN
Oil on Canvas · 24" × 28" (61cm × 71cm)

Harbor Scene:
A Lesson in Using Artistic License

MATERIALS

SURFACE
stretched oil-primed linen

BRUSHES
no. 2 riggers

¼" dagger

PIGMENTS
Ivory Black, Ultramarine Blue, Alizarin Crimson, Cadmium Red Deep, Cadmium Orange, Cadmium Yellow Deep, Cadmium Yellow Lemon, Phthalo Blue, Titanium White

OTHER
medium cup

odorless mineral spirits

painting knife (1")

small triangular painting knife

wooden or paper palette

Harbor Scene is an example of taking various elements you see before you and composing them in a way to tell a whole new story. The reference photo below was shot with a telephoto lens. But the human eye does not see things in this way, and painting from a telephoto shot could create a strange and unnatural look. To counteract that possibility, I decided to add a piece of background that didn't exist in the photo. I added a piece of ocean going into the horizon in order to ensure a less confined composition and tell a better story.

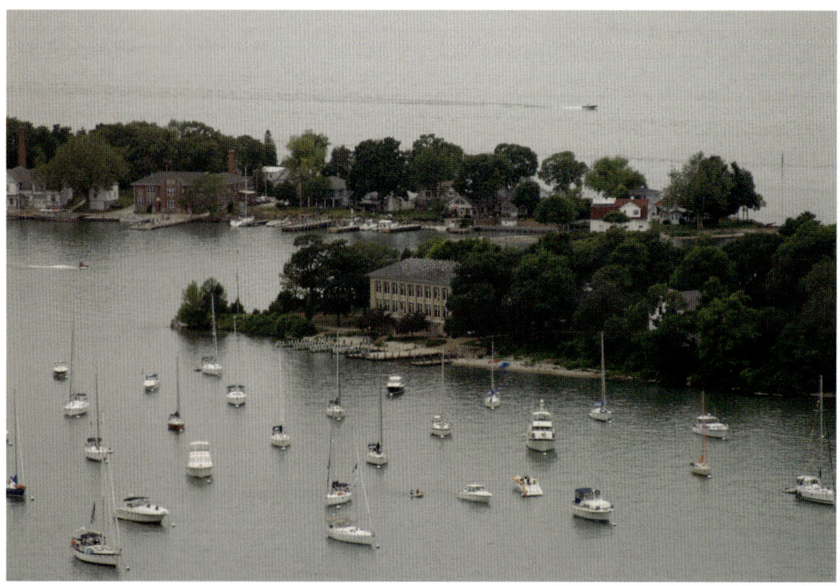

This scene is attractive but for my taste it's a bit too gray and there are too many boats.

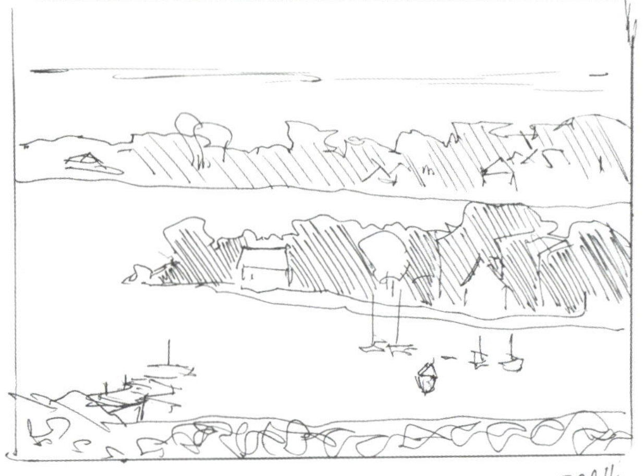

As you can see, I eliminated some of the boats and added a piece of foreground and a pier to give the viewer a sense of where they are standing. Otherwise you might feel as if you are a seagull flying overhead. I also added a horizon line to give the viewer a place to breathe.

1 BLOCK IN YOUR DESIGN

It's important to get this right from the beginning. Take your time sketching in the distant tree line and adding the shapes, values and colors correctly so you don't have to do extra work later. Use Ultramarine Blue, Alizarin Crimson and add mineral spirits to thin the paint. Apply the mixtures to the canvas with a ¼" dagger. For the greens, use Phthalo Blue mixed with a touch of Cadmium Yellow Deep. Always use at least two brushes when painting greens and purples, keeping the same brush for each color so they don't intermix and turn to gray. Establish the basic lines and suggest a few structures.

2 ESTABLISH THE CENTER OF INTEREST

Continue sketching in the trees in the middle distance. Even though they read as one large mass, you don't want them to read as a big blob without any differentiation. Establish the main structure, which is one of the major focal points of the piece.

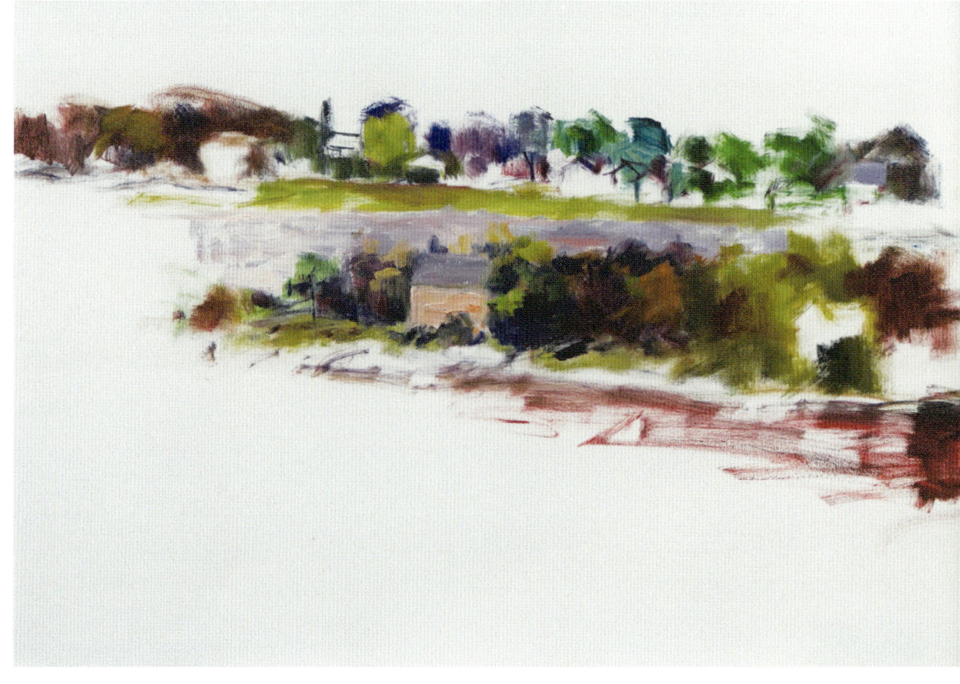

3 CREATE HARMONY

Using heavier paint lay in the background water using Ultramarine Blue, Alizarin Crimson and Titanium White. Add touches of Cadmium Orange to gray it down. Because of all the greens and purples, our gray structure needs to turn a bit red. Do this by adding Cadmium Red Deep to Titanium White and adding a touch of your purple mixture (Ultramarine Blue with Alizarin Crimson). As a result, everything harmonizes well.

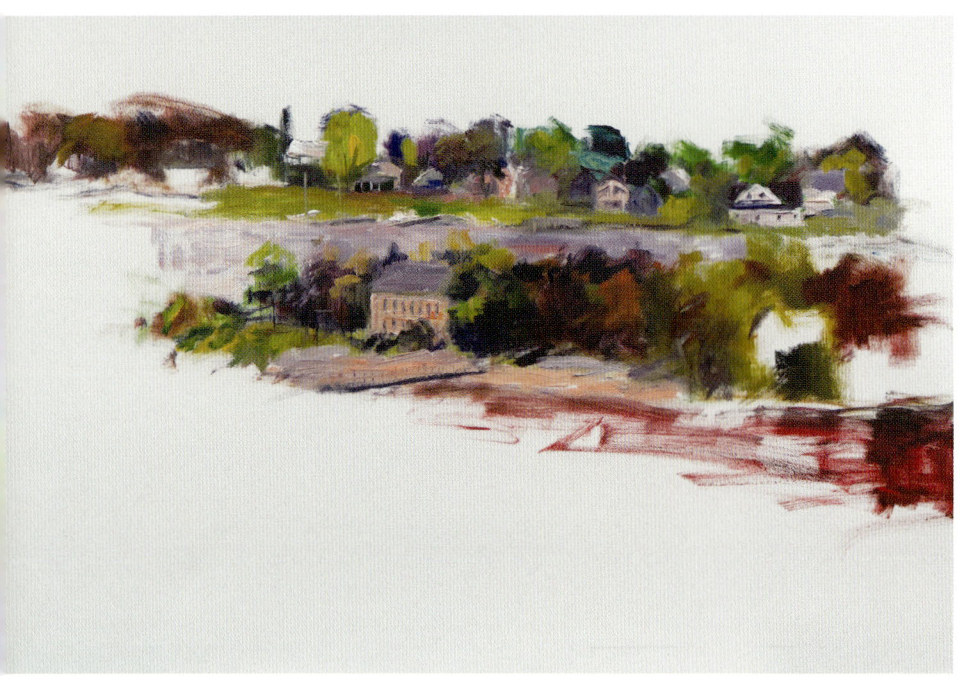

4 PAINT THE BUILDINGS
Continue working on the structures. The grayer buildings are in the blue-purple family. The lighter ones are more in the red family. When something is white and surrounded by lots of green, the rods and cones of the eye read that white structure as red. This is what happens in nature.

Add a few dabs to suggest windows in the main structure and keep the other structures less rendered so they do not fight for interest.

5 TAKE ARTISTIC LICENSE
Here's where you need to take artistic license. Paint the ocean beyond the tree line. It tells a better story and makes for a much more interesting painting. It also gives the viewer a chance to breathe. Continue painting the water, giving it more texture and more color shifts as you move toward the foreground. Use the same mixtures but make them more saturated and more intense. Paint in the sky, keeping it cool by using a mix of Ultramarine Blue, Alizarin Crimson and Titanium White. Use a touch of Cadmium Orange mixed with Ivory Black to make it read gray. Use a 1" painting knife to apply the paint. Keep the sky flat so it will not compete with the texture of the water.

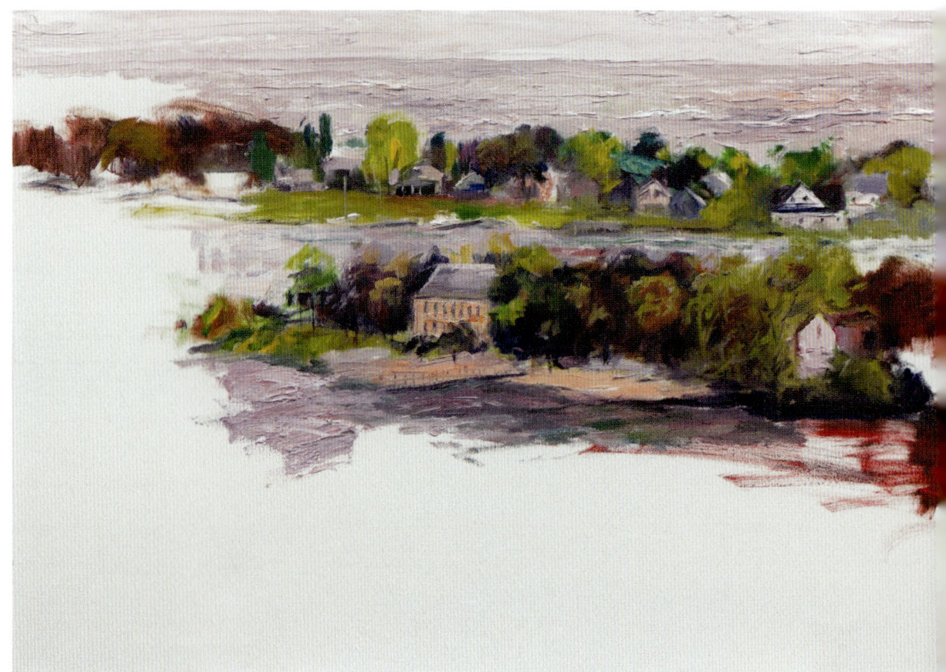

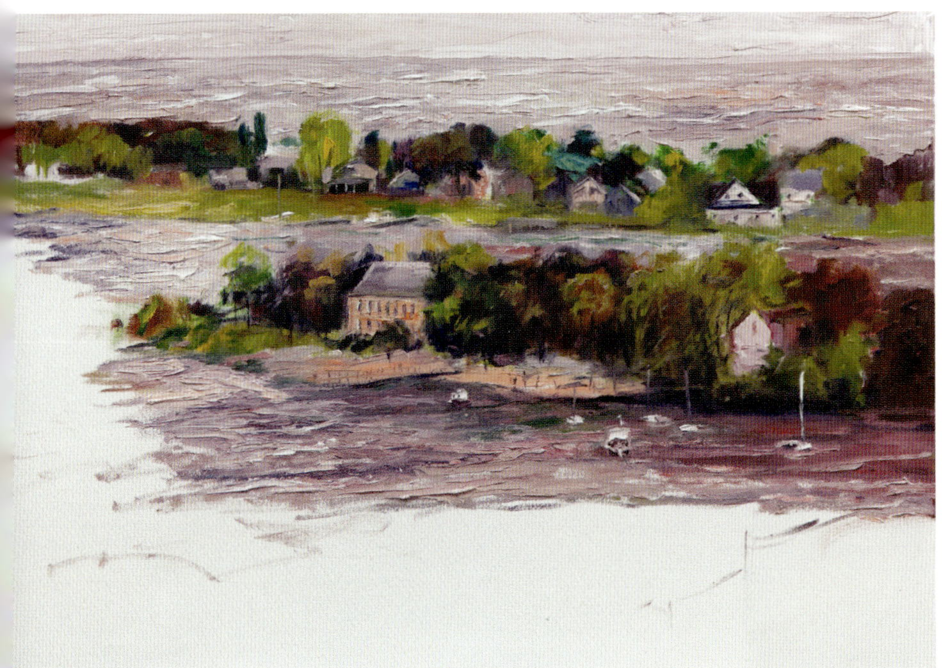

6 PAINT THE BOATS

Render some of the boats. Use a ¼" dagger for the hulls and a no. 2 rigger for the masts. They add interest, but don't add too many boats because you don't want your foreground to be filled with lots of white dots. Keep the boats grouped together so they read as masses and not separate spots of color. Paint the house on the right and make it feel closer than the houses in the distance by making it warmer in tone.

7 PAINT SUNLIGHT ON THE WATER

Using more artistic license, add some warmth to the left side of the painting to give the feeling of sunlight on the water. This helps draw the eye to the foreground. Without these strong choices, the painting could become busy and disjointed. It could also become overwhelmingly dull and gray. Use a ¼" dagger and a lot of heavy texture to suggest light. The textured paint will pick up some of the natural light from wherever you are working and create its own lights and darks.

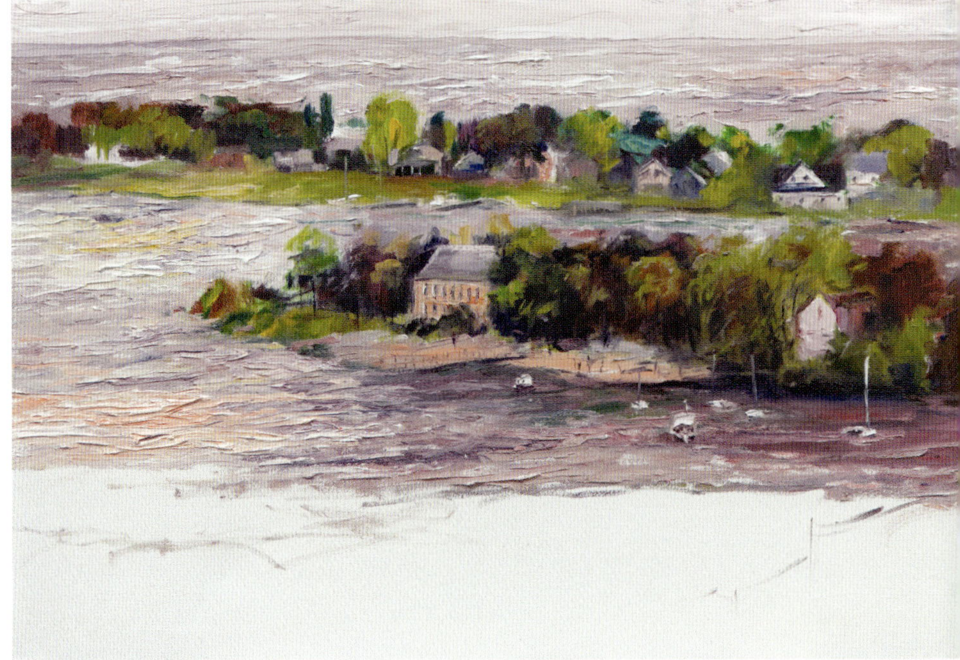

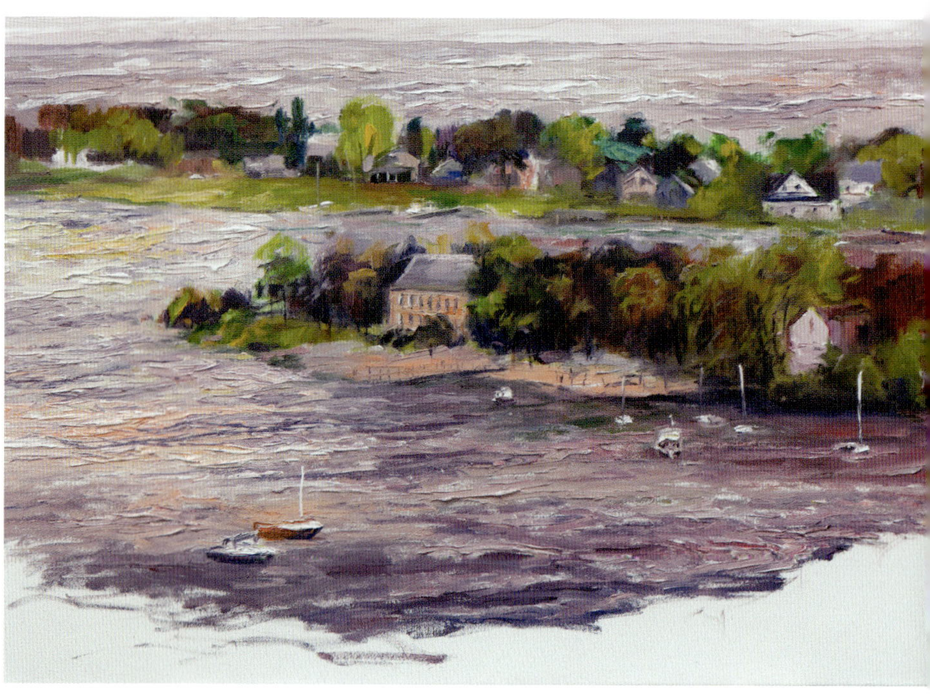

8 CREATE TEXTURE IN THE WATER

Continue working on the water using more texture and more contrast. Change the strokes around to get the feeling of waves working their way toward the shore. Add a few more boats, but again, treat them as a grouping. Paint the boats in the same manner as before, this time using a ¼" dagger for the hulls of the boats and a no. 2 rigger for the masts.

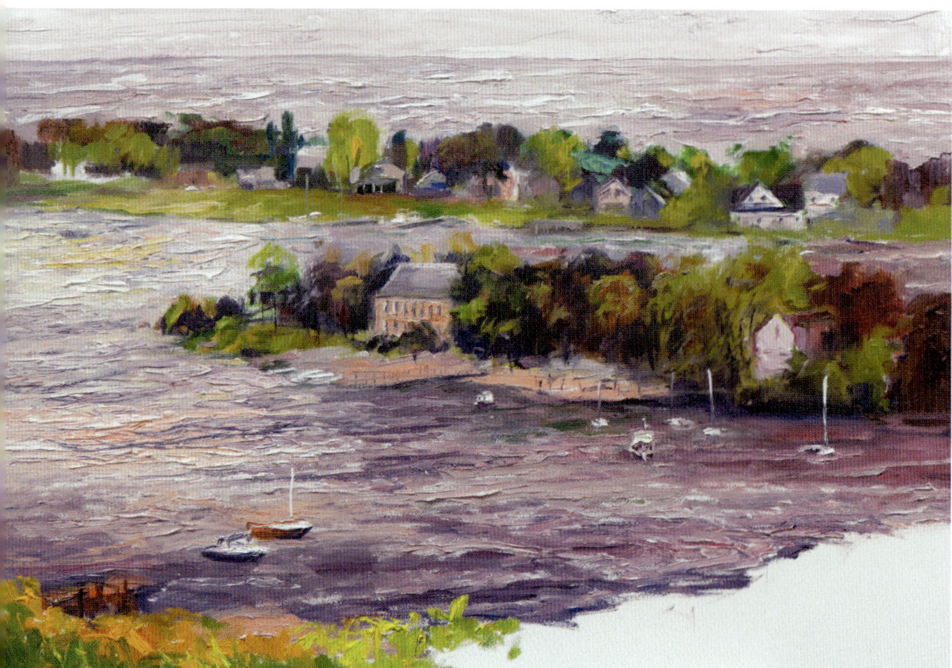

9 USE YOUR IMAGINATION TO PAINT THE FOREGROUND

Use a small triangular painting knife to create a pier and a ¼" dagger to create the pylons and foreground grass. This is a good idea because it's a nice warm note to have in the foreground; adding warm notes to the water and giving the feeling of a little sun breaking through not only cheer the painting up but give the viewer different places to look inside the scene. It also leads the viewer's eye into the painting.

Work on your imagined foreground using lots of warm colors. Cadmium Yellow Lemon, Cadmium Yellow Deep, Phthalo Blue and various purples are used to describe the hedges. These warm notes up front throw the rest of the painting into the background, making the atmospheric perspective even stronger.

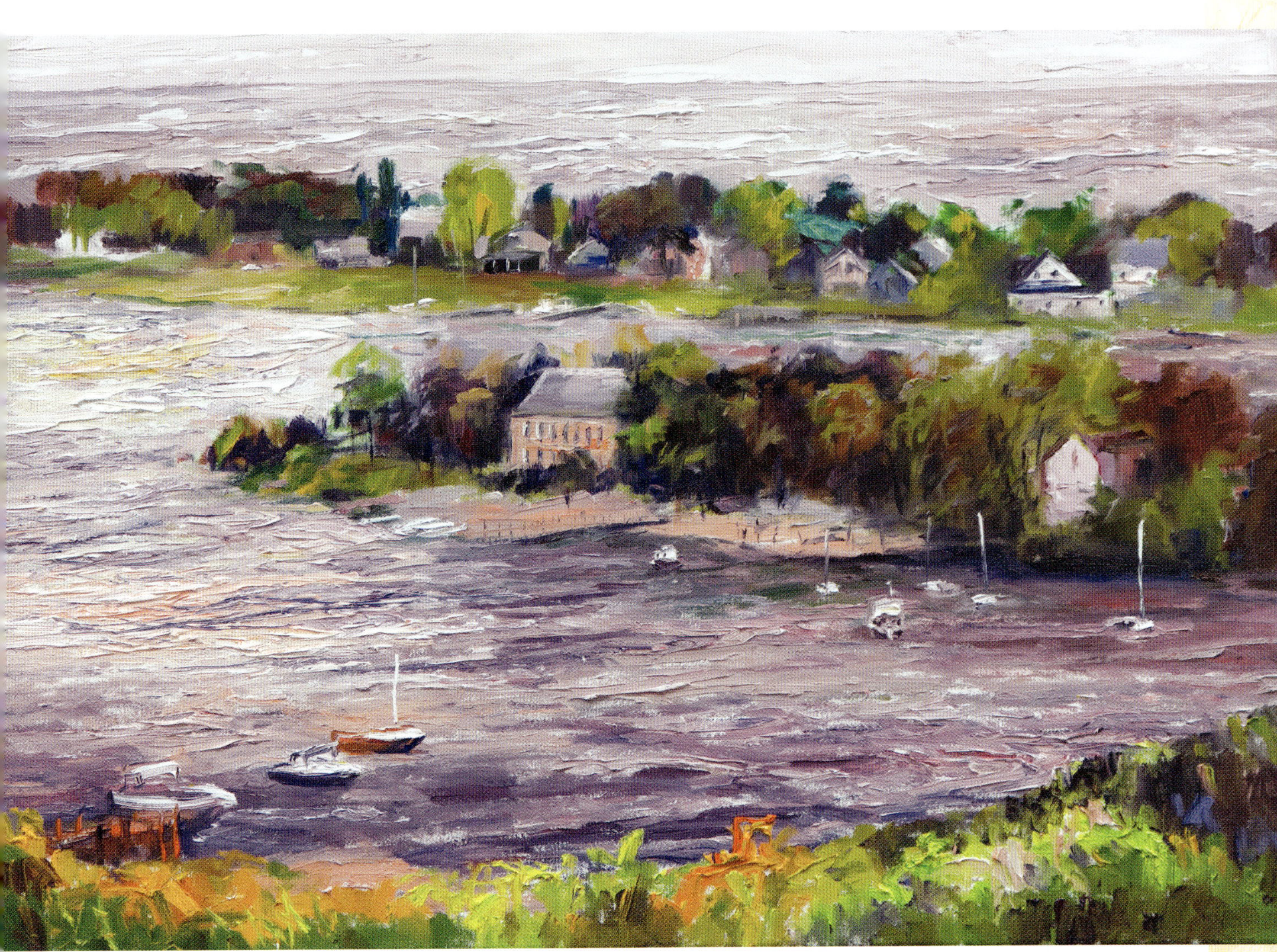

10 FINISH THE PAINTING
Add one last boat and a few spots of color to the foreground. Make a few small adjustments and then stop. The painting is done. By using your imagination and taking artistic license, you will grow more confident in your painting and stop copying exactly what you see in front of you.

HARBOR SCENE
Oil on Canvas · 24" × 36" (61cm × 91cm)

Walborn Pond:
A Lesson in Laying Paint Wet-in-Wet

MATERIALS

SURFACE
stretched oil-primed linen

BRUSHES
no. 6 filbert

no. 2 rigger

¼", ½" daggers

PIGMENTS
Ivory Black, Ultramarine Blue, Alizarin Crimson, Cadmium Red Deep, Cadmium Orange, Cadmium Yellow Deep, Cadmium Yellow Lemon, Phthalo Blue, Titanium White

OTHER
medium cup

odorless mineral spirits

wooden or paper palette

Nearly every painting I do is created in one shot, no matter what size the canvas is. This approach was perfected by the great American Impressionist Edward Willis Redfield. It's not for the faint of heart because you have to layer wet paint over other areas of wet paint. The amount of pressure you apply with your brush will cause the paint to either lie on top or mix with the wet paint beneath. Over time you will get the feel of it and be able to manipulate the paint however you wish to get whatever effect you desire.

This way of painting is not only a great deal of fun, it's also a way to create unique paintings that are full of spontaneity. In this painting I paint trees against the sky, bushes against trees and brightly colored leaves on top of dark, cool areas. I also paint the pond using various colors and values to suggest movement. On top of that I paint reflections in different colors for both the trees and the foliage. As if that's not enough, I also paint the branches of the foreground tree over the already multilayered background. It is this wet-in-wet technique that allows me to achieve all the desired effects I want in this painting.

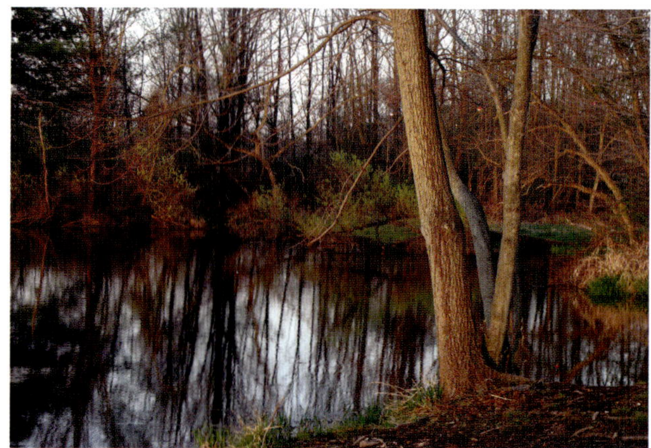

This place has a wonderful contemplative mood. The morning light helps reinforce this notion.

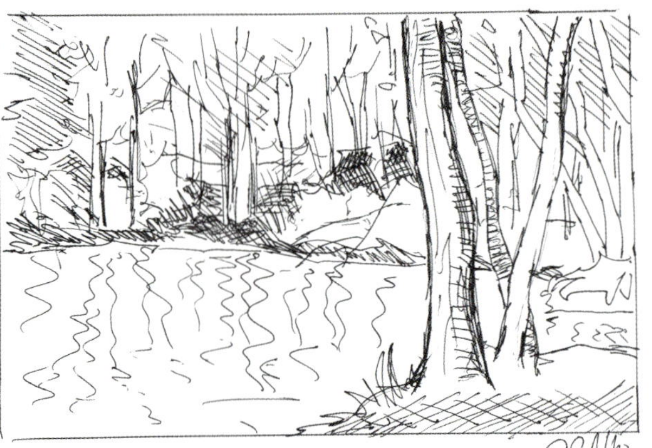

I didn't change all that much in the sketch from real life. I brought the distant bank of the pond to more of a diagonal line than in reality so your eye wouldn't be led off the canvas.

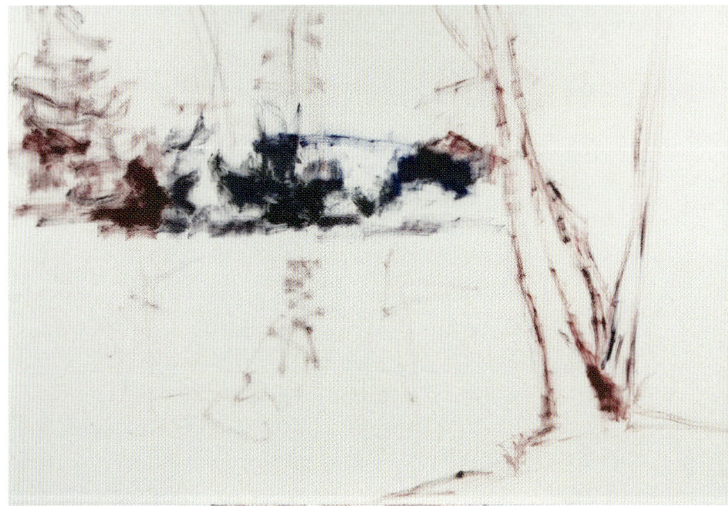

1 BLOCK IN THE HORIZON LINE

Use mineral spirits to thin a mixture of Ultramarine Blue and Alizarin Crimson. With a ¼" dagger, sketch in your horizon line, indicating a few bushes and suggesting where the hillside meets the sky. Raise the horizon line so you do not cut the composition in half. The water will be more important than the sky.

2 SKETCH THE FOREGROUND TREES

Sketch using the same mixture to indicate the foreground trees and the nearest piece of the shoreline.

3 PAINT THE BACKGROUND

Using heavier paints, lay in the background elements to the trees, bushes and distant hillside. Use Ultramarine Blue, Alizarin Crimson and a touch of Cadmium Red Deep for the cooler sections. The yellow in the Cadmium Red Deep makes the purple areas more gray. Add a bit of Cadmium Orange to your purple mixture to make things appear even more neutral. Use Phthalo Blue and Cadmium Yellow Deep to block in the green bushes. At this point you can already see how well these colors interplay together.

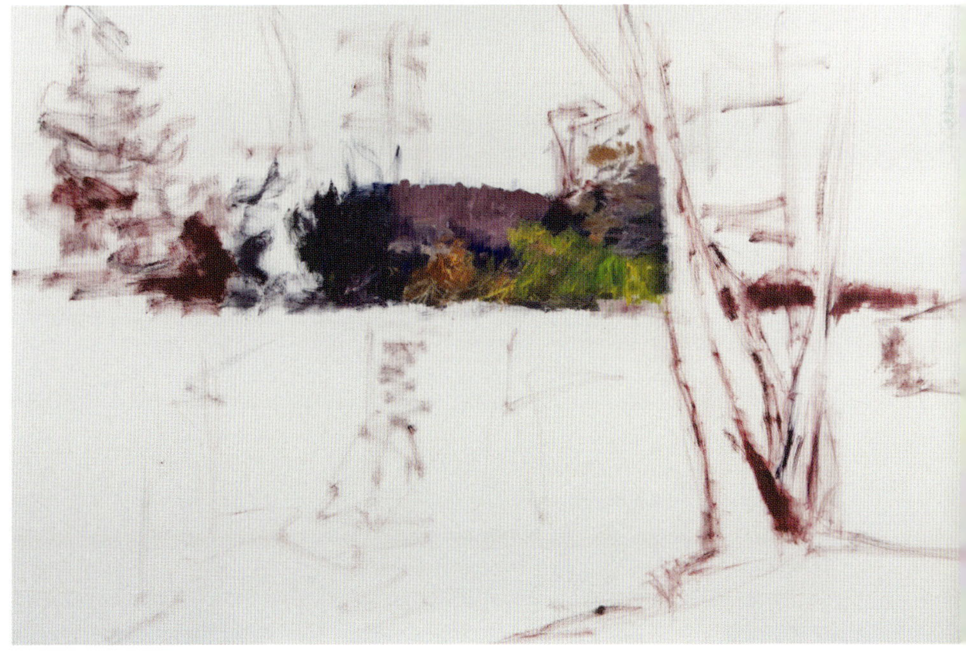

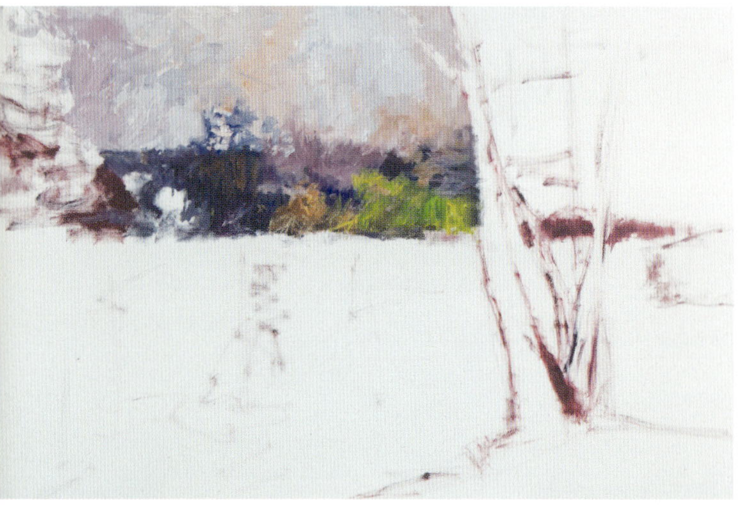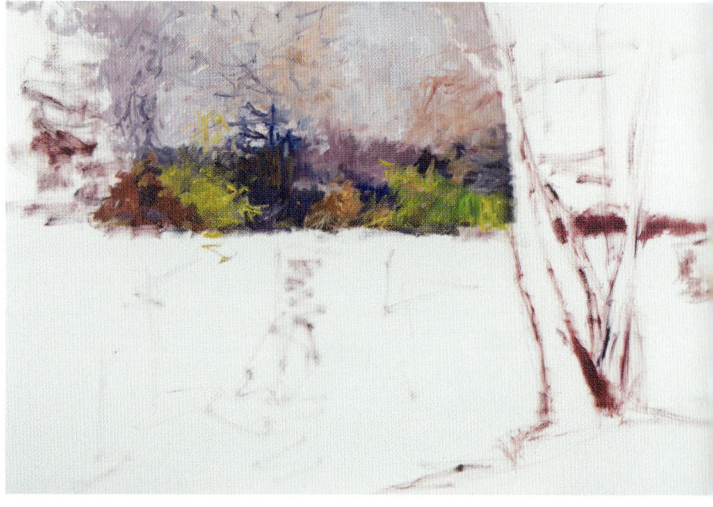

4 PAINT THE SKY

Lay in the sky using a no. 6 filbert and a cool mixture of Ultramarine Blue, Alizarin Crimson and Titanium White. Then warm it up a bit with Cadmium Orange. Since there will be a great number trees against the sky, take your dagger brush, dip it in the purple mixture and lightly add streaks of varying values to indicate what will be the background trees. This is how you achieve a feeling of density in the woods. Keep the value of the sky darker than it really is because you don't want it to fight with the brightness of the water, which will be one of the major focuses of the painting.

5 PAINT THE TREE BRANCHES

Continue laying down streaks with a ¼" dagger to indicate branches against the sky. Make sure you keep everything close in value and color temperature. If any elements of your painting become too bright and warm, they will compete with the foreground tree and the land that is closest to us. This step will ensure atmospheric perspective. The best way to do this is to always make comparisons as you work. Lay down something in the background and ask yourself, *Will this compete with the foreground?*

6 PAINT THE BACKGROUND TREES

Lay in the various trees with a dagger and rigger, using your purple mixture, warming it and graying it where necessary. Use a ¼" dagger for the majority of the trunks, and a no. 2 rigger for the more pronounced branches. Use a ½" dagger to suggest the evergreen tree on the left. If you only paint the trees against the sky without scrubbing in various shades of warms and cools to indicate the background branches, these trees will look very unrealistic, more like cutouts against the sky. With the rigger add a few highlights near the center of the painting using Phthalo Blue, Cadmium Lemon Yellow and a touch of Cadmium Yellow Deep. Keep the highlights to a minimum and centralized so your eye doesn't start moving all over the place.

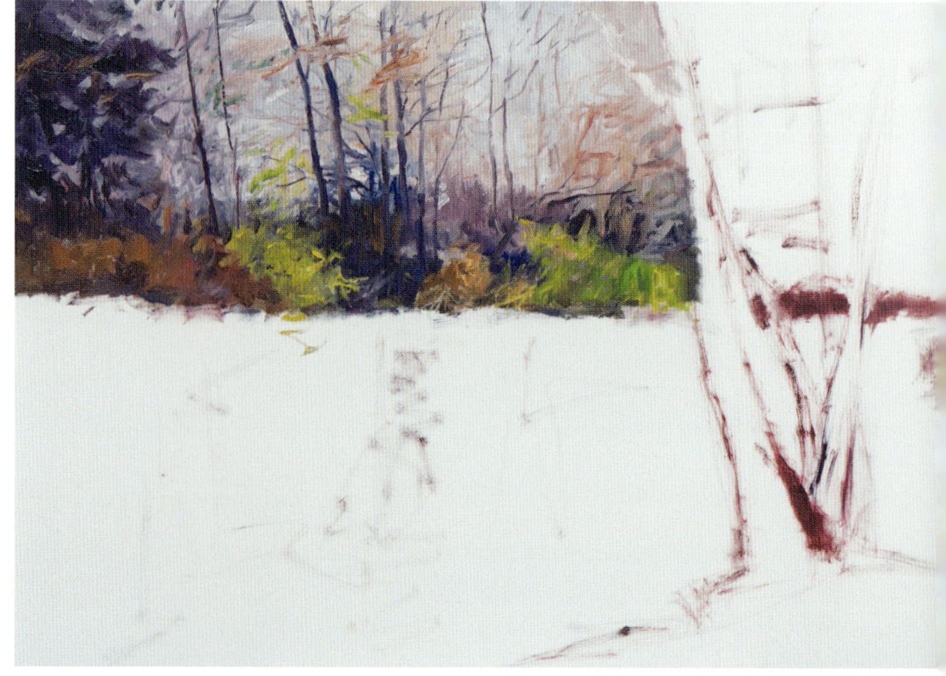

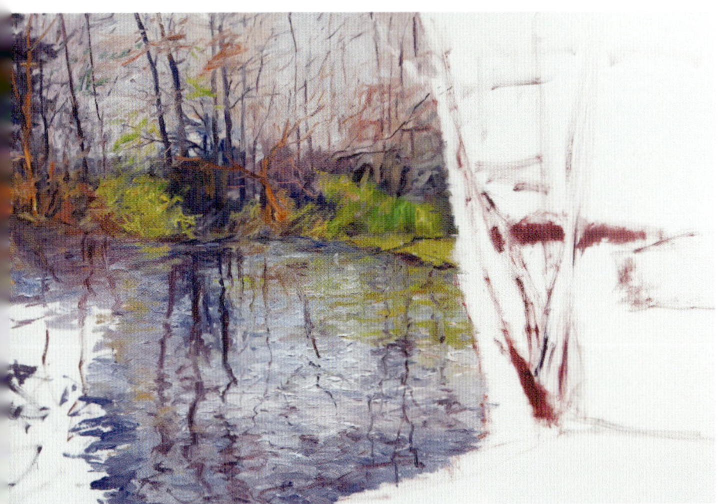
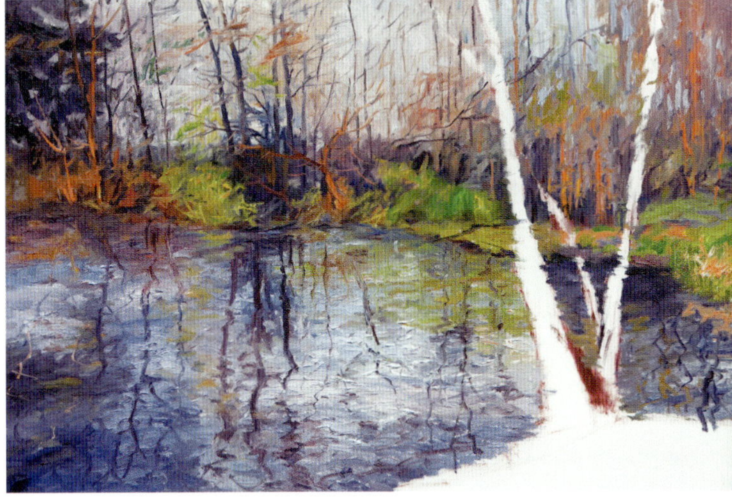

7 BEGIN PAINTING THE WATER

Paint the water using the same mixtures but make adjustments for color temperature. The water is cooler and brighter. Use strong horizontal strokes to indicate the movement of the water. Drag both your dagger and rigger brushes over the wet paint, holding the brush up and dropping your shoulder in order to make a strong line. These lines indicate the reflections of the trees, and you have one chance to get them right. If you overwork them you will lose all the freshness, and your painting could turn muddy. Use Cadmium Yellow Deep and Phthalo Blue to indicate the reflections of the bushes and some of the landmasses. Notice that they are a bit darker and cooler in value, which is what happens in nature. While working from a photo, it's easy to forget that everything in nature is always moving, including still water. Trees, leaves and water, no matter how still, are always being affected by air movement. Remember that and put movement into your strokes to suggest that feeling.

8 WORK ON THE BACKGROUND TREES

Continue working on the background trees, suggesting their shapes, color and value. Here the background warms up, so exercise caution; you don't want anything to compete with the foreground tree.

9 PAINT THE FOREGROUND TREE

Place the main trunk of the foreground tree in the painting with a ¼" dagger. As you can see, it's much warmer than the background trees or for that matter, anything else in the painting. It also has the hardest and most decisive edges. Add a small touch of Ivory Black to your purple mixture to make the shadowed side of the tree look strong. Using your rigger, indicate some lines in the bark. With some of these lines use Titanium White, which you should allow to blend with the mixture underneath. For other lines use the darkest of your purple mixtures. You don't want to go overboard with this because it will not only darken the tree but also fight with the lines that indicate the reflections in the water.

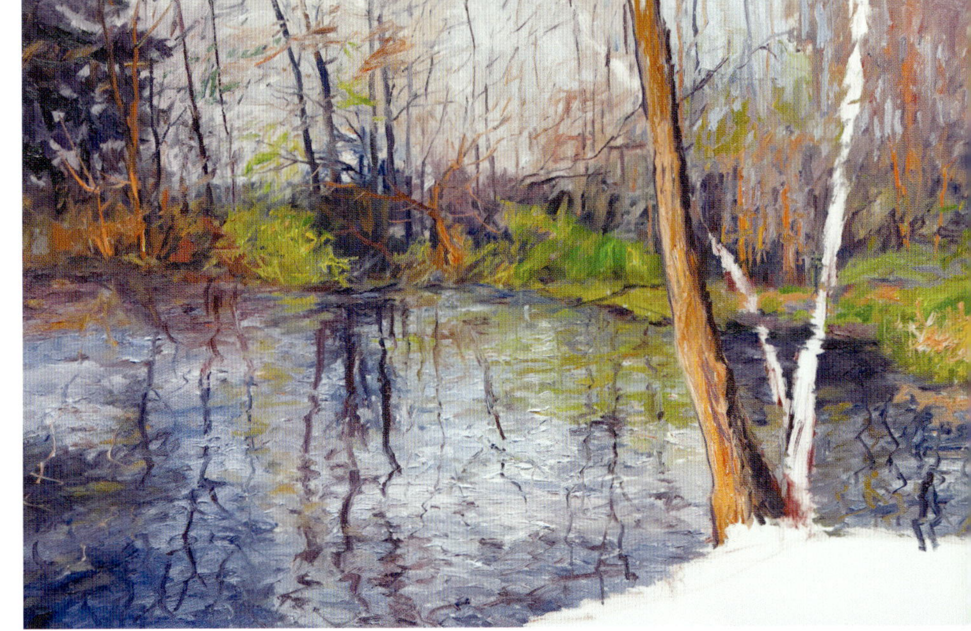

10 PAINT THE BRANCHES

Paint in the branches using the side of your dagger for the thicker ones and the rigger for the thinner ones. Twist your arm and wrist around as you lay in each branch to indicate the way branches grow. At times you should twirl the brush. The idea is to do it once and keep it as fresh as possible. You do not want to overwork this.

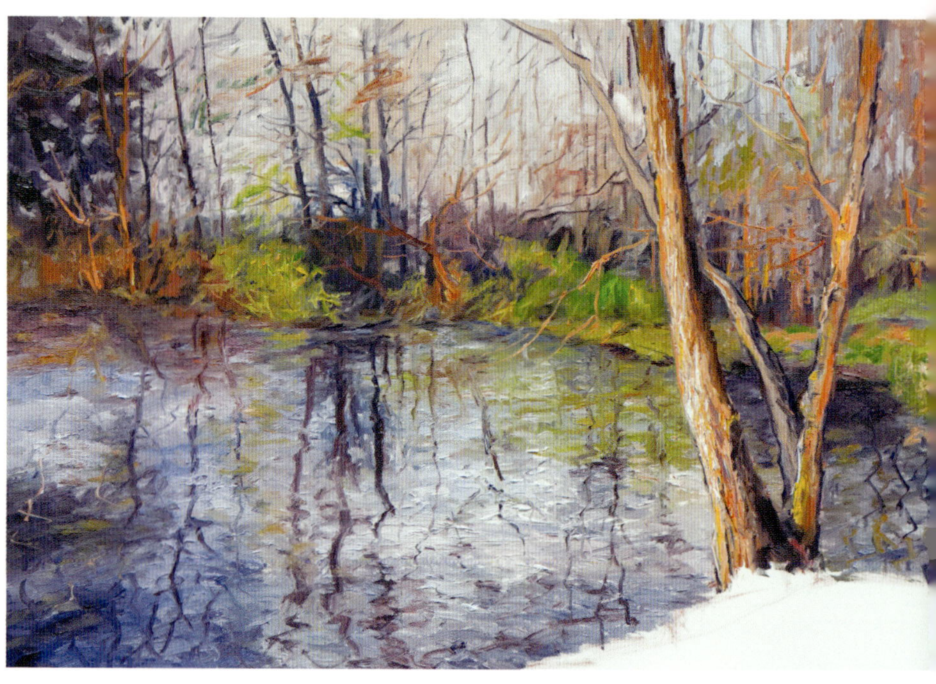

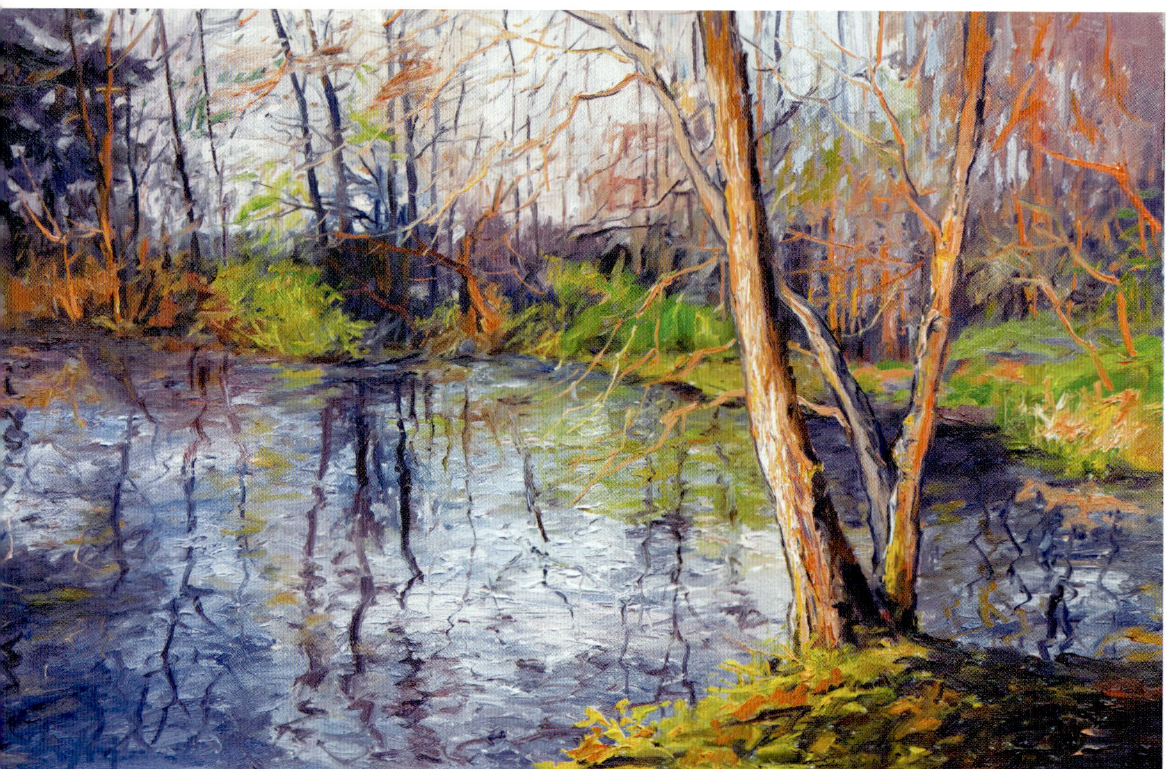

11 WORK ON THE FOREGROUND AREA

Paint in the foreground with a ¼" dagger. Use Cadmium Yellow Lemon, Phthalo Blue and a touch of Titanium White for the brighter areas and Phthalo Blue and Cadmium Yellow Deep for the mid-range areas. Use your purple mixture to indicate shadows. Add a bit more Cadmium Red Deep to make these foreground shadows not only warmer, but also to make sure they don't compete with the very strong cools in the background, especially those at the center of the painting. As a general rule, things tend to be warmer when they are closer.

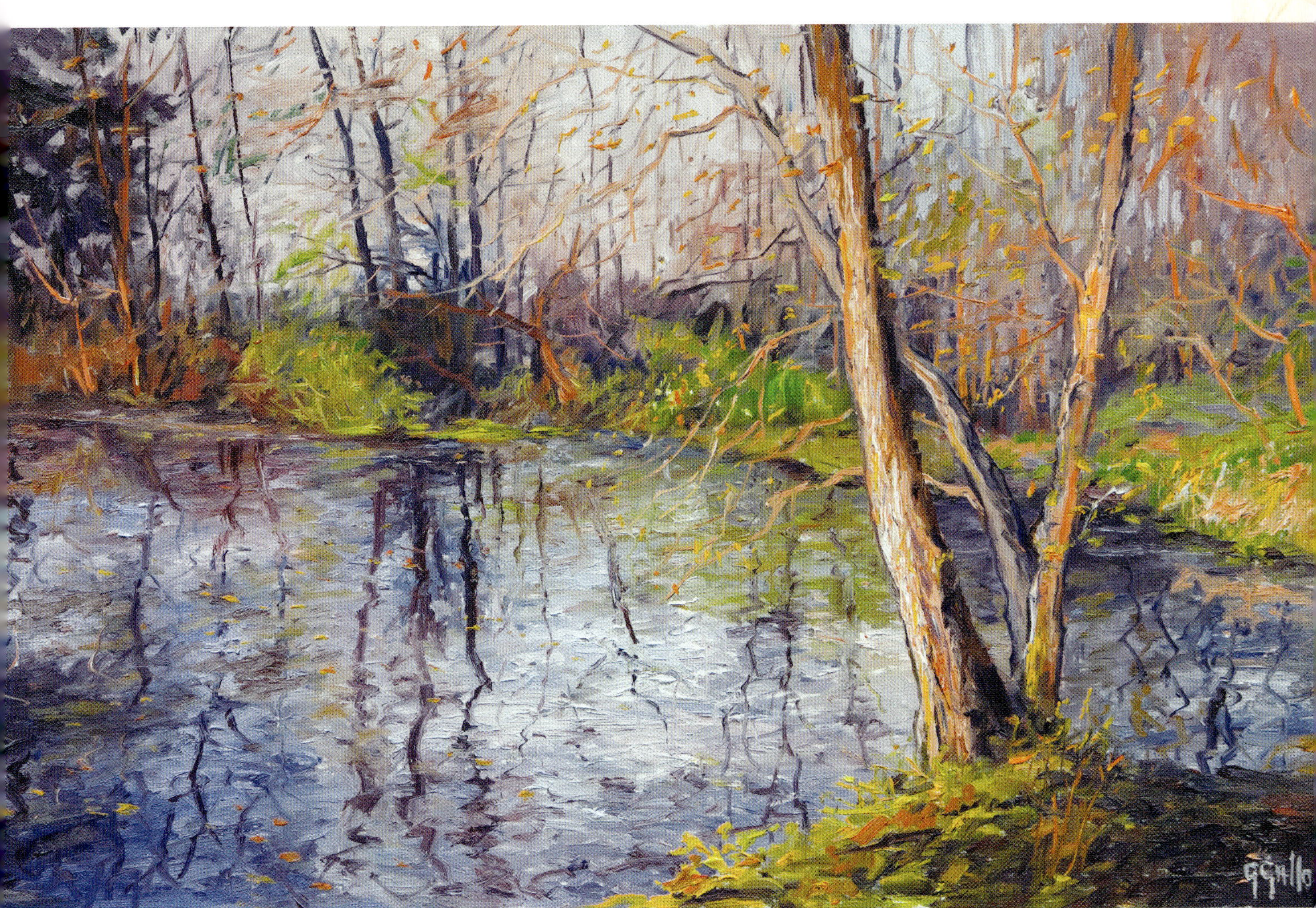

12 FINISH THE PAINTING

To help set the foreground tree off even more, take your no. 2 rigger loaded with lots of paint, and add leaves using Cadmium Yellow Lemon and Titanium White for the brightest ones and various mixtures of Cadmium Yellow Deep, Cadmium Orange and Cadmium Red Deep for the darker ones. Add these touches sparingly. Sign it and you've created a masterpiece!

WALBORN POND
Oil on Canvas · 30" × 48" (76cm × 122cm)

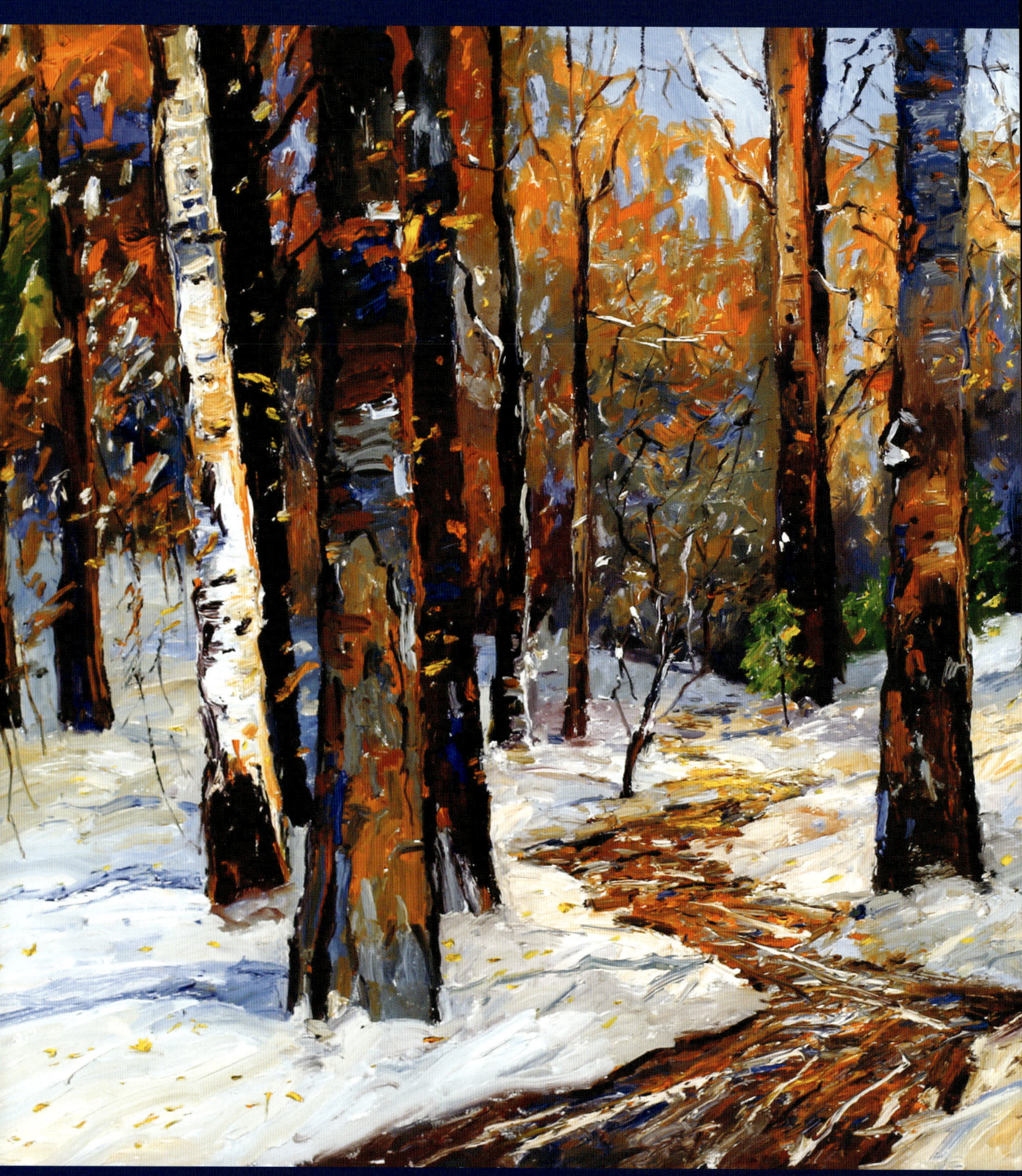

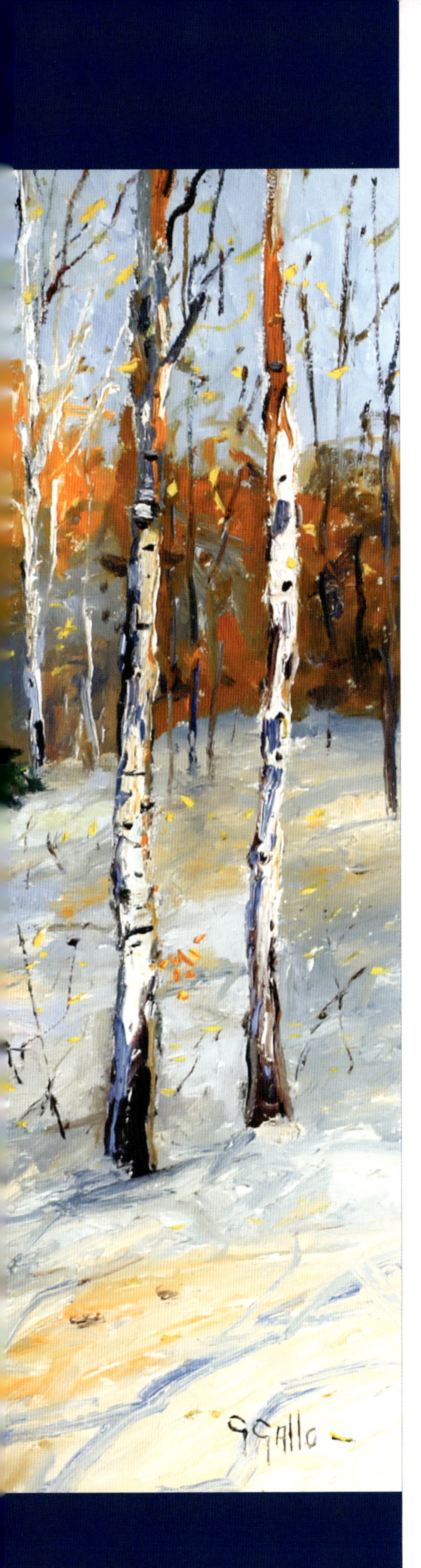

CHAPTER 7

GALLERY NOTES

Writing this book has been a wonderful experience. In many ways it has forced me to articulate openly what is usually a very personal and internal process. My general approach to painting is always the same. First, I come across a subject that moves me. I'm mesmerized as I take it all in, and after I recover emotionally I begin to ask myself a series of technical questions as to how I want to paint it.

Most importantly I want to get across to the viewer how beautiful I think something is. This, by its very nature, is an act of sharing. It is from this place that I start. Then I go to issues of design, values, color, brushstrokes and any other technical question I need to answer in order to create the most cohesive way into the painting so I can finish it with strength and clarity. With the paintings in this chapter I am going to let you into my inner process and explain why I made the decisions I did in each painting.

This painting is a strong study of both design and complementary colors. As evening fell upon the forest, I felt it had a sense of great dignity. The groupings of trees seemed to convey both strength and peacefulness. I played up these emotions by making the trees a bit wider than they actually were to convey their strength. I also exaggerated their height by making them grow right out of the top of the canvas without tapering them all that much. The orange light that bathed the tops of the distant trees was so gorgeous that I decided to push it even further. This allowed me to also push the complementary color of blue in the sky and in the shadowed areas of the piece. The warm and cool greens of the evergreens, along with hints of purple in the shadows, completed the color gamut. As in many of my paintings, I have a spot of pure white. I believe that viewers sometimes need this to feel the full spectrum of values from light to dark.

WINTER EVENING · Oil on Canvas · 36" × 48" (91cm × 122cm)

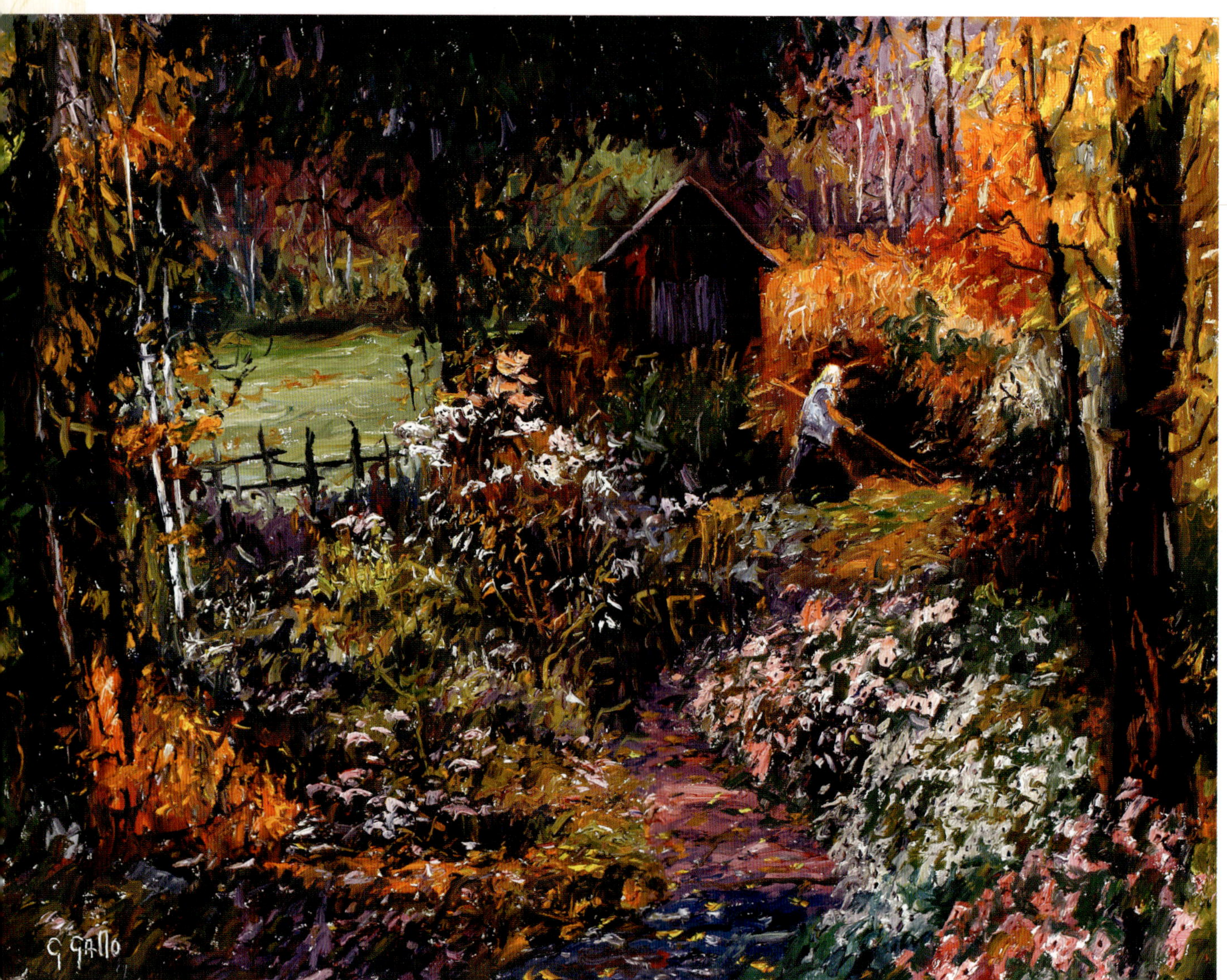

SUMMER'S END
Oil on Canvas · 36" × 48" (91cm × 122cm)

This is an example of pure Impressionism. Much of this painting is nothing more than dabs of color, both warm and cool, stitching the entire composition together. The only solid objects in the piece are the shed and the large tree behind it. You can see that I treated the shed and tree as one large mass. Had I broken this up, the painting would have become too spotty. Painting is about comparisons. We know something is warm because something cool is next to it. We enjoy all the little luscious dabs of color as long as there is a solid mass to complement it. The trees on either side of the painting act as anchors to hold the design together. The figure acts as a place where the eye can rest.

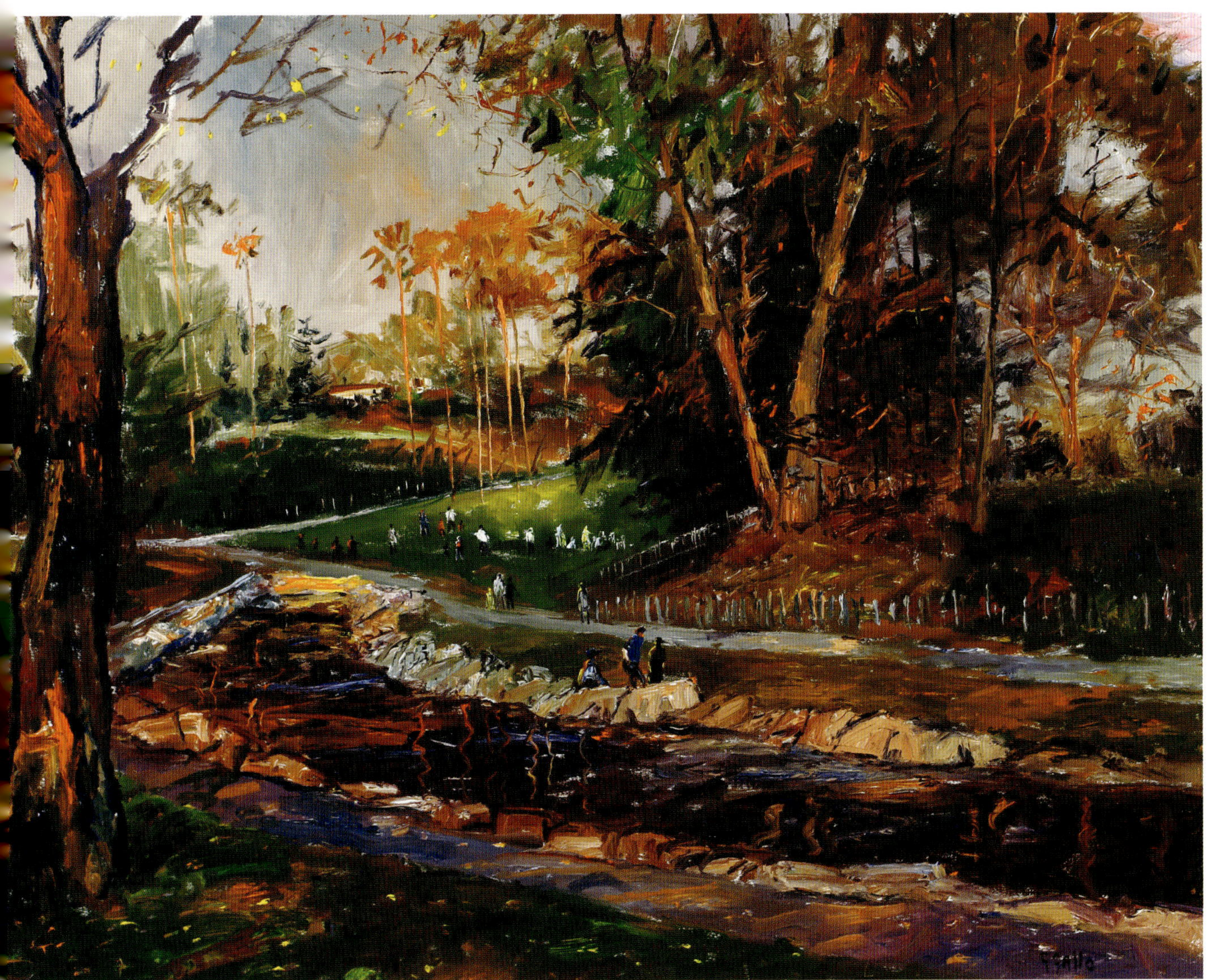

As evening fell on this little park in Orange County, California, the place became magical. It was on a Sunday and as the crowds continued playing and chatting, I became overwhelmed with the notion of stolen moments. There was less than an hour of light left, and it seemed that everyone wanted to get in their last bit of enjoyment before night closed in. Being aware of the emotions a scene brings up is essential to create a painting that is sublime. Ignoring these emotions means you are just copying nature and not saying more about it. You must get past just being a technician if you wish to say something not only deeper but more human. This scene is a study in warm complementary colors. The design is anchored by the large tree on the left, the water that cuts through the center and the large mass of trees on the right. The warm light in the center gives the eye a place to wander to.

EVENING IN THE PARK
Oil on Canvas · 36" × 48" (91cm × 122cm)

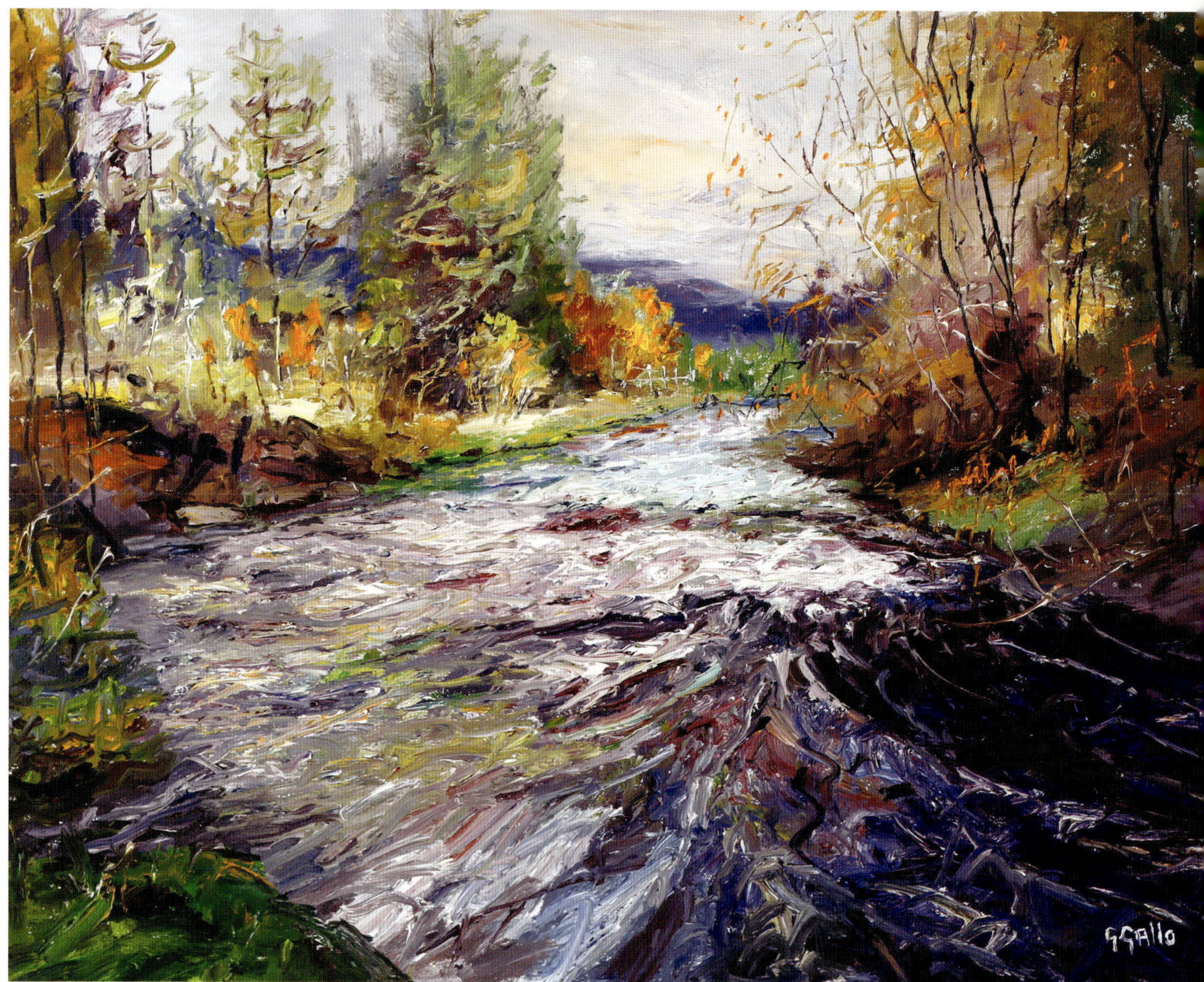

NORTHERN CALIFORNIA RIVER
Oil on Canvas · 36" × 48" (91cm × 122cm)

When choosing a subject you need to ask yourself, *What am I about to say?* Too many students don't know why they are painting a subject as they work. When coming upon a scene, you need to dissect the various elements and find a way to realize them into one cohesive thought. Be clear as to the story you want to tell. Here I featured the river. It takes up most of the composition in terms of space. It is also the area that has the most dynamic shifts in value and color. This is also true of the edges. Some of the sharpest edges in the painting are featured in the ridges of the water. To offset all of that I dealt with the background elements: trees, bushes and brush with less-contrasting values and softer edges. Had I put more extreme value and color shifts into the background, your eye would not know what to concentrate on. A successful painting can come about only by having a clear plan as to what you want to say before dipping your brush into your paints.

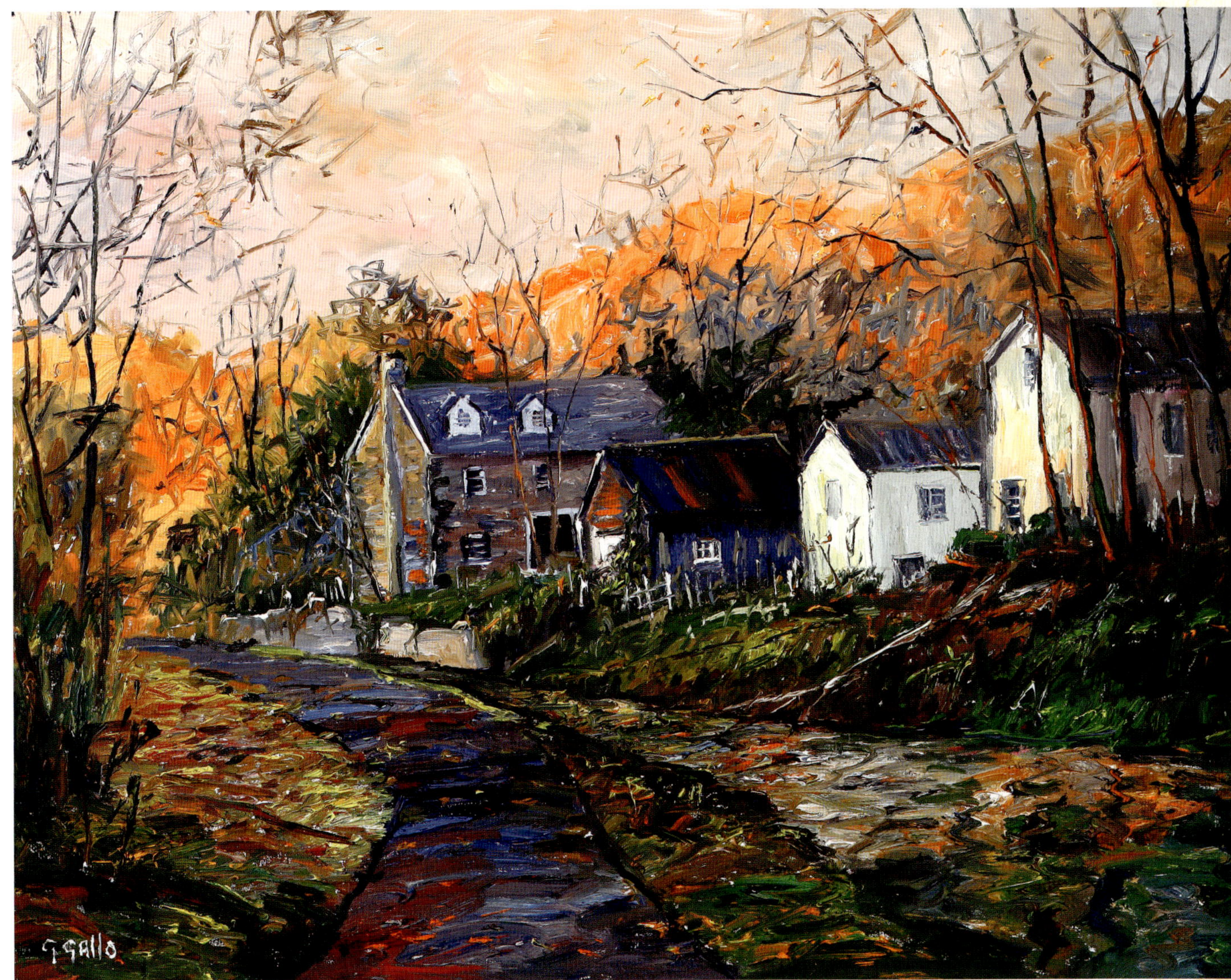

Here's an example of a painting that is all about color temperature. It's a classic rendering of warms and cools. The tops of the trees are catching the last bit of light. I mixed these warm orangey neutrals with Cadmium Orange and tempered them with my purple mixture of Ultramarine Blue and Alizarin Crimson with a touch of white. The sky is a warm neutral of a similar mixture leaning toward white. The cool structure on the left is in the purple family, grayed out with the addition of orange and a touch of Ivory Black. The purple color notes along with the oranges create beautiful color harmony. Adding the additional color spots of the dark green fir trees completes the secondary color triad and makes for a dynamic painting. I stress that this is far from a trick or formula because this is what happens in nature, especially in the evening when all secondary colors become more pronounced. The foreground is a mixture of purples, greens and oranges, all dulled out by combining the complements. This ensures complete harmony because all you are doing is repeating the color mixtures while being cognizant of their temperatures. The white structure is painted with Titanium White, a hint of Cadmium Yellow Lemon and Cadmium Orange. This is important because the Cadmium Lemon, which has a hint of blue, reads not only as a yellow but picks up some of the blue from the sky. The touch of Cadmium Orange adds warmth to the mixture and gives the feeling of sunlight.

ALONG THE TOWPATH
Oil on Canvas · 30" × 40" (76cm × 102cm)

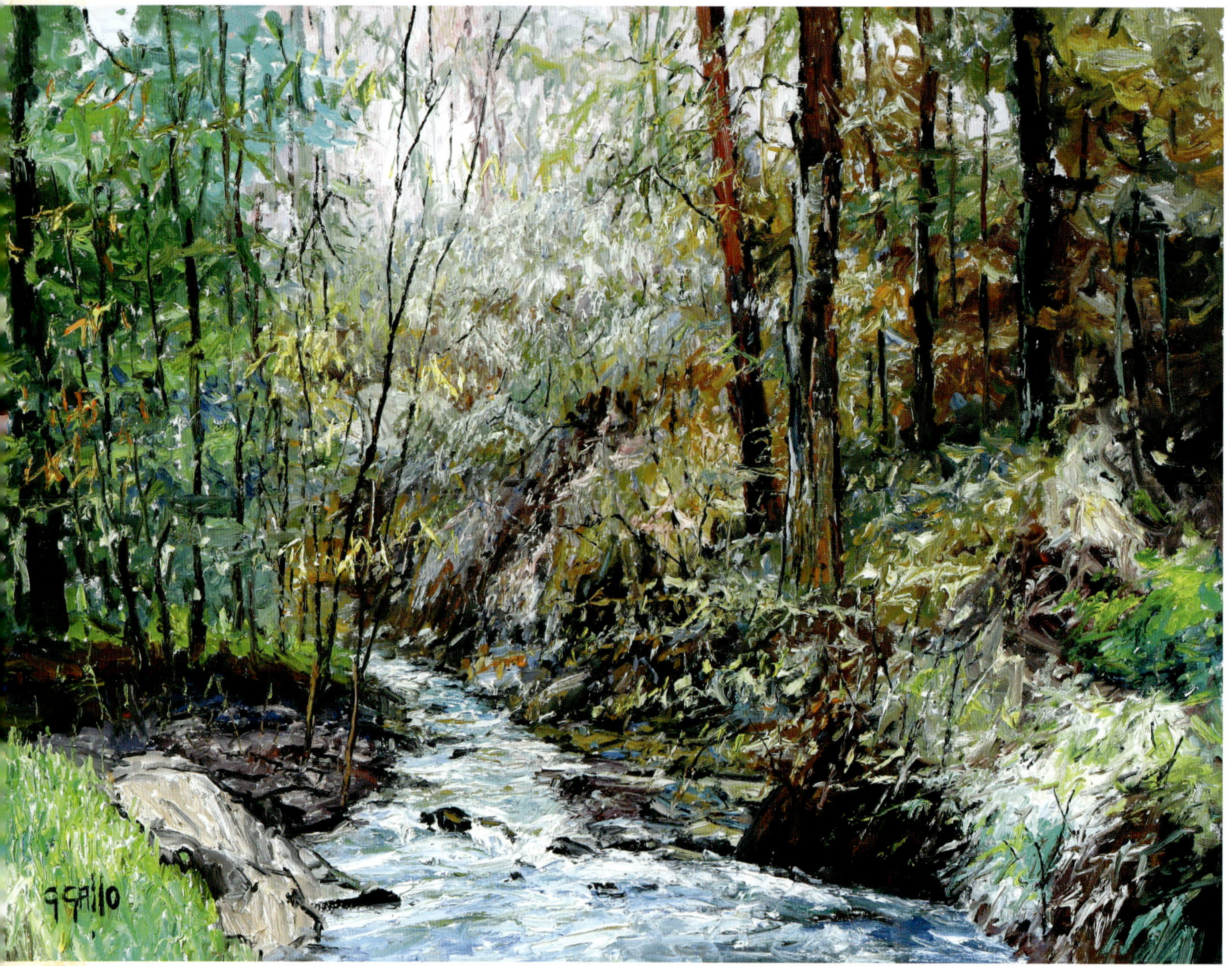

LAUREL CREEK IN SPRING
Oil on Canvas · 36" × 48" (91cm × 122cm)

Years ago I would not have been able to paint this picture. First of all, it's got a lot of green, which can be a very tricky color. You have to find all the variations of greens when working with so much of the same color. The other and more important aspect is that the light is cool because it is a high overcast day. As things get lighter, they also get cooler, which is the exact opposite of what happens on a sunny day. As a result of the cool light, all shadowed areas get warmer. Even though I knew this years ago, I somehow had a hard time bringing myself to introduce these facts into a painting. In situations like this you can use white paint for the light and force even more warmth than you see into the shadows. Because of the harmonious nature of our palette, you can use your reds (Cadmium Red Deep and Alizarin Crimson) for the shadowed areas. Any painting with this much green needs the complement of red. The silvery tones of the creek are created by using violets made with Ultramarine Blue, Alizarin Crimson and Titanium White. A few warm flecks of Cadmium Yellow Lemon in the right places bring the whole painting together. The fact that Cadmium Yellow Lemon has a touch of blue helps create the feeling of the cool light. Knowing your palette inside and out will help you create paintings full of sparkle because of your firm understanding of not only the separate colors but how they will interact with the other colors in your palette.

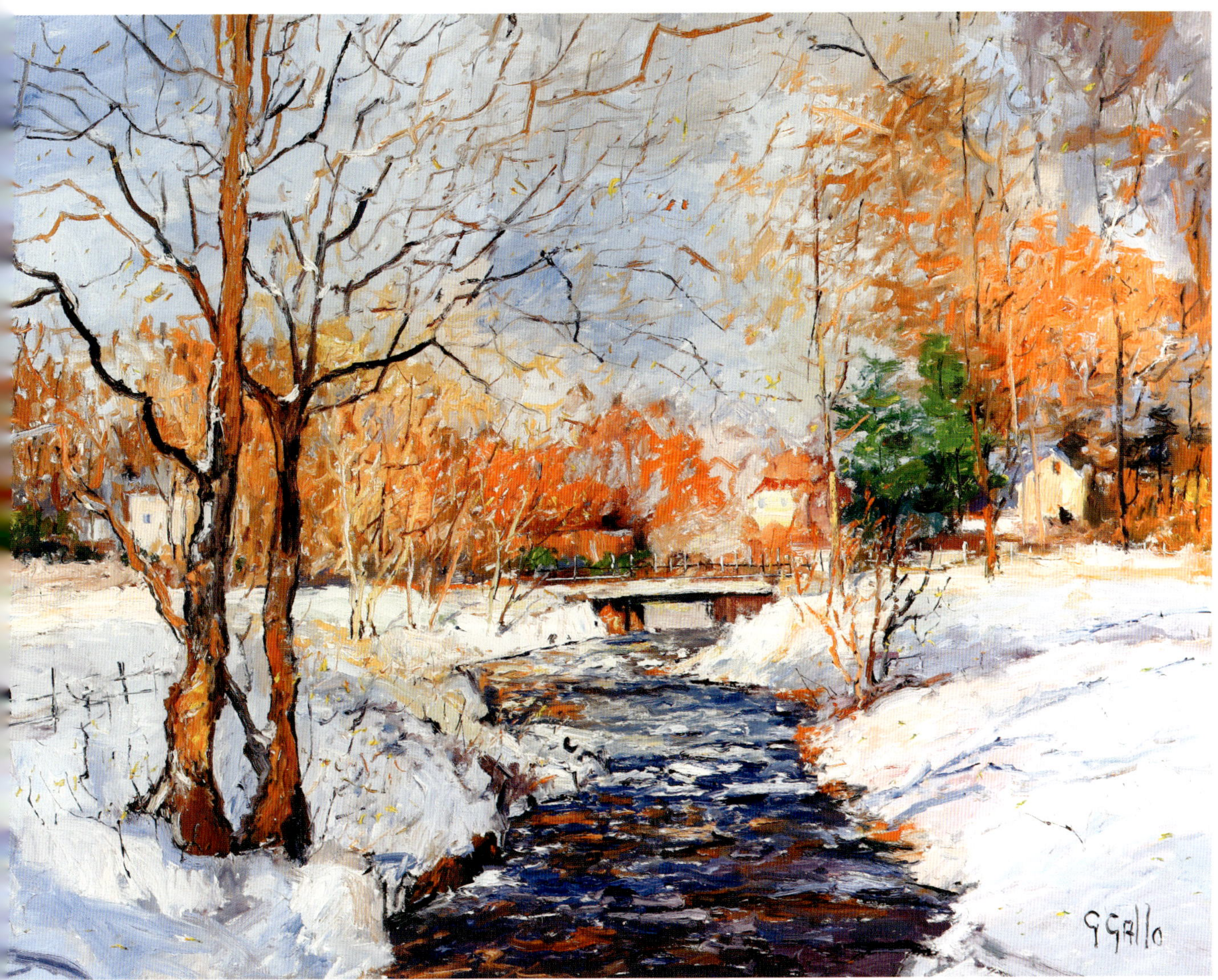

This painting was done in Mamaroneck, New York, where I lived for several years. Painted in the late afternoon, the background trees became a beautiful warm orange. The evergreens were a wonderful orangey green. The shadows were a lovely blue-violet, and the snow took on many different shades of white, both warm and cool. These color combinations were visually intoxicating. With good design and drawing, and knowing how well these colors all interact with one another, you increase the odds of painting something that will work. Just going out there and winging it without any forethought generally leads to disaster. As you paint more and more, you will have a good idea before you start of how the painting will look when it's finished.

COLUMBUS PARK IN WINTER
Oil on Canvas · 36" × 48" (91cm × 122cm)

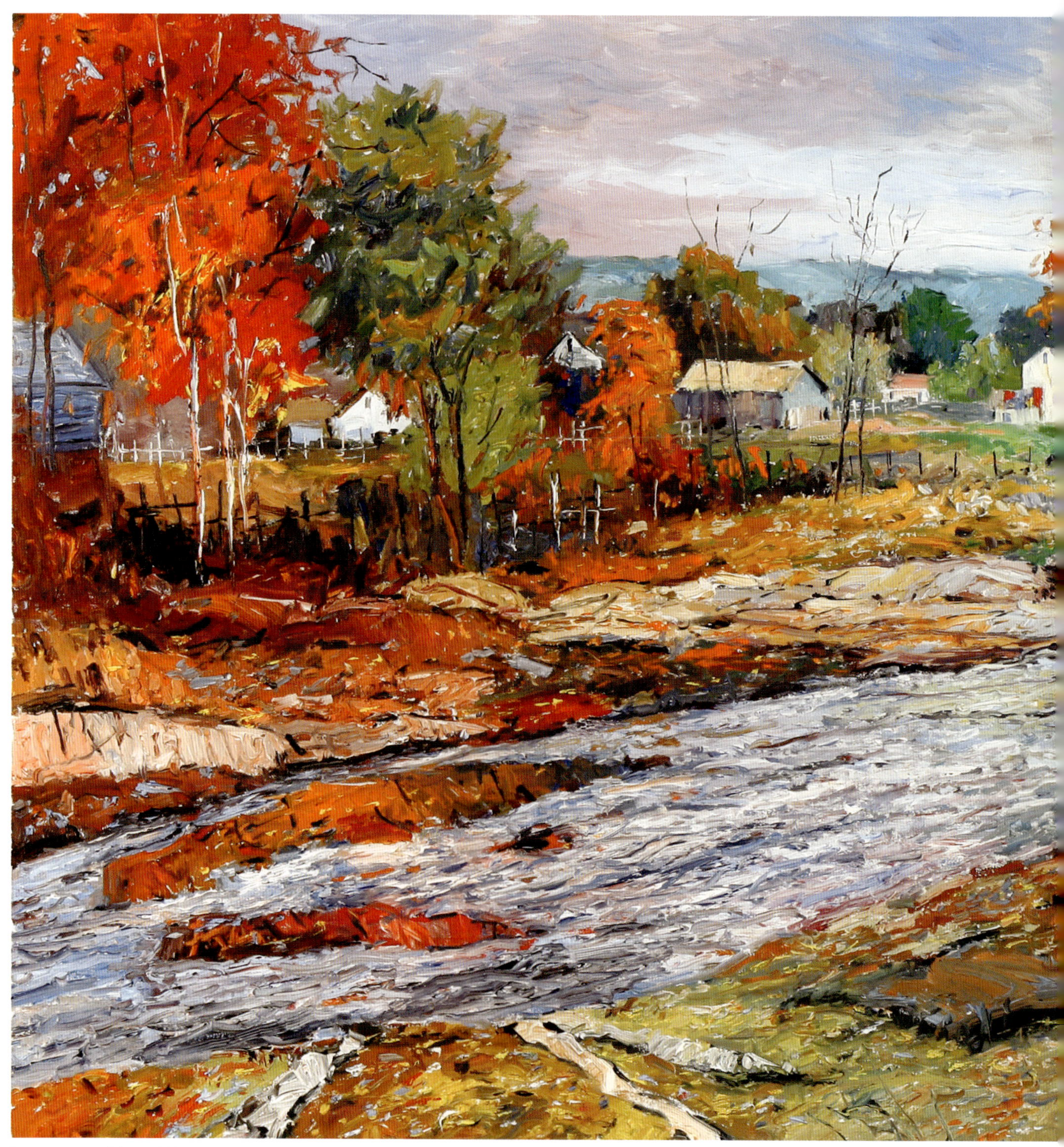

In many ways this could be considered a very complex painting because of all of the elements: several structures of different sizes, colors and shapes; mountains in the distance; many groupings of trees; and a river cutting through the center. The light is shifting between a high overcast day and one with a little warmth creeping through. The key when designing something with so many different objects is to not separate them but, rather, keep them as a whole. See things as big masses. Structures and trees are a mass, not separate objects. The big trees on the right are not only used as a framing device to hold the composition together, but they're one big unit that connects with the ground, rocks and shadows, all reading as one large mass. The darkest darks are placed in the foreground to aid in the feeling of atmospheric perspective. The lightest house in the piece, just to the left of the center of the canvas, helps to hold the viewer's eye in place. It's also painted with a nearly pure white. This helps express the coolness of the light and helps complete the color gamut in the viewer's eye, seeing everything from black to white.

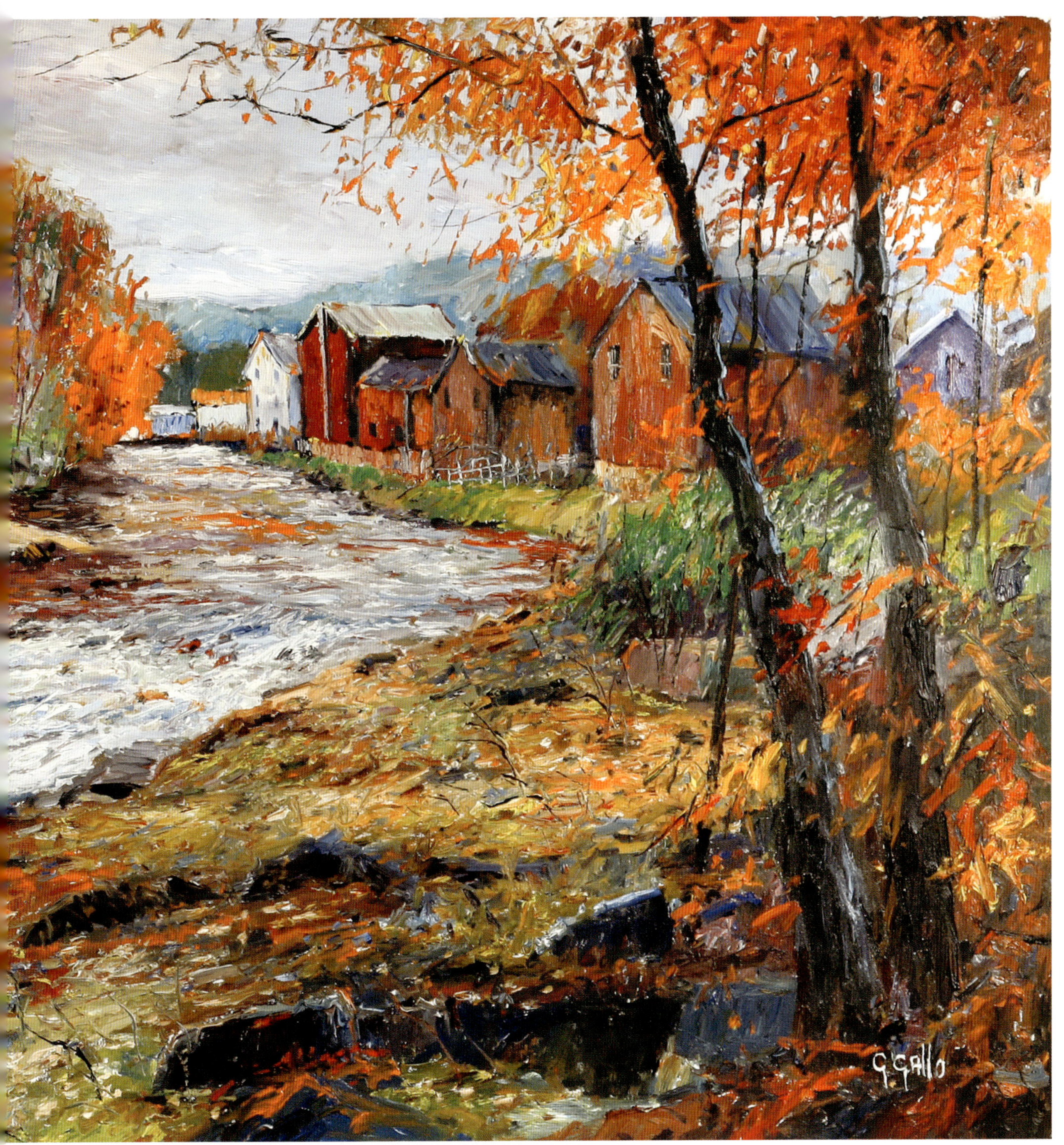

VERMONT VILLAGE · Oil on Canvas · 34" × 68" (86cm × 173cm)

About George Gallo

George Gallo was born in 1956. An only child, he grew up in Port Chester, New York, which he describes as a classic American working-class town. He began drawing when he was about three years old. When his mom saw some of his drawings on the kitchen table, she asked him who drew them. When he said he did, she didn't quite believe him, so she asked him to do a drawing while she watched. So he drew a helicopter. "Oh, my God," she said. "You're really good at this." A few days later she surprised him with a watercolor set.

At the age of twelve, George began to study pictures of paintings in art books. One day he noticed that the paint in one painting was very thick and had lots of texture to it. "What kind of paint is this?" he asked his mom. She glanced over at the picture. "That's oil paint." Overwhelmed by the beauty created by the brushstrokes, he decided to try out oil paints.

The first painting that inspired Gallo was *Autumn Bronze* by Robert Wood. He saw the print hanging over a sofa in the home of one of his father's friends. The painting seemed to reach out to him. He walked up to it, and as he studied it he couldn't believe there were so many little mysterious places in the painting, sunlight hitting spots in the distance, colorful shadows in the foreground, and he thought to himself, *How do people do this?* That was the moment when he really fell in love with landscape painting.

Next to Gallo's junior high school was a building with a sign on it that read "DAC—Donald Art Company." He had walked by the building every day and always wondered what kind of art business it was. One day he went into the building and asked what they did there. A worker showed him around and told him they made prints out of old artwork.

"I could not believe my eyes. They must have had hundreds of paintings by the top artists of that time. I didn't know it back then, but they were the premier printmaker in the United States. I would spend hours in that place because they had all these original oil paintings that they were producing prints from through a process called off-set lithography. They were making these prints for offices and homes, mass producing them."

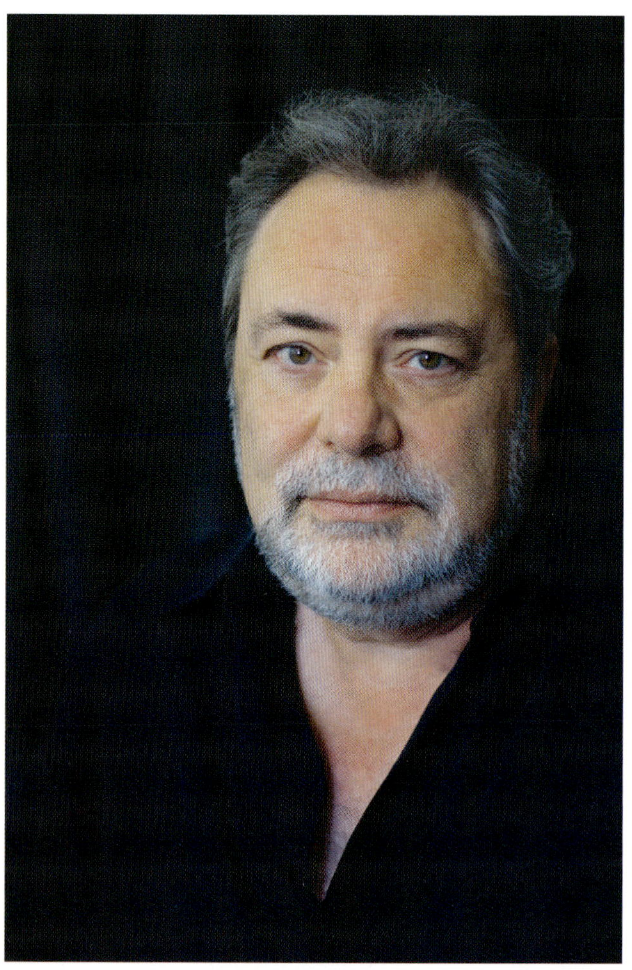

Two people who worked at the Donald Art Company gave him stacks and stacks of prints for free, and he took the prints home and studied them. Then he went to his easel and tried to re-create the brushstrokes. "That was the beginning of me learning how to paint," Gallo says.

During his high school years George used to hang around a little frame shop in downtown Port Chester. The shop was owned by Aurelio Yammerino, who lived in the back of the shop. "He did framing for people but was an incredibly gifted artist. He was one of those men who devoted his life to his drawing and painting but not to exhibiting. Yammerino was in *Who's Who in American Art* at one point. He was a brilliant man, and Charles Durning played him in the movie *Local Color.*" Yammerino taught Gallo about the importance of design, which Gallo feels is highly misunderstood today. "I think that Yammerino, along with the painters who studied at the Art Students League at that time, truly understood that design is the most important thing in a painting. A well-designed painting that is poorly executed will still be interesting and will still hold your interest. But a beautifully crafted painting with a terrible design won't hold your attention for very long. If you have the right shapes and the right values, you don't even need to worry about hitting the right color. I've seen trees in paintings where the artist painted their barks with purple and I still believed it."

Gallo discovered the Pennsylvania Impressionists when he was in his late teens. When he was a high school senior, he would get on the train and go into New York City. He had read about a place called Grand Central Art Galleries on 57th Street that exhibited many paintings by the American Impressionists. On his first visit he walked in to find an exhibit of the works of three of the Pennsylvania Impressionists: Edward Redfield, Walter E. Schofield and Daniel Garber.

"There was this big show featuring the three of them. I had never seen anything like these paintings in my life. The thing I found the most fascinating about them, especially with the Redfields, was how enormous they were. I had never seen 50" × 60" (127cm × 154cm) landscape paintings before, and they seemed to swallow you up when you looked at them. They were so grand and yet intimate at the same time. When I stepped up close to the canvases, it was just gobs and squiggles of paint, and I thought to myself, *How is this possible?* And then I would step back about ten feet (3m) and I could almost smell the pine trees and feel the coldness of the snow and the reeds popping out of the earth. Then I would get close again and say to myself, *No, those are big chunks of paint. How is this possible?* I would go back and forth, and I had no idea it had to do with shapes and values. It just blew me away. So I became very enamored with the Pennsylvania Impressionists.

"There was a man who ran the gallery by the name of John Evans. We became very good friends. And I started asking him all these questions about Redfield, and I wanted to learn more about the Pennsylvania Impressionists. John gave me a book about them, and he also gave me a bunch of transparencies of the Redfield paintings. I took all this stuff home and just studied it and studied it."

George struggled with his painting for years because he had a hard time finishing any of them, a hard time knowing when they were done. "I think this happens to a lot of artists. You're not clear in the beginning as to what you want to do, so if you get something good, it's sort of an accident. Being very clear as to your intentions up front eliminates this problem.

"A lot of students will drop an easel when they see something they think is beautiful, and they'll just start painting. But if you ask them specific questions like, 'What's your real subject?' They'll say, 'Oh, I don't know. I just kind of like all of it.' And they just keep adding things and adding things as they paint because they never really knew from the beginning what the point of the painting was. And this can happen to the best of us, even after we've painted thousands of paintings. When you're working outdoors you really have to be careful because the eye gets greedy and it wants to incorporate everything it's seeing, and you've got to really hold back and say, 'Is this helping or hurting my original intention?' Because if it's not helping the original intention, whatever that may be, it is best to leave it out."

Gallo has had dozens of one-man shows including three at Grand Central Art Galleries. In 1991 he won the coveted Arts for the Parks Top 100 Award. Gallo was a teacher for four years at Weekend With the Masters. Although Gallo has also written and/or directed many Hollywood features, including the classic comedy *Midnight Run*, he says he is happiest when he is outdoors working at his easel and chasing the light.

Local Color—The Movie

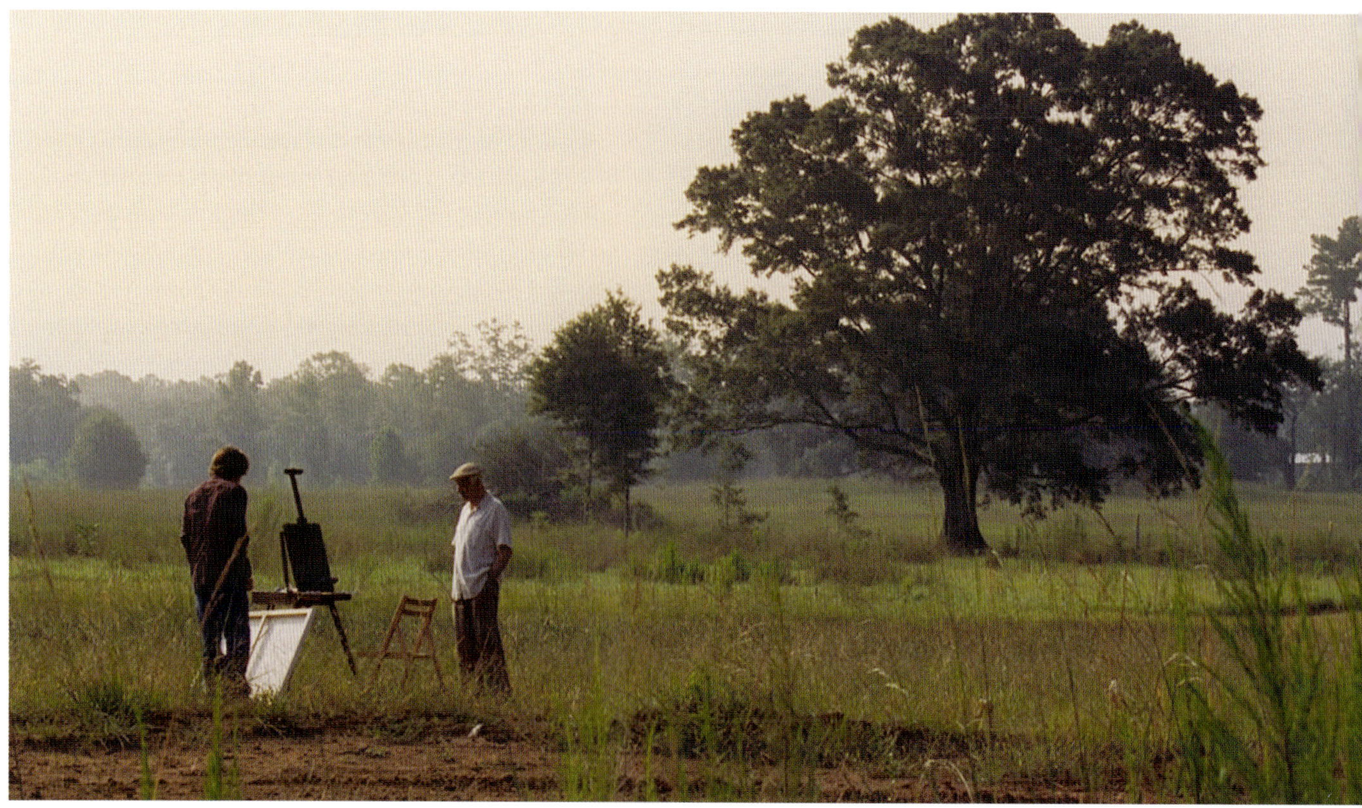

Nicholi Seroff (Armin Mueller-Stahl) instructing John Talia (Trevor Morgan) on a warm summer evening

THE IDEA FOR THE FILM

Local Color is based on the true story of George Gallo's relationship with his mentor, a Russian master by the name of George Cherepov. For years George played around with the idea of writing the script, but it wasn't until he was much older that he felt he could write the older character with any sense of understanding and resonance. "You know, when you're younger and you're around an older person who's that craggy, cranky and foul-mouthed, they can just come off as a crazy old bastard. As you get older, you get a better grasp of what life is really about. And you can look at that person with a lot more understanding and sympathy. So when I got to be about fifty, I got a handle on what made the old guy tick. That's what made me finally write the screenplay."

The movie was a labor of love. It was basically self-financed by Gallo and a few friends. Julie Gallo, George's wife, was determined to make the movie and ended up producing it. "We didn't have children. And Julie kept hearing this story and felt that it should be brought into the world. And it seemed to move people when I

told them the story about it. I also thought it would be a nice gift to give to representational painters because I think as a group they were pretty much forgotten in the twentieth century."

MASTER PAINTER—SCREENWRITER/DIRECTOR

Gallo began his motion picture career by reading everything he could find about writing scripts. "I learned about the craft of writing, then I started writing. And I wrote a few screenplays."

An idea to begin calling people in the film industry led George straight to the phone book, where he found the home number of Arthur J. Ornitz. A famous New York cinematographer, Ornitz shot *Serpico*, *The Anderson Tapes* and *A Thousand Clowns*. "I asked Arthur if he would read one of my screenplays. And he was very gracious. He read my script, and he liked the way I wrote. He gave the screenplay to his friend who was a movie producer by the name of Martin Bregman. Bregman had produced movies with director Sidney Lumet, and so I got lucky. Marty called me up and said he wanted to option my screenplay,

138

and suddenly I had this career as a screenwriter because I sold a script to Universal Studios."

And so Gallo started writing more screenplays. "I kept writing and writing, and I got better and better at it. I kept painting, but I kept my painting more to myself. The writing started to supplement my income, which was great. I could write Monday through Friday and paint on weekends. It's been like a dream come true for me—such a wonderful way to live, and I feel so blessed."

OSCAR-NOMINATED ACTOR—PAINTER

Gallo felt the role of Nicholi Seroff was pivotal to the success of *Local Color*. His wife, Julie, told him that Armin Mueller-Stahl would be perfect for the part. But he didn't know Armin Mueller-Stahl, and he didn't think the Oscar-nominated actor would work for scale on such an intense role. But Julie convinced him to take a shot. George called the William Morris Agency and was told that Armin had retired from acting and just wanted to paint for the rest of his life. Pleasantly surprised, George said, "Well, this is pretty interesting because this movie is about an artist." Gallo was given Armin's phone number in Germany and immediately called him.

"You sound like a very nice man," Armin said. "But I don't want to leave my home in Germany and come to America and work for scale." George asked him if he would just read the script. "Okay. Send it to me. I'll read it." So the script was mailed to Germany. A few days later Armin called George. He was very quiet so George spoke up. "What's going on?" Armin cleared his voice, and then said, "When can we start?" And that was it.

THE THEME OF THE FILM

"Life can be unsettling for many reasons. For me, art has always been the place I go to feel whole again. Maybe that is why I don't have much interest in art that is disturbing. I don't need something on my wall to remind me that things can be very unpleasant. For that we have the evening news. I've always felt that art was a place we could all go to and unite for a bit, forget everything that's negative and just feel good about this very strange and wonderful thing we call life. Seeing beauty is of vital importance for human beings. It reminds us of not only the best things in life, but that life itself is worth living. I would consider it an insult to the Creator to use the talents I've been given to create more ugliness.

"Great art isn't trendy. The modernists saw great success in the last century but found they could no longer sell their works only a few decades after they took the New York art scene by storm. The reasons these artists were given was that their work wasn't cutting-edge enough. I understand how technology becomes outdated, but not great art. Great art can't become outdated for the same reasons that Shakespeare, Greek myths and Mozart still hold up. It's because those works speak the truth and the truth is timeless. If a piece of art is relevant because it's trendy, you can bet it isn't much of a piece of art.

"Many artists working in the representational field today complain that they aren't getting the exposure they would like because the art mavens are still pushing modernists over traditionalists. But I believe the door is open for representational painting to surge and flourish. Someday the tide will turn, but only if we paint revolutionary representational paintings."

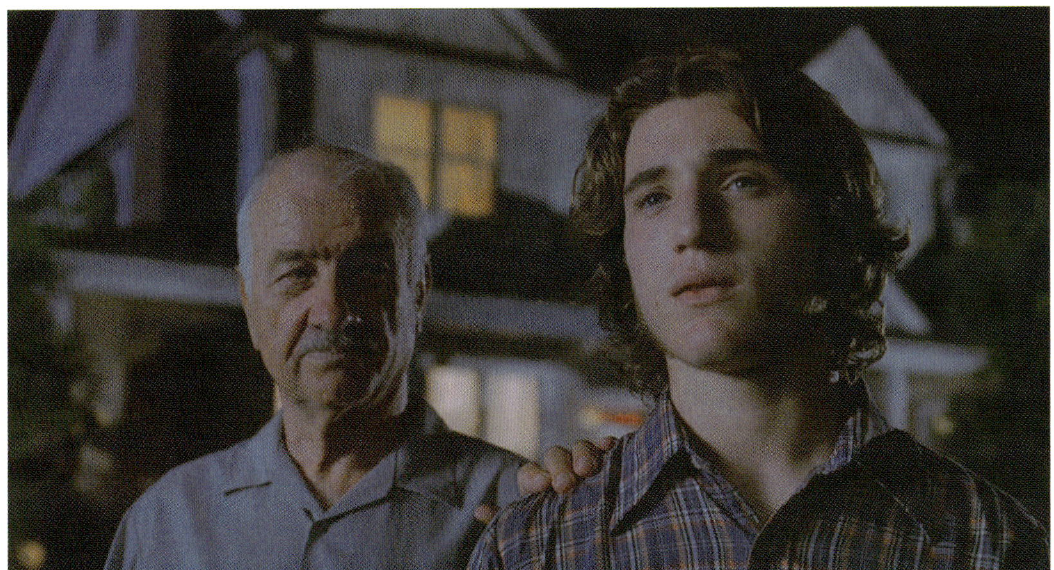

Nicholi and John watch a breathtaking sunset.

Conclusion

I remember struggling one day when I was out painting with George Cherepov. We were standing in thick, beautiful green grass up to our ankles, and just that smell of being in the outdoors made me feel so good. I was painting a scene of a road and a distant mountain, but I was having a difficult time. Cherepov walked over to me, took the brush out of my hand, applied a couple of little dabs of paint, added a cloud, a fence and a highlight on a rooftop, and then walked away. In about three minutes he made the painting just sing! And I thought to myself, *God, how does he know this stuff?* Well, he had painted forever; that's how he knew

There's no doubt that there are moments when you will have breakthroughs. But in general the repetition, the constant work at it will cause you to become proficient to the point where the eyes slowly open.

One autumn I was in Colorado hiking in the mountains with James Van Fossan. The aspen trees were turning bright yellow and orange. The leaves literally looked like medallions, gold medallions strung across the mountainside. And there was snow in the mountains and the fields. And this river was zigzagging through the middle of it all, and I looked at James and said, "You know, I don't care what anybody says, but you'd have to be a moron not to believe in God."

I believe I've been guided throughout my life, guided by something far bigger than man, and I bow to that higher power. I'm humbled by it. And I feel that it guides me every day. I feel that the work I'm doing is my way of showing appreciation for having been here. And I take satisfaction in knowing that I can inspire others to do their best. I'd like to think that there's some kid who'll come down the road and look at my work and find the same joy in it that I found in the works of some of the Old Masters.

Dedication

This book is dedicated to Julie, my wife, muse and best friend for more than thity years.

Acknowledgements

I want to thank David Leffel, Josh Posner, Tony Pro, Leigh Ann and James Van Fossan, Rosemary Thompson and Symi Jackson of Rosemary and Company Artist Brushes, Michael and Karen Harding of Michael Harding Oil Colours, Chris Hauser and the staff of Carter Sexton Art Supplies, Heather Goldstein of Jerry's Artarama and Kyle and Keith O'Brien of New Wave Palettes. I would also like to thank Jenia Hauser for flawlessly photographing all of the artwork in this book. And to Fluffy, greatest cat west of the Mississippi.

About Cindy Salaski

Cindy Salaski is the cofounder and CEO of ArtMatch4U.com. The vision of ArtMatch4U is to enable artists and art lovers quick, easy access to everything in the world of fine art.

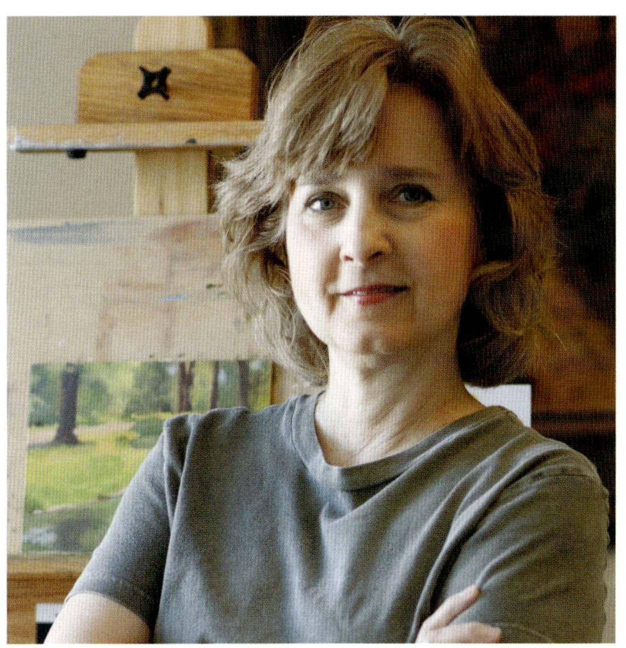

Much of Salaski's career was in marketing and sales. From 1991 to 2006 Cindy was a luxury home specialist with Realty Executives in Paradise Valley, Arizona. However, after studying with North Light author Eric Wiegardt at the Scottsdale Artists' School in 2006, she decided to focus on her first love—fine art.

Along with her duties at ArtMatch4U, Cindy paints in oils, watercolors and pastels. She has studied with Albert Handell, Barry John Raybould and Phil Starke. Cindy was also in a mentorship with world-renowned plein air painter Kevin Macpherson from July 2010 to July 2011.

Salaski also enjoys writing. In 1984 she was named one of the top ten writers in the scripts category of the *Writer's Digest Magazine* Writing Competition. In 1997, she won third place in *Pure Fiction*'s Electronic Slush Pile; winners were chosen by Martin Fletcher, editorial director at Simon & Schuster. In 2012 Cindy wrote the article "Mastering Brushstrokes with Albert Handell," which was featured in issue 88 (Dec/Jan 2013) of *International Artist Magazine*.

Salaski's first book, *Oil Painting with The Masters: Essential Techniques from Today's Top Artist*s, was released by F+W Media/North Light Books in July 2014. George Gallo is featured in that book along with nineteen more of today's top master oil painters.

Index

Impressionist Painting for the Landscape. Copyright © 2014 by George Gallo & Cindy Salaski. Manufactured in China. All rights reserved. No part of this book may be reproduced in any form or by any electronic or mechanical means including information storage and retrieval systems without permission in writing from the publisher, except by a reviewer who may quote brief passages in a review. Published by North Light Books, an imprint of F+W Media, Inc., 10151 Carver Road, Blue Ash, Ohio, 45242. (800) 289-0963. First Edition.

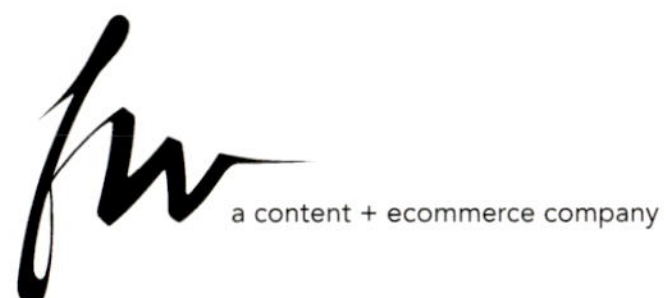

Other fine North Light Books are available from your favorite bookstore, art supply store or online supplier. Visit our website at fwmedia.com.

18 17 16 15 14   5 4 3 2 1

ISBN: 978-1-4403-3727-7

DISTRIBUTED IN CANADA BY FRASER DIRECT
100 Armstrong Avenue
Georgetown, ON, Canada L7G 5S4
Tel: (905) 877-4411

DISTRIBUTED IN THE U.K. AND EUROPE
BY F&W MEDIA INTERNATIONAL, LTD
Brunel House, Forde Close, Newton Abbot, TQ12 4PU, UK
Tel: (+44) 1626 323200, Fax: (+44) 1626 323319
Email: enquiries@fwmedia.com

DISTRIBUTED IN AUSTRALIA BY CAPRICORN LINK
P.O. Box 704, S. Windsor NSW, 2756 Australia
Tel: 02 4560 1600
Fax: 02 4577 5288
Email: books@ capricornlink.com.au

Edited by Kristy Conlin
Designed by Wendy Dunning
Production coordinated by Mark Griffin

METRIC CONVERSION CHART

TO CONVERT	TO	MULTIPLY BY
Inches	Centimeters	2.54
Centimeters	Inches	0.4
Feet	Centimeters	30.5
Centimeters	Feet	0.03
Yards	Meters	0.9
Meters	Yards	1.1

Visit **artistsnetwork.com/impressionist-landscape** to download free bonus materials.

Ideas. Instruction. Inspiration.

Receive FREE downloadable bonus materials when you sign up for our free newsletter at artistsnetwork.com/Newsletter_Thanks.

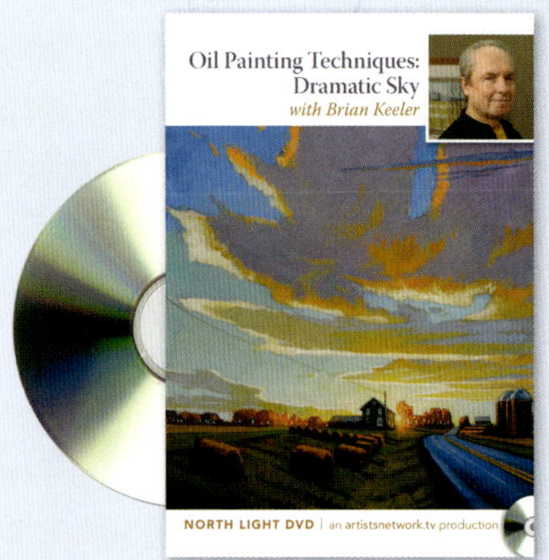

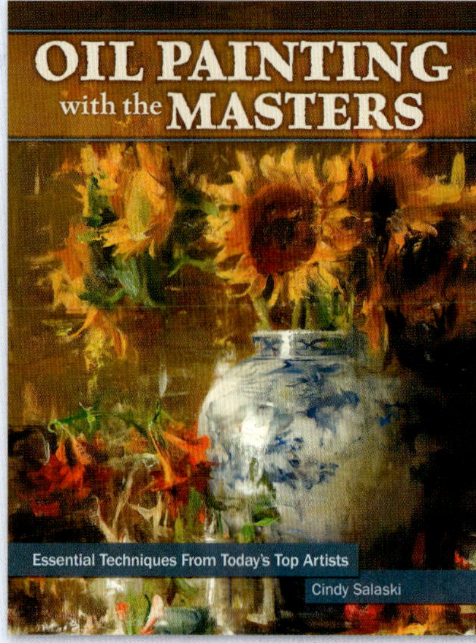

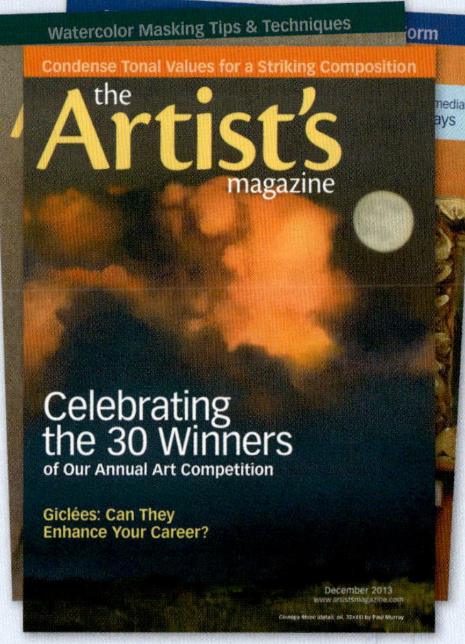

Find the latest issues of
The Artist's Magazine
on newsstands
or visit artistsnetwork.com.

These and other fine North Light products are available at your favorite art & craft retailer, bookstore or online supplier. Visit our websites: artistsnetwork.com and artistsnetwork.tv.

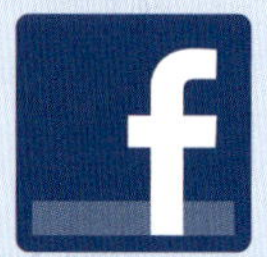

Follow ArtistsNetwork.com for the latest news, free wallpapers, free demos and chances to win FREE BOOKS!

Get your **art in print!**

Visit artistsnetwork.com/competitions for up-to-date information on North Light competitions.

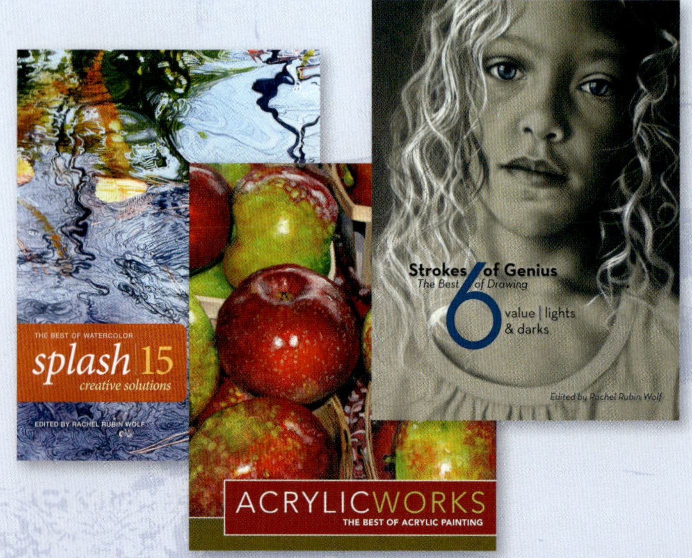